Virtual English

Virtual English examines English language communication on the World Wide Web, focusing on internet practices crafted by under-served communities in the US and overlooked participants in several Asian Diasporic communities. Jillana Enteen locates instances where subjects use electronic media to resist popular understandings of cyberspace, computer-mediated communication, gender, sexuality, nation and community, presenting unexpected responses to the forces of globalization and predominant US value systems. The populations studied here contribute websites, conversations and artifacts that employ English strategically, broadening and splintering the language to express their concerns in the manner they perceive as effective. Users are thus afforded new opportunities to transmit information, conduct conversations, teach and make decisions, shaping, in the process, both language and technology. The subjects of *Virtual English* challenge prevailing deployments and conceptions of emerging technologies. Their on-line practices illustrate that the internet need not replicate current geopolitical beliefs and practices and that reconfigurations exist in tandem with dominant models.

Jillana Enteen is Associate Director and Director of Undergraduate Studies in the Gender Studies Program at Northwestern University, where she teaches courses in New Media Studies, Postcolonial Theory, Cultural Studies, Queer Theory and Asian Diaspora Literature. She has published across a broad array of disciplines, including journals ranging from New Media and Society to Science Fiction Studies to the Journal of Lesbian Studies.

Routledge Studies in New Media and Cyberculture:

Routledge Studies in New Media and Cyberculture is dedicated to furthering original research in New Media and Cyberculture Studies. International in scope, the series places an emphasis on cutting-edge scholarship and interdisciplinary methodology. Topics explored in the series will include comparative and cultural studies of video games, blogs, online communities, digital music, New Media art, cyberactivism, open source, mobile communications technologies, new information technologies, and the myriad intersections of race, gender, ethnicity, nationality, class, and sexuality with cyberculture.

Virtual English

Queer Internets and Digital Creolization

Jillana B. Enteen

Routledge
Taylor & Francis Group

NEW YORK AND LONDON

The Northwestern University Research Grants Committee has provided partial support for the publication of this book. We gratefully acknowledge this assistance.

The author and publisher gratefully acknowledge permission to reprint material in this book that appeared in earlier forms in the following publications: " 'On the Receiving End of the Colonization': Nalo Hopkinson's 'Nansi Web" was published in: Ron E. Shavers and Mark Bould, eds. *Science Fiction Studies*, Special issue on Afrofuturism 101, 33(1) March 2007; "Spatial Conceptions of URLs: Tamil Eelam Networks on the World Wide Web," Radhika Gajjala, ed. *New Media and Society*, Special issue on "Consuming/producing/inhabiting South-Asian digital diasporas" 8.2, April 2006: 229–249; "Siam ReMapped: CyberInterventions by Thai Women," *New Media and Society* 7.4, August 2005: 457–482; "Lesbian Studies in Thailand." Special issue on "Lesbian Studies in the Twenty-First Century." Noreen Giffney Katherine O'Donnell, eds. *The Journal of Lesbian Studies* 11.1/2 (2007). " 'Whiskey is Whiskey. You Can't Make a Cocktail from That': Self-Identified Gay Thai Men in Bangkok," *Jouvert: A Journal of Post-Colonial Studies* 2.1, Fall 1998.

First published 2010
by Routledge
711 Third Avenue, New York, NY 10017, USA

Simultaneously published in the UK
by Routledge
2 Park Square, Milton Park, Abingdon, Oxon OX14 4RN

Routledge is an imprint of the Taylor & Francis Group, an informa business

© 2010 Taylor & Francis

Typeset in Times New Roman by Wearset Ltd, Boldon, Tyne and Wear

Library of Congress Cataloging in Publication Data
A catalog record has been requested for this book

ISBN10: 0-415-97724-X (hbk)
ISBN10: 0-415-99429-2 (pbk)
ISBN10: 0-203-87950-3 (ebk)

ISBN13: 978-0-415-97724-1 (hbk)
ISBN13: 978-0-415-99429-3 (pbk)
ISBN13: 978-0-203-87950-4 (ebk)

Contents

Acknowledgments

I would like to thank Nalo Hopkinson, whose interest in this project, including helping me locate some of her own specific creole constructions, has inspired my thinking tremendously. Similarly, this book would not have been possible without the support of my friends and colleagues in Thailand: Addisak, Khun Tada, and Khun Somrudee Thaipanich, Varaporn Chamsanit, Pui Sangsuriyasilp, Pat Yavajanuwat, Juk, Muk, Sabrina, Pasuk Phongpaichit, Anjana Suvarnananda, Surang Janyam, Suteera Thomson, Peter Jackson, Suvanna Kriengkraipetch, Sanitsuda Ekachai, the Thai Fulbright office, EMPOWER, SWING, the Rajamangala Institue of Technology, and Chulalongkorn University, as well as a more recent Thailand-based friend and scholar, Laurence Davis. Sincere appreciation goes out to Pat and Tom Bransford and Jennifer Bransford White for the opportunities they supplied at Urban Technologies, Inc. I spent many hours thinking, working, developing curricula, and enjoying the responsibilities, trust, and spirit of collaboration that they fostered.

Thank you to three teachers and role models in particular: Cora Kaplan, Elizabeth Meese, and Larry Spence. Each of you, at crucial junctures of my education, emulated what is best about academic work and teaching. You inspire me constantly to think critically and expect the most of myself, and I strive to follow in your footsteps. I also extend my most extreme gratitude to some wonderful mentors, who tirelessly propelled me from Shakespeare Studies at the University of Alabama to Cultural Studies at Rutgers, the State University of New Jersey, to numerous academic posts. Their help with my thinking and writing is immeasurable, and they have taken me from thesis and dissertation writing to faculty work with kind, yet tough guidance: Bruce Robbins, David Lee Miller, Cheryl Wall, Abena Busia, Sharon O'Dair, Ed Cohen, Richard Miller, Marc Manganero, Louisa Schein, and, in particular, Mary Finn, who never stops helping me revise my thoughts, life, and work. And thanks for the education of several incredible professors: Sandy Flitterman-Lewis, Dawn Trouard, Julie Graham, Jonathon Goldberg, Diane Roberts, Harold Weber, Francesca Kazan, Jonathon Goldberg, Diane Roberts, Harriet Davidson, and Ann Coiro.

I appreciate the support of engaged colleagues: Radhika Gajjala – whose constant collaboration over the years has been amazing. Our unusual ways of thinking ceaselessly intersect in productive ways and our ability to clarify each other continues to astound me. Thanks to my colleague-friends – in particular, people who have read my work and helped me grow at many stages of this project: Benedict Anderson, Lisa Gitelman, Jeffrey Masten, Deanna Kreisel, Jennifer Devere Brody, Dwight McBride, E. Patrick Johnson, Dorothy Wang, Hortense Spillers, Carol Boyce Davies, Bill Worthen, and Dawn Marlan. Megan Boler, Anna Everett, Kathleen Fitzpatrick, Susanna Paasonen, and Michele White participated in several conversations that helped me better understand how to articulate my method in relation to internet research as a general "discipline." Also, I've received wonderful attention, reading, and advice from Steve Jones, Mary Bryson, Lisa Nakamura, Judith Halberstam, David Eng, Alondra Nelson, Thuy Linh Tu, Gayatri Spivak, Anna Everett, Michael Moon, John Keene, Megan Sinnott, Ara Wilson, Tamara Loos, and Cecilia Milanes.

I am extremely fortunate to have found colleagues and university members at several institutions that have contributed much to my thinking: Kate Baldwin, Kevin Barnhurst, Nikki Beisel, Martha Biondi, Brian Bouldry, Melody Bowdon, Cynthia Bowman, Jennifer Brier, Jeremy Butler, Peter Carroll, Claire Cavanagh, Carolyn Chen, Evelyn Nien-Ming Ch'ien, Patricia Dailey, Kathy Daniels, Mary Dietz, Nick Davis, Natasha Dennison, Penelope Deutscher, Kasey Evans, Lane Fenrich, Peter Fenves, Marsha Figaro, Lisa Freeman, Reginald Gibbons, David Glover, Susannah Gottlieb, Jay Grossman, Kelby Harrison, Michael Hanchard, Sharon Holland, Bonnie Honig, Darlene Clarke Hyne, Greg Jue, Jules Law, Tessie Liu, Ira Livingston, Vanessa Lemm, Nancy MacClean, Nathan Meade, Andrew Matzner, Rosalind Morris, Ann Orloff, Alexandra Owen, Frances Freeman Paden, Amy Partridge, Susie Phillips, Peggy Peitsche, Öykü Potuogli-Cook, Gayatri Reddy, Sandra Lee Richards, Bill Savage, Regina Schwartz, Joan Sherman, Mike Sherry, Carl Smith, Julia Stern, Helen Thompson, Penny Van Esterik, Tracy Vaughn, Wendy Wall, Dorothy Wang, Michael Warner, Celeste Watkins-Haynes, Katy Weseman, Jane Winston, Ji-Yeon Yuh, Linda Zerilli, and many others left unsaid.

Much of the thinking for this book took place in the homes of my friends: George Hadjidakis, Eliot Blake, Lisa Lynch, Tanya Agathacleous, Chris O'Brien, Tamar Rothenberg, Helen Hurwitz, Anthony Allesandrini, John Welch, Jonathan Kahana, Joseph Chaves, Eve Oishi, Erik Dussere, Stephanie Hartman, Cathy Clarke, Barbara Ballinger, Ben Singer, Ruth Wilson Gilmore, Ben Weiner, Susan Georgecink, and Don Gilliland – I could never have imagined a better cohort of inspired/inspiring graduate students and fellow travelers, each of whom produced fascinating ideas and engaged thoughtfully with my ideas in their formations.

I wish to extend much appreciation to Matt Byrnie, senior editor at Routledge of the Cyberculture Series, for his endless support and patience – presenting me with a book contract that was signed the day before I gave birth to twins, and putting up with years of delay as a result – a better editor one could not have. Tremendous gratitude to Marcus Elmore – he and Colleen Tully supplied me with the support necessary to pull me through the last edit of this book, which took place under remarkably challenging circumstances – I thank you both so much – in different ways – for your friendship, keen intellects, and never-waning dedication. Many, many thanks to Abena Busia for allowing me to reprint her poem, "Caliban," in its entirety as the epigraph to Chapter 2. Her poetry speaks much more efficiently than my words ever could. And sincere thanks to the two anonymous readers who gave me excellent suggestions for the manuscript's revision.

I extend heartfelt thanks and love to Tori Marlan for her encouraging reading of the penultimate draft of this manuscript, but much more, for her friendship – one of the most important gifts that I have had in my life was her insistence that writing, teaching, working full-time, and raising twins were not to hinder our friendship. Her expectation that I would live this full life helped me both manage to do so and think better. I am similarly grateful to Crystal Mandler, who inspires me to be dedicated and concentrate on what's important, particularly through example. Her ability to keep it all in focus, laugh at herself, and follow her passions offers me inspiration; her friendship and deep caring and commitment to others makes me marvel. Zoe Zolbrod has been a kindred spirit and someone I trust, whether it be to choose a book cover, offer a kind ear or helping hand with little notice, or make herself locatable during my vacation time from teaching in Thailand. Knowing that I could find her in Nepal miles from any direct communication lines – through postcard messages stuck to bulletin boards rather than digital texts, is a wonderful feeling. I'm so thrilled our long-awaited books are coming out in tandem! Greg Lanier has offered both unwavering affection and support, as well as technological expertise, constant commentary, and much-needed ego-bolstering in crucial moments. Finally, Marissa Faustini has been my choreographer, my reader, an inspiration, and my co-conspirator; she challenges me to learn, grow, change, and let go, not to mention providing me with both affection and space to breathe within the chaos.

Many students have been a source of inspiration and energy – what more could one hope for than to be constantly engaged with great young minds: Neel Ahuja, Christian Appel, Anayah Barney, Blaine Bookey, Helen Cho, Nerida Cook, Andy Cray, Daniel Crowder, Asher Haig, Kathleen Ho, Annie Lee, Han Lee, Mugsie Pike, Shuyan Pua, Arathi Premkumar, Gary Sapir, Sujata Shyam, Jackie Swiatek, Marina Thomas, and Poornima Yechoor. And Sharlyn Grace, my research assistant, deserves a special mention for her sharp ideas and keen formatting. Special shout outs for the double duties performed by students-turned-friends: Barrak Alzaid, Jessica Mathiason, and Sonia Nelson – whose intellectual engagement with my work as well as whose help – editing for me, being walked by Askar, and entertaining the twins – kept me functioning. This manuscript so much better reveals my often convoluted thoughts because of the questions, comments, editorial advice, and friendship they continually provide.

Having the unconditional love and support of a sister, someone who will drop anything at anytime to be there for me, is priceless and rare. Sharon Enteen Prusso makes me constantly aware of how lucky I am to be her sister. Her terrific husband, Doug Prusso, always, always says yes, and never lets me stop laughing at myself. His help in my life exceeds words. Moreover, my BFF, Wendy Gold, like my sister and like a sister, offers me friendship, love, and support than I never dreamed possible before meeting her.

The Mitzner family gives me amazing strength and confidence. As I have often said, I can be anywhere in the world and, knowing I'm a Mitzner, never question that I should forge my own path and follow my instincts. Belonging to this incredibly quirky family filled with love, neuroses, passion, and originality is something I carry with me – they have helped me define who I am both in their own many ways of being and in their unconditional love and support (not to mention challenges), throughout my life. Bob Levy, Billie Mitzner, Isador Mitzner, Melanie Mitzner, Ginger Levy, Marci Mitzner, Nicke Gorney, Robin Levy, Mindy Mitzner Anastos, Kenzie Mitzner, Sheryll Mitzner, and of course, Mitzi, I love you and thank you for being there. Grandma Henrietta – who was by far the most original and inspirational woman I know. You, and my beloved Grandpa Morris, made sure I inherited your love of learning, stimulating me to push myself further in every direction. Their first daughter, my mother E. Nancy Markle, is truly a woman warrior. As the Chief Information Officer in several large corporations, she has shown me that women and technology suit each other – a major tenet of this book – as well as providing me with a model for smashing glass ceilings. Moreover, her love for me cannot be understated. My mother has given me invaluable life skills and enabled me to live a better life than I ever could have without her, supporting me in all my endeavors although they were not always her preferred routes.

I extend love and gratitude to my father, George M. Enteen, who inspired me to become an academic, as well as to embrace seemingly difficult languages, make unusual choices, and venture to faraway places, making them home. His constant grappling with new ideas – even after retirement – illustrates to me the value of this profession. More importantly, my father's love is profound. He holds dearest his role of father; it is wonderful to know this and realize that his love and support – of such great benefit to me – are one of the pillars of joy in his own life. Thanks also to the wonderful family that he provides, each one amazing and supportive: my Aunt Alice Learman, Michael Alevy, Jonathon Alevy, Adam Alevy, Sabrina Learman, Alejandra Palma, Gina Guilano, and Deb Alevy and, of course, the witty, special Julie Kagno, who has jumped so many barriers, all the while spreading her love and keeping the seriousness of life as light as is possible. Further gratitude to family members Rebecca Bitterman, Andrea Bitterman – in her quiet strength, and my two deceased grandmothers: Ruth Enteen and Sylvia Levy, and grandfathers: Robert Enteen, Morris Mitzner, and George Levy.

Thanks for the support and love I've received from my extended family, whom, through my daughters, will always remain close to my heart: Asli Julia

Weheliye, my "Swegie," and Barbara Weheliye, who for over a decade made Berlin a home for me. I am continually in awe of the strength Barbara has to live an uncharted life and constantly forge for herself Eine Heimat, a place to think, learn, live, and share with others. I furthermore extend gratitude for the affection and kindness I receive from Nur Achmed Weheliye, Samatar Weheliye, Daud Nur Achmed and Kadija, and Said Weheliye. And sincere thanks to Alexander G. Weheliye, who, for many years, shared his wisdom, experience, keen intellect, and humor, along with providing countless readings of my work, supplying my most useful suggestions and critiques.

Similarly, I thank my support system beyond the confines of the university: Gilla Davis and Judy Mendels-Peterson have provided emotional support that has enriched all facets of my life, and for that I am so thankful. Judy's insistence that I need not be overwhelmed, and her many strategies and daily support for helping me navigate through the small pieces that led me to the book's actual completion cannot be understated. Meredith Wu made sure, as a new mother of twins, I could do anything – and continues to both push and inspire me through support and through her own strong choices and convictions. Peace and love to Michael Faith, Dorie Silverman, Geri Blier, Lourdes Parres, Chris de Lizer, Patricia Hyland, and Jessica Friedberg, whose lives – on and off the mat – have made be realize that I am part of everything and can find everything I need and more within myself.

Special thanks to Valerie Conway, who has been the companion and best friend of the girls for years, growing from their caretaker to someone whose opinion and friendship I value deeply. And love to Arndt Weisshuhn and Mike Protevi – the greatest friends and godfathers there can be. Mike, you are my pillar, and I hope I am yours. Much affection to many amazing friends: Andrea Wiedermann, a terrific pal with a warm heart, great stories, and fantastic design skills, as can be seen from this book jacket which she created. Acki, Christian, Jamila, Patricia, Patrick, Roya, and Miriam – you've provided me with much support and kindness. Yves Clément, Michelle Koszuchowski, Denise Nunes, Sylvia Parker, Kelly Cassidy, Alexandra Silets, Suzanne Ryan, and Marnie Beilin, have, over the years, shared friendship in so many ways, each helping me with their unique strengths and their willingness to be with me at the drop of a hat. Heather Slonaker lives in my heart and always will. Chris Franko gave me more than a decade of support and friendship, knowing before I did that I could do all the things that enabled me to live the life and learn the things necessary to see differently.

Place and location, as the following pages argue, are crucial to consider alongside production and communication. For this I thank the Writers Work Space – Amy Davis, and the anonymous fellowship donor, in particular – for time in a great writing space. The Coffee Studio in Andersonville also serves a congenial atmosphere where I was able to work on this book. These locations are filled with kind writers that make writing work. In addition, material support in the form of grants from the Fulbright Scholars Foundation and Northwestern University were crucial to the production, research, and printing of this manuscript.

Finally, my love and gratitude for the unconditional love provided by Askar (who can't read this, but knows), Aaliya Rae, and Marlena Fanon, each of whom fills my life with intense happiness and keeps me joyfully engaged with the present moment as they bark, sing, and grow. They have been so patient, most of the time, as they waited for me to complete these pages – even if, as they often note, they've finished their own books many times over.

1

Introduction:
Life Skills

"Did you learn some computers today?"
(Grandma to Shawna, "Dirty Laundry")[1]

The idea for this project came to me at a part-time job I started in 1997 during my final years of graduate school. I was hired to develop a "Life Skills" curriculum to accompany a technology training course for twelve-to-sixteen-year-olds at Urban Technology Incorporated's[2] "Youth Leadership Academy." This engaged my interests in technology, urban youth, and popular culture, and afforded me a break from the long, isolating dissertation process. This project would lead to *something* and quickly – the program would be taught within days of its completion. Co-writer Jennifer Bransford White and I were to update and expand the "Life Skills" modules, incorporating information mandated by the State of New York for child foster care education programs while simultaneously imparting cutting-edge technology skills and captivating the attention of this challenging age group.

When the first group of students gathered in a basement room of the Concord Family Services foster care organization in the Bedford-Stuyvesant neighborhood of Brooklyn, most had never been in a room with a computer. Upon entering the lab, several of the eager novices raced to the computers, picked up the mice, and placed them directly on the screen. My co-writer recounted this event months later as proof that the participants had made great leaps in their technological literacy as a result of the Youth Leadership Academy. By the end of the six-week program, this group was able to produce more sophisticated spreadsheets than I can to date. But rather than the beginning of a trajectory of technological literacy, the students' initial impulses struck me as the reverse: why shouldn't a mouse elicit a direct response from the place it touches on the screen? What is logical or self-evident about the movement of a mouse on a rubber pad unattached to the rest of the hardware? Furthermore, what is obvious about clicking? Double-clicking? Suddenly, mouse technology seemed very counterintuitive, and it became clear to me that these teens had better ideas for the application of technology from the onset. A decade later, the iPhone is celebrated for allowing the user to interface directly with the screen, and Steve Jobs and his team at Apple are credited with the innovation. At Concord Family Services, not only were students taught to use technology in predictable ways, but their potential for technological innovation based on their own "life skills" was ignored. Their success in the Youth Leadership Academy depended on lowering their expectations about computer technology, curbing their imaginations, and accepting a cultural interface that did not reflect their lives or interests. Technology was demystified, yes, but in the process, creative inspiration that could have led to innovation took a back-seat to memorizing Microsoft iconography.

The following summer, I witnessed first-hand how these young people responded to their opportunities to acquire technology skills. Several students wanted to program sound into their personal webpages. Urban Technology, Inc. responded to their demands by drafting a musician to teach music software. The results were strictly local – they placed themselves "on the Web" sonically in a way that mirrored their self-perception. The pages they produced, therefore, ended up mimicking one another's. Like many of the other early personal webpages that littered the Web, they were full of smiley-face animations, lists of likes and dislikes, shout-outs to family members, and links to hip-hop sites.

When faced with an exercise to be completed without the help of a template, these "youth leaders" forged creative solutions. The online resources they found to accompany each "Life Skills" module, for example, showed inspiration rather than information regurgitation. Google had not yet begun to crawl, and the major search engines of the time had a reputation for delivering partial, suspect results, so participants were encouraged to use a combination of these algorithms and the ubiquitous "Links" pages to present fresh takes on oft-repeated topics (i.e. their annual nutrition class). One student provided a journalist's account of local-rapper-gone-global Lil' Kim and her diet. An examination of her idol's eating habits was fodder for a lively discussion with peers rather than a monotone report that mimicked school activities. The exercise not only required students to demonstrate a working knowledge of the World Wide Web and search methods, but it inspired them to conduct further research in an effort to substantiate their claims. The students discovered, through a review of Lil' Kim's regimen, what *not* to eat. The habits she claimed – perhaps in jest – had the students in stitches. Not only could they recognize the lack of balance in her candy-centered diet, but they were able to provide alternative meal choices that met Lil' Kim's lifestyle: frequent touring and few chances for home-cooked meals.

In the first year of the Youth Leadership training, instructors distributed paper manuals that guided students, step-by-step, through the technology modules. Impatient pupils often skipped steps in order to finish the lesson with time left to surf the internet. Often, the final product – a table, graph, or spreadsheet – would be missing some part that was included in the directions but overlooked in a stu-' dent's haste. Rather than returning to the text to retrace the missing steps, participants played with the application and figured out how to produce an identical final project on their own. Each assignment would inevitably contain as many variations in its production as there were students at computers, and, as a result, the class had a collective knowledge about the workings of the software that far exceeded required competencies. This information would be shared as students visited neighboring monitors to assist their friends. The following year, manuals were replaced by PowerPoint presentations; participants sat away from the computers and watched the slides projected on the wall. As a result, the students produced projects that more closely adhered to the steps outlined in the learning module. Thus the viewing-then-reproducing approach better facilitated the goals of the Youth Leadership Academy: students did indeed learn standard operating procedures and became fluent in officially sanctioned vocabulary, but gone were the creative deployments that stretched collective understanding and exposed the software's breadth and depth.

By the late 1990s, computer use was increasing exponentially, but websites and software were not necessarily performing as expected. At the time, usability studies were the central gauge for measuring the success of computer-related material. Energy was devoted to development rather than deployment. Furthermore, it was assumed that technological innovations and digital communication were enacted as their developers had envisioned them. The adoption of Microsoft's collective mind was taken for granted. In the introduction to their edited collection *Technicolor: Race, Technology, and Everyday Life*, editors Hines, Nelson and Tu note the limited criteria used by technotheorists to designate technological advancements.[3] They recommend "Casting our nets farther and wider" in order to "more fully realize the different levels of technical knowledge and innovation that individuals and communities" exhibit (Nelson *et al.* 2001, 18). They subsequently suggest that widespread attention paid to the "digital divide" may distract from the recognition of innovation by precisely the populations such discussions seek to address. Consequently, if the "digital divide" is the only lens for viewing the position of people of color vis-à-vis computers, and black urban foster kids are expected to be technologically illiterate, they will be treated as such and may internalize this belief (Nelson *et al.* 2001, 5). Moreover, talk of the "digital divide," important though it is, inhibits alternative formulations and discussions of non-dominant practices.

While Urban Technologies, Inc. was following a strict definition of innovation and literacy through their curriculum, they also encouraged their participants to take on the mantles of innovators, crafting websites for themselves and their communities. Between 1996 and 2000, I interviewed many young technorati from this program and others in New York. Their comments suggest that urban youth using internet technology shifted their view of the world within the Web. While initially optimistic about the internet as a medium for innovative ideas and community formation beyond physical borders, the youth I interviewed were becoming disillusioned with its liberating potential. Rather than giving up on the internet, they rethought its purpose and went local: representing a particular club or school, connecting with neighborhood friends, file sharing, and designing ground-breaking forms of expression using non-standard features of popular applications. New York based websites from programs such as Urban Technologies' Youth-on-Line, Youth Radio, Teen Voices, and Harlem Live![4] were crafted by low-income youth of color intent on forming communities and sharing experiences that originated in their homes, schools, and community centers and reached youth with similar interests. They educated their peers and built networks that united a population often depicted by mainstream media as unreachable, divided, and violent. In order to do so, they employed a specific style of language and used a range of strategies I term "digital creolization." Put simply, digital creolization is the adaptation and amalgamation of English-language terms in online spaces that intentionally modifies prior meanings in order to serve alternative, and often subversive, purposes.

Noting a dearth of similar websites in urban Chicago, I supervised interviews and observations between 2002 and 2004 concerning the online practices of Chicago-based, low-income, African-American youth. These teenagers perceived the Web as a "non-interactive" archive useful only for information retrieval. During the summer of 2002, my research assistant Anayah Barney spent four weeks at urban Chicago locations asking about and observing young people's computer use. The young people she interviewed gave her the information they *thought* she wanted to hear: they provided sometimes (false) email addresses they said they used to keep in touch with distant relatives and friends, and reported doing research for school projects, looking things up in the library catalog, and playing the occasional corporate-sponsored game. What she observed told another story. These youth were not using the Web to journey outward and explore the "wide world." Many of them did not even have email accounts. Instead, they used a familiar interface to send messages to their friends, often at the next computer, and talked about their friends on their profile pages located on portals geared toward Black or Latino populations, such as Black Planet (www.blackplanet.com) or Mi Gente (www.migente.com). Although these portals were marketed as forums for meeting new people and dating, these twelve-to-twenty-one-year-olds were not interacting with people they didn't know, but instead communicating with people they saw or talked to daily, e.g. leaving messages for their cousins or their classmates. They used the templates provided on the sites to represent their blocks, neighborhoods, or schools, and only responded to communication from their friends, family, and neighbors. The internet was another mode of local interaction, not a vehicle for outward voyages and novel encounters. Chicago urban youth in these venues did not want to use computers to forge non-local connections or reach a broad, virtual audience. Instead, they used public computers and the internet to deepen their connections with people they knew in their local, real-world environment. Years later, the wide adoption of social networking applications such as Friendster.com and Facebook.com confirmed that many users had identical desires for communication via digital technologies that enhanced their connections to friends and relatives in close proximity.

During the summer of 2003, Sonia Nelson, a second research assistant, observed eight-to-eighteen-year-olds at StreetWorks, a not-for-profit organization on Chicago's West Side. The organization sought to provide young people, mostly Black and Latino, with access to networked computers, as well as to introduce them to a range of digital media technologies. Located near public transport, the organization had established itself in the community as a meeting place; students on summer recess often dropped in to play Web games. Over time, Nelson noticed that, despite the set-up of the facility – approximately 15 desktop computers arranged around the perimeter of the room – visitors at StreetWorks chose to gather at only a few of the available terminals. Often, when playing single-user online games, one player would sit in front of the computer with a group of three or four peers standing behind, coaching and advising the seated student so that s/he might advance. The youths' approach defied expectations of how a desktop computer was to be used: one chair in front of a monitor positioned at eye-level, with a mouse and keyboard within arm's reach of a single user.

This collaborative approach was also employed when visitors sought information online. Although the computers at StreetWorks were public, the traffic was modest enough that youth found it worthwhile to wait for specific computers. Why wait when all browsers lead to the World Wide Web? Nelson discovered that the StreetWorks computer users had different senses of the local and the global than those touted by browser creators and internet service providers. For them, each computer held specific data: they relied on browser histories and caches to access websites they had visited in previous sessions or to learn where other visitors had been. They had created local banks of proven Uniform Research Locators (URLs), indirectly and inadvertently referred by peers. While they also used search engines to locate websites of interest, these were not the primary means for online exploration. Instead, they navigated the internet through traces stored in individual plastic PC boxes and shared by peers in a non-traditional, yet technologically sophisticated, manner. Rather than collecting favorites, bookmarking pages, or refining their ability to query the various search engines available, StreetWorks users displayed a grasp of specific browser application features that most casual internet users do not possess. Nelson's observations illustrate yet again that computer users may possess literacies that are not immediately legible as such. There are manifold ways to understand the internet; its location is not self-evident, and there is no necessary consensus among the digitally connected as to what constitutes the local and the global.

The uses of the internet by members of the "analog" side of the "digital divide" show, in these instances, that focusing only on a divide precludes recognition of unique or unexpected engagements with computer technologies. Those studying the digital divide must not be satisfied with the conclusion that some people do not have access or literacy. Instead, we must unearth the biases embedded in western culture, exposing the racist and gendered suppositions that continually proliferate, yet receive scant attention. What is considered technology and which cultural artifacts provide the inspiration for research and development are not neutral matters. The internet's current configuration is neither global nor universal. The "digital divide" is more accurately expressed as the gap between normative and non-normative practices than an inability or disinterest on the part of low-income users. Non-normative practices need not be considered less skilled, less literate, less strategic, or less effective.

Digital Communication and English

It was useful for earlier studies that fell under the rubric of Communication to place television in a category that considered issues ranging from broadcasting to spectatorship, and telephony in another that examined the implications of sound transmission or disembodied speech. At the current historical juncture of media convergence, however, interpretation of digital technologies must take into account the rapid shifts and flexibility of digital and analog transmissions. One might as easily be watching a downloaded television show on a portable personal viewing device as watching a cathode-ray tube emit light in the form of a live news event on network television. When we answer the ringing telephone attached to the wall, where analog sound waves travel through wires suspended between home and telephone poles, the voice that responds to our greeting may just have likely made its journey in multiple forms and following non-identical routes, whether as bytes from a cell-phone or via VOIP (Voice Over Internet Protocol). The end results of these transmissions are now integrally related.[5] The study of digital networked communication must acknowledge the complexity of these new vehicles for digital transmission and the increasing variety of interfaces possible for their consumption.[6] Yet these shifts of shape, sound, and configuration render the delineation of digital technology or computer-mediated communication (CMC) increasingly difficult. Computer-to-computer information exchange seems self-explanatory at first, and sending photographs and texts through email or Internet Relay Chat (IRC) is unqualifyingly accepted as CMC or Internet Communications Technology (ICT), two common denotations for categories of study. Yet, does the transmission of a digital image from a mobile phone to a computer count as digital communication? If so, shouldn't sending an SMS (short message service, also known as a text message) between mobile phones also be considered computer communication? Finally, why would text and image exchanges count as computer-mediated communication when the exchange of sound bytes that constitute cell-phone conversations does not? It must also follow that, if all cell-phone communication is necessarily ICT, then landline use must also fall into this category, particularly since, at present, computer interactions, at least when considering the majority of connections worldwide, still often take place via land-based dial-up connections.

Then again, what constitutes digital space? Like communication, the space of the digital serves to privilege placelessness over location – occupied, culturally imbued understandings of some bounded parameters. Cyberspace, which I discuss in greater detail in Chapters 3 and 4, posits a disinterested spacelessness, enabling greater-than-light-speed travel, an epistemological oxymoron. It imagines itself as nowhere, despite the geographical footprint of huge warehouses housing digital servers – not to mention the natural resources necessary for their continued maintenance. At the moment, much worldwide communication is digital, though the majority does not occur on the internet. Not only is the internet frequently considered solely in terms of information exchanged via email and the World Wide Web, but other forms of digital interaction have not received sufficient consideration – among them digital music sources, cell-phones, and e-pets. When including all forms of digital communication, it seems obvious that digital space is where many people are right now: we hear the ringtone we've programmed to denote a call from a friend; we watch PowerPoint presentations; we read our news from an RSS (Really Simple Syndication) feed. Delimiting the boundaries of the digital may no longer be possible; however, cyberspace is not some parallel dimension where we conjure a non-space linked securely to a place – such as a country – by typing in a URL with a country code Top Level Domain Name (ccTLDN) – ".uk," for example. No longer can we assume that at a ".com" suffix situates a company in the United States; in fact, such a website may not be a business at all. It may not have a location beyond the server that houses its digital domain.

Despite the many variances, digital communication has one surprising commonality: its connection to English – both as language and as cultural underpinning. English is embedded in almost every form of digital communication, from html and cell-phone programming to domain-naming practices. Worldwide participation by users from communities and nations where English is not the primary language outnumbers participation by English-speakers, regardless of how digital communication is defined. English serves as the de facto lingua franca of the computer-related technologies, particularly the internet and the World Wide Web. Similarly, the centrality of the US in World Wide Web and internet development and communication often facilitates the reproduction of hegemonic western discursive practices. Linguistic and geographical inequalities result from internet involvement, and the medium often extends the practices of earlier US-based English-language media such as television and film. This study recognizes the colonial and imperial histories of English-language spread, but does not assume that current English-language use in digitally networked environments is singly informed by these histories. Navigating between the critical-applied linguistic theories and the celebratory framework of appropriation linguistics, I move away from the all-or-nothing proposals that obfuscate most discussions of English-language use. Digital creolization is the process of English-language use rehearsed in formulations of nation, gender, and/or sexuality in or regarding computer-mediated technologies.

The English language is not a fixed, static means of communication in which grammar rules are to be respected and conventions duplicated. Non-standard English not only develops, it sputters, fizzles, spurts, oozes, morphs, travels, dis-assembles, and reconfigures – embodying adjectives that have been used to understand the mal-functioning of other "technologies" of movement, from steam and gas engines to electric currents and data bytes.[7] Locating English as a master language renders its non-normative users, in Gilles Deleuze and Felix Guattari's words, as "becoming minor," and, as a result, undergoing the process of deterritorialization. In "Minor Literature: Kafka," Deleuze and Guattari posit deterritorialization of a major language as a characterizing element of minor literature, written in the major language from a minoritarian position. As an a subjective assemblage, the "minor no longer designates specific literatures but the revolutionary conditions for every literature within the heart of what is called great (or established) literature" (Deleuze and Guattari 1993, 18). A minor literature is a "revolutionary force for all literature" (1993, 19). Expanding the tetralinguistic models of Henri Gobard, Deleuze and Guattari suggest that minor literature combines vernacular, vehicular, referential, and mythic languages. Becoming minor means being multilingual in one's own language, thus employing different language systems based on context. The process of becoming minor within the writing-machine of a "minor literature" involves voicing the multilinguistic resonances within language. To make a "minor literature," one must oppose "the oppressed quality of this language to its oppressive quality" (1993, 27). When a writer can become "a sort of stranger within his [or her] own language" (1993, 26), s/he creates minor literature through deterritorialization. Deterritorialization of language

> can have ambiguous edges, changing borders, that differ from this or that material.... Each function of language divides up in turn and carries with it multiple centers of power. A blur of languages, and not at all a system of languages.
>
> (1993, 24)

Deterritorialization occurs with language deployment by people who "live in a language that is not their own," occupying the "disjunction between content and expression."[8] The notion that literature becomes minor by being made strange through deterritorialization is an apt way to mark the moment where English is engaged strategically for online communication.

Cyberculture, Postcolonial, Queer: A Methodological Challenge

The internet seduces its users into believing that the entire world can be reached by clicking a mouse; yet the majority of users traverse only a fraction of available pathways. In what is often envisioned as virtual travel, most cyber-voyagers perform a limited range of online activities – email, electronic commerce, gaming, chat, and data-collection. Moreover, despite the myriad possibilities that connectivity offers, email and World Wide Web participation flows primarily to, from, and through US-based corporate aggregators such as search engines, television-related websites, and news portals. Assessment of computer-mediated communication (CMC) as it is practiced is often overlooked, yet it is crucial to study digital dialogues in their complex and multifarious deployments. Importantly, more expansive awareness of the scope and types of online interactions can influence not only corporate, but more inclusive development of internet features and functions.

Internet use has become standard both for communication and for knowledge transmission throughout the world. Vital to the way we now understand information production and retrieval, the internet was initially celebrated as a revolutionary medium affording distinctive possibilities for communication. Often thought of as more democratic than previous media, the internet has been cited by many academic and journalistic sources as housing the potential for community formation beyond national boundaries and identity construction freed from the material constraints of gender, race, and class. Taken at its broadest, the internet – a digital medium that invites convergence with almost every other form of media – is indeed central to the way those with access understand communication, time, space, information production, and its retrieval. While the internet's ability to reach beyond national borders calls to mind umbrella terms such as "globalization," it is necessary to note that globalization has no single definition, nor is there such a thing as globalization in the abstract sense. Still, many contemporary understandings of globalization ignore the contours of the unbounded internet and gloss over the persistent inequalities embedded in its use. For the purpose of this book, globalization is not simply the acceleration of pre-existing circuits of trade and migration, or the spread of ideas and the conquest of territories. Instead, globalization marks a qualitative change in technology, communication, and social relations while increasing the influence of once-remote people, markets, and ideas. Fortunately, more in keeping with this perspective, recent scholarship has moved beyond utopian pronouncements and has instead evaluated user experience with respect to specific iterations of the internet such as World Wide Web use, email, or IRC.

While innumerable studies address how digital technologies influence identity and mediate a variety of social practices for groups in the mainstream, populations that take up different instantiations or relatively little bandwidth are rarely considered. Scholarship vacillates between two extremes, on the one hand arguing that New Media abolishes racial, ethnic, and national boundaries, and on the other contending that online practices conform to, and even enhance, contemporary geopolitical inequities, amplifying, rather than rearticulating, dominant forms of expression. Internet-based cultural practices are indeed shaped through hegemonic discourses that emanate from western-derived conceptions of individual subjectivity and identity-based politics. These culturally skewed configurations are also embedded in hardware and software.[9] Global finance under-girds internet interaction, so that only particular bodies are linked and only particular discursive formations are rendered legible.[10]

The narratives and conversations taking place in cyberspace relay the complex interconnections of participants' conceptions of culture, race, gender, and nation,[11] yet New Media scholars' concentration on dominant internet practices and their capitalist-based logics inadvertently overlooks these interconnections in order to render visible the complexities of US-centered and corporate-based Web presences. Furthermore, CMC tend to treat digital communication, and World Wide Web sites in particular, as static documents in predominantly English-language environments that possess unchanging and atemporal geo-political coordinates. English is presumed to be the lingua franca of the World Wide Web despite the rapidly increasing linguistic cacophony within the confines of Web browser technologies. Thus the coexistence of sites and conversations not concerned with commerce, US-based institutions, or world events monitored by the US media are less often the object of statistical and/or theoretical attention and marginal users were, until recently, overlooked. Important contributions made to Internet Studies by Radhika Gajjala, Ananda Mitra, Chris Berry, and Fran Martin, among others, reveal this oversight and decenter the United States by considering a range of alternative practices and participants in online environments.[12] As a result, the communicational, dialogic, dispersed, and constitutionally non-unified aspects of websites are beginning to be recognized as crucial areas for scholarly attention.

Internet scholars' lag in recognizing practices and populations not clearly speaking the language of top-down, US-centric global capitalism can be partially attributed to the disciplines that house this newly emergent field. Initially, the methods used to analyze digital communication reflected two sides of a disciplinary divide. Since Internet Studies often resides in Communications departments, quantitative approaches that generate statistically driven outcomes abound. This model privileges the collection of large amounts of data that is analyzed using algorithms, providing content analysis and resulting in definitive conclusions. Alternative approaches derive from a Cultural Studies framework and rely on anecdotal evidence to excavate the ideological apparatus that gives meaning to texts within specific cultural milieu. According to this method, objective conclusions are ontologically impossible. Cultural Studies consists of a diverse set of practices and forms of evidence, as described and enacted at length by Dick Hebdige and Stuart Hall.[13] For the social scientist, however, anecdotes do not constitute evidence. This reduction, meanwhile, is for the humanities scholar untenable, as any claims to objectivity can only be understood as naivety. Rather than recognizing disciplinary differences and attempting to build bridges, the two sides of Internet Studies initially argued this methodological impasse, too distracted to incorporate other knowledges.

Consequently, Internet Studies stands at a peculiar, but potentially powerful, juncture of disciplines and means of knowledge production. As the field has matured, the subjects of scrutiny, as well as the disciplinary frameworks for analysis, have blossomed. As critical race theorists and anthropologists, feminist/gender theorists, and postcolonial scholars enter the field, they bring with them the tools and ideologies of their disciplines. This leads, in the best-case scenario, to what queer theorists have described as the "lack of fixity" that enables a dynamic, responsive analytical model without rigid methods or pre-articulated subjects. Eng, with Halberstam and Muñoz, considers this the political promise of queer theory: "its broad critique of social antagonisms, including race, gender, class, nationality, and religion, in addition to sexuality."[14] For Internet Studies, this might be recast to include digital media that can reveal "social antagonisms" in their many instantiations – competent as a field in displaying a range of subjects and realizing what seems to remain potential, if not virtual, in terms of interdisciplinarity.

The above list of "new scholars" is purposely problematic. Putting feminists and gender theorists, for example, in a single-word formulation is extremely reductive. The subject of what constitutes first-wave, third-wave, or post-feminism has been the subject of many book-length studies. Similarly, "postcolonial" is not meant to signify an easy alliance, even among those who situate themselves squarely within the rubric of the term. The field has never been cohesive, and quickly after it assumed an external sense of coherence, Postcolonial Studies fragmented and overlapped into studies of diaspora, colonization, coloniality, and more.[15] I put these categories together to strategically signal the complexities of all conceptually dynamic fields – similar to the disciplinary dynamics that might be embraced as Internet Studies. Feminist/gender and postcolonial theorists, in particular, recognize that any form of data collection reflects those involved in the process and that local conditions must be more than briefly considered. They not only foreground the ubiquitous grasp of European thought, particularly when construed as reason, logic, universal, and objective, yet persist in presenting their projects from the constraints of comfortable binaries: self and other, online and real life, center and margin, first world and third world. While in many ways useful, the critique of knowledge acquisition from a Cultural Studies perspective can lead to an unending self-critique and apologism which functions to dismiss rather than decenter its position.

Postcolonial Studies turns its gaze to what has been situated as the margins of knowledge production, creating, in effect, new centers. One shortcoming is that this preoccupation with centers and margins overlooks the dynamics different from those presupposed in this formulaic configuration. In her seminal essay,

"Under Western Eyes," Chandra Mohanty demonstrates that good-hearted, well-researched western feminist interpretations of non-western women are built upon assumptions that necessitate new processes for analysis that carefully examine the relationship among studying subjects, subjects of study, and results, i.e. data, information, and interpretations that are gleaned and circulated as knowledge.[16] We see in Critical Race Studies that problematizing rather than generating knowledge may lead us down interesting avenues. For example, Hazel Carby advocates, "black feminist criticism be regarded as a problem, not a solution, as a sign that should be interrogated, a locus of contradictions."[17] All forms of data are contradictory and multifarious: information is messy – from the ways and motivations of subjects that provide it to the results generated through its analysis. Data interpretation must be seen as always in process and ideally should face scrutiny from multiple theoretical lenses. Recent works in Internet Studies that incorporate critical race, gender, and postcolonial theory from the onset have produced remarkable readings of human involvement with digital technologies.[18]

Virtual English is situated within the framework of Cultural Studies, queer theory, gender theory, critical race theory, and poststructuralist accounts of the possibilities of technology. As borders, boundaries, and online practices are inscribed globally by the ever more consolidated new world media, the examples in this study query what constitutes the international, the national, and the local. Current global inequities are reinforced by widespread conventions for naming, locating, and conceiving of digital media. Queer theory is the guiding theoretical apparatus for this study – perhaps precisely because it lacks form.

In "More Queer: Resources on Queer Theory," Elia, Swanson, and Goldberg discuss the interdisciplinarity of queer theory, and the relatively late integration of queer theory within Communication Studies.[19] While queer theory too often imagines universal theories of gender and sexuality, it was, in its inception, radically opposed to a fixed subject or practice, a political metaphor without a fixed referent.[20] In Lauren Berlant and Michael Warner's essay, "What Does Queer Theory Teach Us About X?" the authors refuse to define queer theory, asserting instead that queer should take the form of commentary.[21] The main thrust of inquiry under the mantle of queer, they suggest, should "sustain awareness of diverse context boundaries" (Berlant and Warner 1995, 344). They argue:

> unlike some varieties of traditionalism, queer commentary refocuses to subordinate emergent cultures to whatever happens to pass for common culture. We want to promote the building not of culture in general but of a culture whose marginal history makes it inevitably controverted...
>
> (Berlant and Warner 1995, 349)

I am attempting to account for the existence and expression of a wide range of positions within several distinct cultures, not interconnected through globalization, but certainly in dialogue with US and European conceptions of gender, the heterosexual/homosexual binary, national culture, and nationalism. I use the term "queer" to mark a flexible space for non-dominant cultural reception and production. Queer is manifold in my deployment; it not only reveals heterosexism, but unearths the western identity constructions that under-gird much of gay and lesbian online productions originating in the United States.

As both critics and fans of "queer commentary"[22] have noted, while initially imbued with radical potential, queer theory has stagnated in practice by refusing to note the embedded, yet not identical, intersections of race in heteronormativity.[23] This occurs when the object of queer theory becomes identity-based. By using the term "queer," I hope to reassert a sense of difference that takes the "marginal," particularly the erotically "marginal," as, in the words of bell hooks, "a site of resistance" and a "location of radical openness and possibility."[24] In the instances of cultural production and reception I examine, queer erotics are already part of the producers' and users' centers, occupying positions other than those of dominant, US- and Euro-concerned frameworks. Potentially, queer theory could disrupt the teleological model of sexual identity formation fostered by the presumption of a unified global sphere of desire and its articulation, proving that sexuality is organized in tandem with other cultural forces such as race, ethnicity, and nation. It is from this angle that queer theory guides my analysis.

Put differently, Eve Sedgwick writes, "Queer is transitive – multiply transitive."[25] Positioning communication as the means for locating queer effects, Sedgwick states, "Speaker and interlocutor reflect on ways in which language really can be said to produce effects: effects of identity, enforcement, seduction, challenge" (Sedgwick 1993, 11). Taking up Sedgwick's challenge to excavate language and the effects of communication on queer-theory-related concepts, I scrutinize the English language, with an eye toward locating its functions and their effects in non-normative contexts; this marks how queer methodology might usefully position English as the primary axis for my analysis and communication as inherently a medium where English might be queer. Consequently, English in digital communication provides the structural adhesive in the pages that follow, and sexuality acts as a secondary vector. This allows me to unveil some of the racisms, ethnocentricisms, and unexamined commitments to globalization and nationalism intrinsic to some internet sites, and, more importantly, to reveal where website producers are resisting, reframing, and recasting the dominant assumptions thought intrinsic to these terms through their use of queer practices. In this way, the impetus that Sedgwick identifies may be ongoing: *queer* describes "the experiential linguistic, epistemological, representational, political adventures" of sexual identities and interpersonal communication (Sedgwick 1993, 8).

Cobbling together personal correspondence, formal interviews, content analysis, ethnography, and close textual analysis, this project might be said to deploy what Judith Halberstam refers to as "scavenger theories."[26] Class and caste are, perhaps, the weakest of the issues I examine since the majority of the producers I discuss live outside the US yet have access to computers, internet connections, and enough education to write English-language texts. Ethnicity, gender, sexuality, geography, and national belongings are the axes that are extended or demand reconsideration as a result of what I claim to be emerging non-dominant practices online and their ideological implications. The economies of place, space, gender, race, sex, sexuality, nation, and location are powerful constructions – constructions that, as Lancaster and Di Leonardo write, "carry long and complicated histories of conquest, resistances, exploitation,... and neocolonial structures."[27] By analyzing this range of material, I hope to effectively render visible some of these structures and economies as well as their normalizing forces.

Attending to material practices that appear in digital representations, I pay close attention to the local by examining single pages displayed at a moment in time, while also taking into account the broader contexts reflected by these texts. Recent collected works in queer theory have taken up the call for a "transnational turn," one that stops positing the nation-state as antithetical to the global, globalization, or globalisms.[28] Rather than placing the nation and the global in a hierarchical binary, I explore how the reach of digital communications, presumed at least potentially global, can trouble our understandings of geography and the nation. In a McLuhanesque sense, the global village means that social and cultural life and identity flow through increasing media connections, not only money and commodities. Recognizing the inability to divorce the nation from the global, Tze-lan Deborah Sang points out in her study about Chinese women and same-sex desire, "even when a particular non-Western space for inquiry is ostensibly identified as the nation, it is always already shot through with colonial, imperial, transnational, cosmopolitan, global – whatever we call it – presence and valence."[29] I seek to not only recognize the persistence of historical domination but illustrate its complicated and contradictory traces in current formations of transnational interaction.

Virtual English examines the ideological implications of current conceptions of the internet and the World Wide Web. It bridges the chasm between the glorified perception of the internet's potential and the everyday use of emergent technologies by investigating alternative practices rarely charted in considerations of digital environments. By analyzing the internet activities of overlooked populations, this book reveals that corporate intersections are circumvented and dominant communication practices are subverted in response to the agendas of users. As Nina Wakeford states, "Whereas the production and consumption of cyberqueer *activities* is flourishing, cyberqueer *studies* in general are at risk of lagging behind by ignoring economic and political conditions which are inevitably intertwined with the social and cultural features of their representations."[30] Thus this discussion could be considered a kind of double negative: I hope to, in effect, "queer," or de-naturalize, what appears to be a proliferation of normative gendered roles, gay identities, and national and international belongings available to internet users, as well as reveal the moments where economic and political conditions allow for their recasting. I use the World Wide Web to queer, or trouble, assumptions about gender, sexuality, and, nation, remembering that digital spaces are real-life places we inhabit and not the special haven cyberspace narratives promise.

In fact, globalization – both online and off – is not simply homogenization. A visit to one of the many Thai, men-seeking-men websites or to a Bangkok mall complicates the notion that globalization flows from a single source – be it the US or Japan – or remains authentic in its consumption and effect. Irony, affect, camp – all of these play a role in the dialogue that accompanies the arrival of globalization and the circulation of global commodities, languages, and identities. *Virtual English* contributes to and expands this emerging field by locating instances where non-mainstream participants use digital creolization to resist the hegemonic norms of cyberspace, computer-mediated communication, nation, gender, and sexuality. This study investigates contemporary internet participation as unevenly coterminous with the expanding forces of global capitalism, potentially, though not inevitably, magnifying current postcolonial structural inequalities. Digital media have provided the means for individuals and small organizations to recast their community membership, forming local, national, and international coalitions. These subjects are appropriating, broadening, and splintering the English language, extending local patterns of communication, and discussing alternative agendas. Furthermore, artists and Web designers from these populations have responded to the internet by proposing alternate versions of digitally enhanced futures and deploying digital media strategically. The rarely examined work of these producers is often aimed at and accessible to dominant populations.

Concern about the validity of conclusions drawn from the lens of postcolonial theory is especially relevant when considering countries that have never been colonized or countries that, like Thailand, have experienced colonial pressure without sacrificing their independence.[31] Until Thailand's recent shift to an outward-looking economy, Thai was the primary language and regional languages such as Isaan, a dialect close to Lao, and Hill-Tribe languages eclipsed the use of western languages. Thais themselves controlled the internal production and interpretation of cultural practices, national identification, and historiography. Discussions of "the postcolonial condition" must therefore take into account Thailand's specific circumstances.

Overlooking the perpetuation of economic disparities between the first and third worlds in favor of celebrating the breakdown of geographical boundaries and gender restrictions further entrenches imperialist economics. Extending postcolonial theory, internet theory should "foreground a politics of oppression and struggle, and problematize the key relationship between center and periphery" (Mitra 1997, 276). Anne McClintock considers how postcolonial theory may fall short:

> If postcolonial *theory* has sought to challenge the grand march of Western historicism and its entourage of binaries (self–other, metropolis–colony, center–periphery, etc.), the *term* postcolonialism nonetheless reorients the globe once more around a

single, binary opposition: colonial–postcolonial. Moreover, theory is thereby shifted from the binary axis of *power* (colonizer–colonized – itself inadequately nuanced, as in the case of women) to the binary axis of *time*, an axis even less productive of political nuance because it does not distinguish between the beneficiaries of colonialism (the ex-colonizers) and the casualties of colonialism (the ex-colonized).[32]

McClintock worries that the term "postcolonial" re-centers considerations around the ex-colonizer's axis of time. To indiscriminately apply a western theory based on the experience of colonialism to countries with different colonial circumstances can only lead to false conclusions. Yet even this falls short of current conditions, as it renders the inevitable, simplistic dualism of colonizer and colonized as a monolithic circumstance wherein power flows unilaterally. The creolization that accompanies colonization and reveals change, resistance, and instability is not at all visible here.

With similar concern, Rey Chow asks:

> Is the "post" in "postcolonial" simply a matter of chronological time, or does it not include a notion of time that is not linear but constant, marked by events that may be technically finished but that can be fully understood only with consideration of the devastation they left behind?[33]

Time, accompanied by language, is dramatically redeployed in internet use and digital communication, and Chow marks the potential schism in its understanding. Internet Relay Chat is instantaneous, yet non-interactive instantiations online hold a peculiar notion of permanence. While Twitter supplies every movement of its users, and IRC and text messages require immediate attention, early webpages were presumed permanent and static. I examine this and other disjunctures through my exploration of Web pages and how they do not adhere to predesignated notions of time.

Despite the self-consciousness and what Charles Taylor describes as "melancholia"[34] of postcolonial practitioners, the emergence of postcolonial theory and its attendant studies have produced new understandings of the margin, centering the margin, one might say, in its content and analysis. Gayatri Spivak argues:

> Postcoloniality as agency can make visible that the basis of *all* serious ontological commitment is catachrestical, because negotiable through the information that identity is, *in the larger sense*, a text. It can show that the alternative to Europe's long story … is not only short tales but tampering with the authority of storylines.[35]

Of course, once the margin occupies the center as the primary subject position, it rejuvenates the centrality of this position, where knowledge as positive knowing is made possible. Kalpana Seshadri-Crooks is attentive to the consequences that accompany the use of an undefined or uncritical notion of the margin.[36] As she writes, "the exploration of postcoloniality from the point of view of the margin (as the excluded and the limit) can be thought of as the realm of scholarship … that energy [of postcolonial studies] arises from its indeterminate location and failure to recoup the margin" (Seshadri-Crooks and Afzal-Khan 2000, 18). In a similar fashion, the lack of specificity in generalized internet discussions re-centers the United States, making the experiences of its subjects represent those of all internet users.

In order to disrupt this, Internet Studies must specify which geographical boundaries are being corroded, and in what contexts. Moments of gender slippage must be examined alongside examples of gender reification. This study complicates the assumptions of postcolonial theories, the fixed notions of what constitutes community and national belonging, and general assertions about internet communication. The presence of stereotypes of Thai women on the World Wide Web illustrates the continued dominance of western-based ideologies about gender and nation in this medium. However, by examining the dynamics of this image production, analyzing the ways in which such representations are engaged with and refuted, and isolating the practices of the Thai women who communicate in the midst of these images, I offer a complicated, and, at times, contradictory, interpretation based on specific instantiations.

This book contemplates instances where internet practices intersect with and reinscribe local environments, noting the confluence of offline and online boundaries as they pertain to specific groups that might be labeled "minorities," even within minority-centered discourses. In other words, while most current writing considers how identity and community are constructed in online environments and comment on radical differences between online and offline identities, this study queries how collective formulations such as political movements, ethnic communities, and groups that distinguish themselves vis-à-vis genders and sexualities represent offline realities through their online interventions and how the online and offline coexist unevenly to produce online discursive formations.

Rather than postulate how identity might shift in new ways, I provide concrete considerations based on specific populations: a futuristic, fully wired community based on the histories of its Caribbean ancestors, Sri Lankan Tamils in diaspora dedicated to creating a virtual nation-state/homeland, participants in an online forum concerned with gendered assumptions regarding Thai women, and Thai men in Bangkok who identify as "gay." Each iteration of computer-mediated communication offers unexpected responses to the forces of globalization and predominant US value systems, disrupting the notion that the internet produces a singular articulation of time and/or space. Focusing on the contributions by these doubly-displaced yet still at home groups reveals that, although the internet might function as a central means of communication and reflect offline culture, the effects vary widely. Radhika Gajjala sets forth a challenge I endeavor to meet:

> With almost everyone on the Internet now claiming to be marginalized voices that are being "empowered" to speak back to the center – where and how are we to locate the center? It becomes more important than ever, therefore, for Internet and cyberculture

researchers to re-examine conceptual categories and frameworks such as "diaspora," "globalization," "new media" and even "empowerment," "multiculturalism" and "voice/voicelessness."[37]

The participants and their contributions to our digital imaginary augment both our understanding of what occurs on the internet and in real life. Finally, the issues I consider are not at the forefront of non-European-centered itineraries. While gender has achieved global attention, gender concerning Thai women is suspect,[38] as is nation with respect to subjects considered to be terrorists, and "gay" with respect to men considered to be imitating the western, "global" gay.

Virtual English: An Overview

The chapter that follows provides the framework for the practices I dub "digital creolization"; subsequent chapters clarify digital creolization through its specific instantiations. By exploring particular authors, worldviews, sets of webpages, or populations based on geographical/internet correlations and identity constructions where ethnicity, gender, sexuality, and national membership provide intersecting junctures that are rarely isolated in dominant digital practices, I conjure four instances that fall under the rubric of digital creolization. The examples I provide should not be considered a full account of digital creolization and its processes; they, instead, gesture to the myriad ways that digital creolization might be imagined. I hope that the moments I've outlined provide a starting point, inspiring the recognition of digital creolization in arenas where it was formerly not considered. To this end, the next chapter, "Booting Up: The Languages of Digital Technology," defines digital creolization by putting into dialogue analyses of the globalization of English and linguistic, social, and cultural theories of the rise of Caribbean Creoles. I suggest that English is constantly creolized in its digital deployment. It undergirds both our conceptions of hardware and software, as well as their relationship, and it is also stretched to meet the needs of its users. Although the internet reproduces western ideologies and practices, buttressing the values and inequities of current social, economic, and political formations offline, it also supplies a venue for a broad range of transmissions.

After the groundwork for the practice has been laid, I examine the four specific articulations of virtual English creolization. Chapter 3, "'On the Receiving End of the Colonization': Nalo Hopkinson's 'Nansi Web" analyzes appropriation and adaptation of English in Nalo Hopkinson's novel *Midnight Robber* (2000). By situating herself "on the receiving end of the colonization," Hopkinson provides unconventional predictions for technological development and correspondingly unorthodox outcomes for relationships between humans, technology, and their environment. She achieves this through creolizing the English language by incorporating Jamaican and Trinidadian Creoles. Like Hopkinson, the characters she conjures, located on a distant planet, break and create code, "hacking" in their mode of narration as well as in their conception of a technologically mediated community.

Positing certain notions of cyberspace as more logical than others is not a "disinterested" aesthetic strategy; the envisioning of space or networks inscribes particular relations of power. In Chapter 4, "Configuring a Nation," I argue that current procedures for identifying the location of electronic data, URLs in particular, situate the internet and the World Wide Web as geographically based systems with corresponding geopolitical reference points in the physical world. The prevailing archeology ties individuals to physical locations, perpetuating the idea that the Earth consists of a conglomeration of nation-states with bounded territories and national subjects. Some websites, however, resist this model, such as those launched by citizens of Tamil Eelam, members of what might be termed a stateless nation that use the World Wide Web to argue their agenda, organize, and inform electronic visitors. These Tamil Eelam websites perform digital creolization to exploit the Web in order to constitute a citizenry and nationality without territorial confines. Tamil Eelam websites invoke chronological narratives ranging from (pre)historical accounts to late-breaking news reports; they strategically deploy domain-naming conventions and dominant metaphors of the internet, space, and networking. Nationalism and national membership are inspired by and exceed the linguistic and information-gathering standards of international journalism. By doing so, these websites both utilize and exemplify strategies that influence national recognition and inspire nationalist sentiments.

Many internet theorists suggest that when Web users create virtual personae, the social constraints of the "real world" are diminished. Yet, more often than not, the narratives and conversations taking place in cyberspace relay participants' conceptions of culture, race, gender, and nation, as well as the intersections that occur when each complex individual with distinct histories and identities comes into contact with remote locations. Chapter 5, "Mixing Up Siam," considers how Thai women's contributions to a particular website, the Thai-managed, English-language SiamWEB.org, function to simultaneously renegotiate and reinscribe conceptions of community formation, gender, and nation. SiamWEB.org supports intercultural communication, presuming that conversations between Thais and non-Thais interested in Thailand will adjust how Thailand is understood and will revise inappropriate characterizations. Through processes of digital creolization, particularly evident through the strategies they use to encourage non-native English involvement in conversations surrounding these dominant representations, SiamWEB.org challenges the status quo, reformulates the western sex/gender regime and nomenclature, posits always-in-process subject positions for Thai women, and questions the conventions circumscribing national membership.

In my final chapter, "Bangkok Boyonthenet.com," I considered whether, and in what ways, Gay.com might be recognizing the specific circumstances of Thai gay men rather than reproducing a universal model of gayness that ignores nuanced circumstances inherent to varying localities. Although the site Gay.com claims to incorporate Thai gay men in contemporary Bangkok, some of whom do visit the site, Thai gay men more often visit websites that reflect their identity with greater linguistic and cultural specificity, such as Palm_plaza.com. This chapter examines some of the sites these men report frequenting, with an eye toward elucidating the larger implications of location and representation. After interviewing over 100 Thai men who identify as gay in Bangkok (June 2004), I found that being gay in Bangkok usually includes the use of the English language and initiating cross-cultural interchanges, and, as a result, many of these sites are predominately English-language, yet the ones reported by these men are not categorized or listed by Google.com or other search engines. Instead, word of mouth in the physical gay locales of Bangkok and links between sites serve to spread the knowledge of their existence. Not only does this chapter acknowledge that the needs of Thai gay men are changing, but it seeks to answer how popular websites are responding to and accommodating them. Rather than acceptance of gendered, racialized, supra-national, primarily sexual identities that are assumed of gay Thai men linguistically and geographically on Gay.com or by Google.com searches, I find processes of negotiation.

The epilogue, "The Medium Massages," points out that all media function as movement – whether through vocal-chord vibrations or the rapid switches of electronic flows that embody digital connectivity. All messages require manipulation of medium, and neither the medium, the message, nor, for that matter, McLuhan's "massage," can be separate elements from one another. Remembering that every time someone uses hip new programs forged by some young American guy for converging communication in some new way (be it via Skype, Second Life, or Google), HIV-positive sex-workers at dirt mines in the Congo or World of Warcraft gold-farmers in China contribute to digital communication. Examining how these normally overlooked contributors apply digital creolization helps to see beyond what the World Wide Web is said "to be," marking a few of the crosscurrents of virtual English in its manifold functions.

2

Booting Up:
The Languages of Computer Technologies

> This tongue that I have mastered
>   has mastered me;
> has taught me curses
>   in the language of the master
> has taught me bondage
>   in the language of the master
> I speak this dispossession
>   in the language of the master
>
> ("Caliban," Abena Busia)[1]

His Master's Voice:[2] Three Examples

Example 1: No terms exist independently of the cultures from which they emerge. While technical terms are often presumed to be objective – merely naming that which they delimit – nominal acts reflect specific histories and desires that intersect with technology–culture–human interfaces. Sexuality, sex, gender, and race are inextricably encoded into computer-related nomenclature, even in the language describing the most basic hardware. For example, the cables that attach computers to peripheral devices such as printers, monitors, projectors, mobile phones, and cameras end with interlocking connectors, designated "male" and "female." Naming these connections as such posits a productive pairing as male and female, a choice that renders this a seemingly natural or obvious coupling (more obvious than, say, 0 and 1, the on/off binary pairings that underlie all computer functions). That a "productive" pairing occurs in the union of male and female connectors perpetuates heterosexism, the belief that heterosexuality is

"His Master's Voice."

superior to other forms of human relationships. Female connectors are imagined as a series of holes always ready for penetration by male protrusions – corresponding pins extending outward from a base. Cables connecting the Central Processing Unit (CPU) to other devices generally have *two* male ends or connectors, ensuring that the monitor, printer, scanner, and Ethernet cables that attach the computer to a network are exclusively male. The female is confined to the "receiving end" located on the devices themselves. In other words, the network is intrinsically male – its winding, phallus-like cables penetrate devices in order to control them. Without penetration, these devices remain barren.

Male and female ports.

This lexicon was drawn from earlier vocabularies of the electrical and mechanical trades. Thus computer hardware, instead of functioning as the vanguard for new imaginative frontiers,[3] replicates the restrictive sexed and gendered assumptions underlying earlier "wired" technologies, reinforcing electrical and mechanical paradigms rather than reformulating them. Despite the male and female designations, gender, not sex, is the word used to describe the pin and socket designation (see "Gender changer," image below). In this scenario, newer paradigms of understanding are rejected, and no fresh vocabularies are forged around how sex, not gender, might better circumscribe these techno-genitalia or how male and female pairings need not be productive or originary. In the last 20 years, under the banner of Gender Studies, gender, sex, and sexuality have been effectively destabilized – revealed as constructs embedded in

Gender changer (source: www.cable-trader.co.uk).

specific, local, historic, and cultural containers rather than as universal norms. In the wake of this profound shift, connector-cable terminology demands closer scrutiny. Situated at the intersection of technology and language – what is often called the human–computer interface (HCI), or more accurately for my purposes, technology–culture interfaces – gender conforms once more to sex-organ homology. A "gender changer" is required if two female or two male parts are to be connected.[4] Not only does this validate male-to-female pairings, it suggests singling out same-sex pairings as unnatural because they can only occur with the help of a technological mediator. Increasingly, however, Bluetooth, wi-fi, and other non-cable-based connections threaten this order. As a result, the winding phallus no longer occupies an essential, or even central, position in the pairing of wireless devices.

The gender of connectors is the first of three examples concerning hardware that I provide to unveil the lingering traces and fundamental non-dualism of hardware, software, and notions of interface. The overlap of digital with analog, language with meaning, and technology with culture, problematizes the discreteness of naming, meaning, and history. After considering the use of English, particularly in computer-mediated environments, I will survey theories of language creolization, noting how English might productively be understood as continually undergoing such a process. The practices I investigate suggest that "digital creolization," my term for this English-language engagement in digital networked communication, occurs not only as a means for operating in transnational computer-mediated environments, but also for communicating strategically, refusing to blithely accept supposedly standardized data-entry procedures and the accompanying terminology.

In the chapters that follow, I rely on this foundational blurring to reveal alterations in the English language as a result of conversations ensuing from contact via digital technologies. I view technology, particularly computer-mediated, digitally networked communication, as enmeshed in the cultural, political, social, and economic concerns of its users. Interpretations of this technology navigate between New Media theories that seek to dismiss the "newness" of New Media communication by yoking it to cinematic representations and those that celebrate it as an unprecedented epistemological break that heralds an entirely novel set of circumstances and effects.[5] Instead, I emphasize that linguistic apparatuses are not received identically by all who encounter them, and that traces of meaning are embedded in digital communications.

In general, humans encounter the world analogically. Vision, for example, is an analog experience because we perceive infinitely smooth gradations of shape and color. Most analog events, however, can be simulated digitally. Examples that are presumed digital, for instance the words on the pages you hold in your hand or the photographs in newspapers, consist of an array of dots that are either black or white. The pixels cannot be seen unless under a microscope, and thus what you perceive is necessarily analog. Although digital representations are approximations of analog events, they separate into bytes, discrete units of binary code, and thus travel differently, take up less storage space, and are easily manipulated. The trick that is touted as the wonder of the "digital age" lies in the conversion: from analog to digital to analog, or simply from digital to analog. Accompanying this wonder is what Otto Imken calls "cyberbole," or anxiety about this conversion and its blurring of the opposition between real and virtual.[6] The binary systems that support both digital technologies and western epistemologies necessitate the imposition of artificial distinctions, posited as extremes of one another. This imposition of binaries – and their constant need for maintenance – stimulates anxiety concerning what is "authentic" and what is "other." But precisely because these distinctions are contrived to begin with, they can never be kept fully separate.

Example 2: In order to experience the cacophony of techno-enhanced possibilities that define our "digital age," one must first "boot up." The metaphor is clear: this chapter should feel like those moments after you press down the power button on a personal computer: anticipatory. You start reading, (hopefully) get engaged, wait patiently while you accrue background information, and gain the competence necessary to understand the chapters that follow. When you *boot up* your computer, you wait for it to become not only different than before, but better prepared to carry out the functions you desire. Less obvious, however, are the layers that are embedded in this term from histories of western conquest to the influence that fiction writers have on how we imagine technology.

Booting up is the period after switching on a computer and before the operating system is fully functional. During this time, a "fixed sequence of instructions … initiate the loading of further instructions and ultimately of a complete program" that launches the operating system, enabling a computer to appear and act as expected.[7] Initially called "bootstrapping," booting up suggests the paradox of getting something from nothing, as an entry in Wikipedia.org (the popular Web-based, participant-authored encyclopedia) describes: "It is the problem of starting a certain system without the system already functioning … solutions,… called bootstrapping,… are processes whereby a complex system emerges by starting simply and, bit by bit, developing more complex capabilities."[8] In order to commence its functions, a computer is figuratively expected to pull itself up by its bootstraps.

Booting up or bootstrapping exemplifies "faulty" translation, with dubious origins and questionable veracity. In most cases the origin of the term "bootstrapping" is attributed to the adventures of German nobleman Karl Friedrich Hieronymus, the Baron of Münchhausen (1720–1797), about whom tales of wonder were circulated throughout Germany and Britain. The genesis and authorship of these tales, however, are contradictory and confusing, and bootstrapping is not, in fact, mentioned in any incarnation of the original Münchhausen publications. The brief account that follows illustrates how the historical traces that adhere to vocabulary infuse current uses with rich, layered meanings. While most computer users do not ponder the roots of the term "booting up," the sense that it originates elsewhere supplies an aura of cultural history that adds resonance and depth to the mere pressing of an on/off button.

Karl Friedrich Hieronymus served in the Russian cavalry during two Russian campaigns against the Turks. These campaigns are purported to have led to the crumbling of the Ottoman Empire; as a result of these victories, the Russians gradually amassed land during this period. Multiple accounts of European history chronicle these campaigns and the accumulation of land as the beginning of the European alliance among Russia, Poland, Austria, the United Kingdom, and later France. These Russo-Turkish conflicts mark the shift from eastern domination to western/European supremacy. Due to the long decline of the Holy Roman Empire of the German Nation, also known as the end of the First Reich, Germany would not join this alliance for some time. Hieronymus' participation thus signaled particular initiative on the part of a German to commit himself to the creation of the occident at the expense of defining the Orient. The Ottoman Empire was the only non-European power to seriously challenge the growing influence of the West between the fifteenth and twentieth centuries, functioning, in effect, as an integral part of the European balance of power.

Baron Münchhausen's stories cast a European protagonist against the Turks, who were depicted as barbarians threatening a civilized Europe. In Edward Said's well-known argument concerning Orientalism, the production of texts that originated in England, France, and then the United States depicting Arabs, Turks, Islam, and the Middle East during the nineteenth century actually created a divide between the East and the west. Orientalism fixed the west as culturally superior to the East. Notably, Said's work fails to include Russian Orientalism and pointedly excludes German Orientalism, both of which he suggests had "clean" pasts,[9] yet the stories surrounding Karl Friedrich Hieronymus in the name of Baron Münchhausen depict strategic positioning vis-à-vis Russia, Germany, and the Turkish Empire that pre-date Said's study. The tales recount eighteenth-century conflicts that are predicated on an alignment that would eventually articulate a cohesive Europe, one that is superior and in direct opposition to the Turks and the Ottoman

Empire. These tales therefore serve as prototypes for the production of Orientalism, the very process detailed by Said. The Baron, a clever European individual, single-handedly outsmarts leagues of unintelligent, war-mongering Turkish battalions; other tales range from improbable feats achieved by the Baron during his time in the Russian cavalry to voyages to the heart of Africa, the Americas, the moon, and the land of cheese. These stories supply justification for Europe's imperial project and construct non-Europeans as others unfit for self-rule, whose territories deserve to be conquered.

The Münchhausen stories have no clear origins. Although authorship is generally attributed to the oral recollections of the Baron himself, the printing and dissemination of the tales are sometimes described as direct transcriptions and other times considered to have served as inspiration's fodder. While extant manuscripts printed in Germany between 1781 and 1783 still exist, British copies from this time are also found in some archives. Early versions were also circulated as children's books, appearing first in English (1785) under the title *The Surprising Adventures of Baron Münchhausen* (or *Baron Münchhausen's Narrative of his Marvellous Travels*).[10] The children's tales are likely to have been translated from English to German by Gottfried August Bürger in 1786. It wasn't until 39 years later that the author of the first English edition, which most bibliophiles consider to be the first publication, was revealed to be Rudolf Erich Raspe (1737–1794), a German scientist and librarian. Raspe's edition inspired enlarged collections: in the same year that the British children's version appeared, a German edition was published claiming to be a translation of Raspe's version. The language, location, and authorship of the original tales were a source of argumentation that appeared in the prefaces of the printed versions of these early editions.

Gradually, Münchhausen's name became associated with the amusingly preposterous story or the lie winningly told. Later, authors used these stories as source material to exaggerate still further or to compose other tall tales of a similar mode. Even the attribution of the term "bootstrapping" to Münchhausen's tales is unverified. In what is often recounted as the most famous account of his improbable battle tales, the Baron avoids drowning in a marsh by pulling himself up by his own hair.[11] It wasn't until the nineteenth century that the bootstrapping tale was featured in most German and English editions. Accuracy, language of origin, authorship, not to mention the content of the tales themselves, have been debated since their initial incarnations.

In fact, the word "bootstrapping" may have originated in the United States.[12] Despite multiple attributions concerning its initial meanings that have been traced back to the mid-nineteenth century, by the late nineteenth century, pulling oneself up by one's bootstraps referred to a quotidian expectation rather than a fabulist feat of remarkable ingenuity. One key example in the US context is the phrase's use as a rallying cry for racial reform. Booker T. Washington, founder of the Tuskegee Normal and Industrial Institute in Alabama, suggested that former slaves might pull themselves up by their bootstraps, although the exact phrase does not appear in any transcription or in his autobiography, *Up From Slavery*.[13] In his famous 1895 address at the Cotton States and International Exposition in Atlanta, Georgia, entitled "The Atlanta Compromise," he summed up his bootstrapping philosophy without using the term directly:

> The wisest among my race understand that the agitation of questions of social equality is the extremist folly, and that progress in the enjoyment of all the privileges that will come to us must be the result of severe and constant struggle rather than of artificial forcing.[14]

Pulling oneself up by one's bootstraps was the prerequisite for access to the rights and privileges of citizenship. Other African-American leaders and intellectuals, most notably W.E.B. Du Bois, contested this proposal. They criticized what was referred to as "Washington's Bootstrapping Plan" as apologist and far-fetched, given the almost non-existent resources held by former slaves in the South.

In many instances, science fiction has provided fodder for technological designers as they visualize and name their innovations. The term likely entered computer jargon by way of Robert A. Heinlein's short story, "By His Bootstraps" (1941).[15] A pioneering text on time travel, it helped bring acclaim to Heinlein, who, along with Isaac Asimov and Arthur C. Clarke, was one of the most widely read science-fiction writers in the United States. The first such writer to publish in mainstream newspapers like the *Saturday Evening Post*, Heinlein reached a broad audience that included technological developers.[16]

Even a term as innocent as "booting up" possesses deep cultural (mis)references. European noblemen simultaneously mapping and conquering the Orient lie at its root. In the United States, where the majority of computer hardware and software was initially designed, the overcoming of systemic racial and economic inequities is also intrinsic to the term. The expression "bootstrapping" might be said to have multiple, scattered origins, all of which reflect the vexed issues central to the particular historic situation of its enunciation. Although the term's historical sediments encode the tensions between German and British publishing, the creation of a unified Europe, and its attendant colonial projects, bootstrapping also has particular resonance in the US context, one that recalls the struggles surrounding slavery and its aftermath. In US parlance, the term does not suggest superhuman capabilities, but rather encapsulates the conviction of many that immigrants or people from impoverished backgrounds have the same potential for socio-economic achievement as those more prosperous, if only they apply themselves. The term has circulated worldwide, carrying with it German folklore, British worldviews, US race relations, and, now, US-based digital capitalism – all encapsulated in the pushing of a button on a byte-caching, electronically stimulated, all-too-often white,[17] rectangular box. "Booting-up" in most contemporary English-language venues conjures personal computers and anticipates technologically advanced environments while retaining inflections from previous deployments.

Example 3: As can be seen in discussions surrounding the "digital divide," US-based issues concerning race persist when considering computer imagery. The choice of nomenclature for digital devices reveals efforts to manipulate and massage objects – such as storage drives – or supposedly opposing ontological categories – such as hardware and software – into their hierarchical relations. Because hardware and software do not function as discrete categories, much like human bodies refuse to conform to precise racial designations, terminology created to designate the relational aspects of hardware and software must account for overlap with regard to computers' physical capabilities (hardware) and coding (software) in order to express mutual interaction. My third example is the use of "master" and "slave" to refer to the structural procedures prescribed for the interaction between data-storage units. When more than one hard drive is installed on a computer, each drive potentially competes for control. To allow multiple drives to function in harmony on a single computer system, the controlling (or start-up) drive is designated the master drive and the other drives become its slaves. In effect, the master hard drive is no more than the first drive the computer recognizes in the process of initiating system procedures, including booting up. Information Technologies expert Greg Lanier explains:

> On a functioning computer, the master drive contains the operating system and the control mechanisms to reach and access the secondary drives. . . . Without the master drive, the system would be useless because the underlying operating system is mandatory for everything. If you try to place your [operating system] on a secondary drive, trouble ensues.[18]

The "trouble" suggested by Lanier has been a preoccupation of philosophers, those sold into slavery, slave owners, and all involved in its resultant economies since the inception of the transatlantic slave trade.[19] Considering the internal operations architecture of those devices networked with personal computers, US-based developers' word choices indicate complicated historical circumstances. In 2003, after complaints from its employees, the County of Los Angeles issued a formal request that computer vendors stop using the words "master" and "slave" in all computer documentation. Imagining a master/slave relationship among hardware components anthropomorphizes the computer's structure in ways that echo imperial conquest, colonial response, and the history of slavery in the United States, much in the same way male and female connectors demonstrate and reinforce heteronormativity.

Nomenclature carries associations of prior and future uses, infusing referents with context, history, and anticipation. Jacques Derrida suggests that the "presence" of writing inherently contains traces of both the past and the future.[20] The idea of a meaning-full present depends on this trace, which is an effect of writing. Derrida builds upon Sigmund Freud's discussion of the trace as an effort of life to protect itself through deferral, thereby constituting a reserve. As our present changes constantly, the traces of writing are unfixable. The present moment is rendered "meaning-full" only through the reserve of past and future meanings that coincide with an encounter of a word within the text surrounding it. Thus, our word choices for such mundane activities as pushing the "on" button to start our personal computers privilege certain histories over others, reflecting past uses in new configurations. The constant redeployment of culturally specific languages in New Media reifies the histories from which the terms were derived, reasserting the foundational position of these cultures and rendering them eternal truths.

This key juncture of technology and language, where gender, sex, sexuality, race, ethnicity, nation, and other modes of thought form a networked relay chat, operates in digital technologies on at least four levels. The first, as I've just illustrated, occurs at the level of semiotics, when a word taken from a historical lexicon such as colonialism or racial slavery names a computer-related object or procedure. Since all words have traces, they are not neutral but rather infused with many lingering meanings. Consequently, when words are imported into computer-related linguistic registers, their meanings are not contained by that which they name. With digital transmissions, a second level of meaning-making occurs: binary code is translated into analog images for human perception. This is referred to as the human–computer interface but is, as I have said, more appropriately described as a string of technology–culture interfaces in which human subjects represent one of many links. In *The Language of New Media*, Lev Manovich replaces HCI with "cultural interface" as he finds it better represents how we are forced to interact with cultural data when using computer technologies, whether coding an operating system or interpreting a "desktop."[21] With internet communication, the interface extends beyond desktops, files, docks, and stacks to include websites, most of which follow a series of once arbitrarily, but now conventionally, formatted "pages" (including a "homepage," the default start page specific to the browser), "location," or "directions" (where the website is anchored to an offline location). As syntagmatic chains of signifiers, particularly those delineating spatial relations, are redeployed in New Media lexicons, their signifieds are rendered entrenched in earlier spatial and temporal syntagms.[22] We now expect that a blog will look a certain way and provide information according to the conventions of information architecture, just as we know that a personal webpage will present information differently than a social networking site. Moreover, although individual sites are expected to "improve" or add "features," optimizing their appearance and functionality over time, websites with similar functions move in conjunctive ways. Social networking websites such as Friendster.com, MySpace.com, and Facebook.com do not vary tremendously from one another, yet in the past five years there have been remarkable shifts in their overall appearance and functionality; a Friendster profile from 2003 can no longer be read on the 2008 version of the site. Thus icons suggesting a computer's operations and internet generic structures form two additional interfaces where the digital and the cultural collide.

Finally, English-language terms used in or about computer-related environments often reveal traces of United States histories and Eurocentric worldviews.

Even when no historical referent can be found, the graveness of these encoded western ideologies should not be overlooked.[23] Catachresis renders them visible while simultaneously destabilizing a term's pasts, exposing the overall tenuousness of meaning. Some of these instances also indicate examples of digital creolization, and concept metaphors. When non-standard English is employed online, it is often dismissed as faulty by linguistic gatekeepers. However, I contend that many of these instances are not mistakes but, rather, demonstrate acute attention to shifts in language, form, current and historical circumstances, and power. By invoking yet altering particular words or phrases that have several entrenched meanings, online users can consciously evoke more traces. Thus, these catachrestic instances reclaim codes and can be recognized as communicative utterances of strength, strategy, and coherence. I now turn my attention to less monolithic, yet meaning-full, presents by positioning together linguistic accounts of the globalization of the English language and those of Creole language development. Comparing these to literary and philosophical examinations of creolization as a form of poetics suggests how we might begin to conceptualize innovative internet-related English-use concerning gender, sexuality, ethnicity, race, and nation as digital creolization.

Globalized English, Cultural Collisions

The potential of the English language to be understood as a creole – and not specifically English as deployed by digital networks – is suggested by the chapter's epigraph, "Caliban." The poem, by Abena Busia, a US-based Ghanaian poet, critic, and professor, intimates the vexed relationship of the English language to the majority of those who adopt it. Busia's "Caliban" reminds us that the acquisition of English involves violence, subjugation, power, and an audience. The title recalls Shakespeare's infamous monster, underscoring the perpetuating cultural capital of canonical British literature. Busia's poem gives fluency to the frustration of *The Tempest*'s Caliban, making explicit the play's historical context of conquest, the slave trade, and the Caribbean-based plantation system.[24] The creoles that emerged from the Caribbean, as the poem's narrator suggests, not only "mastered" her and "taught" her "bondage," but also gave her the language to resist ("curse") and rearticulate ("speak this dispossession"). Shakespeare's English has not simply subjugated those upon whom it has been inflicted; rather, its adoption has resulted in linguistic changes that reflect the conditions of enunciation. The poem maintains that English has both been mastered by the speaker and become her master. While the language has been an imposition, a forced procedure for enunciation, it allows her to speak of dispossession – a state that might not have existed had it not been for the imposition of language, but one that surely now exists and requires a tongue for its expression. The master's language is thereby the vehicle through which Caliban's dispossession can be articulated. Busia ties English explicitly to the Caribbean slave trade and the resulting emergence of Creolized English – the welcoming/imperializing bind. While creolization is often used to describe processes of hybridization, diaspora, mimicry, and mixing, I want to stress its unique suitedness in describing the contacts of cultures, the linguistic results, and the potential for different futures gestured toward in Busia's "Caliban."

Assertions about English's spread by popular linguists such as David Crystal posit standardized English as a *naturally* global language. Crystal reasons that English possesses a "'welcome' given to foreign vocabulary" and an "absence in ... grammar of a system of coding social class differences."[25] Such overarching, unqualified suppositions infer that English-language spread is a result of its superior qualities. Crystal implies that English somehow entails a critique of ethnocentrism and hierarchies articulated through social class. The ethnocentrism of US foreign policy and tourist practices are not qualities within the language itself, according to Crystal's assessment. However, the embedded class markers of British English have been thoroughly remarked upon by scholars and represented in endless productions of popular culture. Crystal's theory of English implies neutrality, ignoring that its use privileges native speakers. Claiming English's suitability as a world language suggests that the cultures from which it evolved are highly advanced and appropriate for global domination. Crystal dismisses the histories of imperial and capitalist forces that have mightily informed English language spread and, consequently, disregards the continuing colonial and military aggression initiated by English speakers on behalf of their nations and specific group interests. The cultural superiority conferred to the language cannot be severed from the structures of cultural and economic dominance employed by its speakers.

The line of thinking asserted in much of critical applied linguistics recognizes that English-language use is not neutral; instead, such linguists focus on the imperial effects of English-language teaching. Taking a similar approach to Ngugi wa Thiong'o's influential *Decolonizing the Mind: The Politics of Language in African Literature* (1986), these linguists reason that English cannot be severed from colonial pasts. Thiong'o argues against the use of English for African writers' expression. Building an African literature in native languages, he explains, is the only way to break the colonizing effects of English. In a similar manner, Robert Phillipson in *Linguistic Imperialism*, Alistair Pennycook in *English and the Discourses of Colonialism*, and other linguists concentrating on English-language acquisition presume that English as a Second Language is a direct response to the aggressive practices of English-speaking cultures.[26] Their studies assert that the spread of the English language entails unidirectional domination and imperialist control. This position, however, renders non-native English speakers or English speakers outside the US and UK pliable and powerless victims of continued subjugation.

Janina Brutt-Griffler rebukes theories that position English as unilaterally aggressive, critiques the presumption that learning English necessarily entails submission, and objects to terms such as "imposition, dominance, subordination, hegemony."[27] Other linguists who reject the tenets of linguistic imperialism employ a framework of appropriation. Linguistic models of appropriation, however, provide an equally reductive model. English is taught and acquired in monocultural transmission: either Anglocentric ideology accompanies the study of the language or locally specific contexts that reject a broad notion of "western values" are presented via the study of language. Once again, students are assumed to receive and digest the cultural tenets present in the course material rather than to negotiate the language as they study it.

Instead, Brutt-Griffler reasons that English is constantly remade as an international and locally responsive language. This resonates with Homi Bhabha's influential assertion that the "ambivalence of colonial rule" inherently contains the capacity for resistance through mimicry. Because Bhabha insists colonial subjugation be recognized as an interactive struggle, and mimicry entails language acquisition, "linguistic multivocality" can disrupt processes of domination through re-interpretation and re-deployment of received discourses. This creates an "agonistic space" (Bhabha 1994, 181) that exists on the borders where cultures meet. By extension, as new speakers for Bhabha, colonial subjects in particular – speak the language, they reconfigure it, but it is also theirs. Complicating Bhabha's generalization concerning mimicry through language acquisition, Vicente Rafael details the different effects of language acquisition felt by Spanish and by Filipinos during the Spanish colonization of the Philippines: "For the Spaniards, translations were always a matter of reducing the native language and culture to accessible objects ... subjects of divine and imperial intervention" (Rafael 1988, 213). For Tagalogs, translation held a profoundly different meaning; it was "a process less of internalizing colonial-Christian conventions than of evading their totalizing grip by repeatedly marking the differences between their language and interests and those of the Spaniards" (Rafael 1988, 213). Pushing this further, Brutt-Griffler contends that English's widespread use has required that the language no longer has "owners" – English must surrender its claim to a single point of origin (Brutt-Griffler 2002, 32). Thus creolization, the new language emerging from the antagonistic space of English (or Spanish) by non-English speakers and mixed with intention with other languages, is distinct from mimicry, recognizing the asymmetrical relations inherent in the contact of peoples and cultures produced through language.

Bhabha's description of mimicry does not mean that opposition is clearly articulated, but rather that it adheres to enacted conformity by those oppressed. Bakhtin finds hybridization to be "a mixture of two social languages within the limits of a single utterance ... separated from one another by ... social differentiation, or by some other factor" (Bakhtin 1981, 358). Hybridity, and by extension, creoles, are thus posited as two languages of differing status mixed. My discussion of creolization does not assume such an easy relationship. Many languages come together to form a creole, which itself becomes a language with a unique vocabulary that no longer can be simply located by an originary set of languages. Furthermore, one cannot assume that there is a unidirectional relationship between the components of the language. Many competing factors affect the dynamic development of language, and linguistic consciousness is not a singular positionality. Creolization explains the gaps in the English book, described by Bhabha as rightfully "one of the most elusive and effective strategies of colonial power and knowledge" (1994, 85). Moreover, calling into question the authority of the English book is essential to recognizing the work being done by those speaking "bad English" and presumes that mimicry repeats rather than replicates through the very act of enunciation. Leaving a trace, the second-hand, and the artificial in its utterance usefully disrupts the ability to claim monolithic colonial power and a stable, dominant culture. Yet while this instability is produced, the discussion stops there. My consideration of creolization comes from a standpoint that hybridity and ambivalence are a priori, but also problematic in their simplicity. Creolization for this study will take the next step, queering these a priori postcolonial moves in order to show language as dynamic, multidirectional, and no longer laying claim to an irreducible original. As a result of the mixture of cultures and peoples, as well as changes in the landscape and communication media, language happens; it is responding to present circumstances and is dynamic just as much as it is reliant on pasts and traces.[28]

Similarly, Ronald Judy argues that the widespread use of English by former colonies renders meaningless the claim of a singular point of origin, insisting that the language has cleaved from a particular cultural or national referent. In his list of national English-language cultures, however, Judy does not sever English-language use from imperial and colonial pasts:

> English as a global language … does not indicate any particular national culture. It is neither English nor British, neither North American nor Australian, neither South African nor Indian, neither Jamaican nor Singaporean, nor does it stand for anything like a cultural aggregate of all these. We simply have no idea what English stands for except the global market – itself a vague reference – which is to say, we have no idea what it stands for culturally.
>
> (Judy 1999, 4)

While the English language, for Judy, suggests globalization and capitalism, English is deployed by so many people that it no longer can be assumed to mimetically reflect single cultural anchors. Octavio Paz echoes this sentiment when he claims that every text is unique – not merely a translation of something before it: "No text can be completely original because language itself, in its very essence, is already a translation" (Paz 1992, 154). Thus there is no original, no copy, no essence, no singular culture in any deployment of English.

Even "native" English use contains indeterminable mixtures of cultural signification. Judy's examples position English users in a complicated nexus of dominating and dominated histories. For instance, while Singaporean English-language use is the result of British colonialism, Singaporean dominance over foreign, less-fluent guest workers reflects linguistic hierarchies privileging native English speakers. For Rafael, Judy, and Paz, globalization is not primarily economic, uni-directional or representative of a monolithic culture; rather, it is a complex mix of practices entwined with language use. Both Brutt-Griffler and Judy eschew either/ or models of English-language spread, understanding English use by non-native speakers as not necessarily transferred following the patterns taken for granted by many linguists where knowledge is bestowed from fluent native speaker to lan-guage learner.

Creole connotes a rich and varied geographical, cultural, and linguistic history. The circumstances that lead to creole development are extreme disloca-tion and the will to survive: creoles develop when their speakers are wrested from native languages and practices. Creoles emerge when several cultures are force-fully brought together, consequently manifesting properties that reflect cultural collisions and new social relationships.[29] The politics that correspond to earlier linguistic interpretations of creole communication reflect creole philosophy that emerged in the early twentieth century among French colonial subjects such as Martinican René Maran, Georges Garros of Cochin-China, and Paul Dussac from Madagascar, each of whom critiqued French colonial racism in favor of a cultural sense of creole that combined the effects of colonization and slavery with an ancestry from Africa, Asia, and Europe. As Firdous Azim points out in his discus-sion of Bertha Mason from *Jane Eyre*, a Creole occupies a complicated, racialized position, one that is neither white nor black/South Asian/Asian:

> As a Creole, she is differentiated from the "authentic" native, and represents multi-ple points of dislocation that the colonizing venture had brought in its wake…. The racial classification is based not on colour alone but on displacement from the place of origin.
>
> (1993, 182–183)

With no native land and no fantasy of origins, Creole subjects could imagine a social body that is primarily dislocated, and without fixed coordinates: this body potentially bridges the African, Asian, Caribbean, and Indian Ocean worlds.[30]

Creole was historically considered to be the body of linguistic practices used by non-Europeans inhabiting European colonies; today, it most often designates the forms of communication that emerged on Caribbean islands controlled by the French and British during the installation of the plantation systems that exploited slave labor. Formerly identified by linguists as oppositional to language, creole was considered a non-grammatical response to colonial dynamics, an incomplete form of communication created by inferior thinkers that deserved enslavement and domination. This designation as a non-language incorporated Europeans' disdain of colonial occupants and non-Europeans. Defined as oral languages with no standard written form, creoles were generally seen as degenerate forms of language, or non-language, until Derek Bickerton's work on creoles as analogous to the primary language acquisition of children. While positing creoles as languages, Bickerton's model positioned them as primitive models of language that effectively mimicked the practices through which children acquired speech and comprehension.[31] By yoking creole to primary language acquisition, Bickerton enlivened the study of creole, marking its importance as a linguistic model. Still, this link between creole development and early linguistic acquisition rendered creole inherently less sophisticated than European languages and condemned its speakers to forever occupy an infantilized position.

Users of English increasingly dismiss grammar and words they find irrelevant, crafting a language that expresses the particularities of local situations.[32] A broad range of authors who have published substantial bodies of work in English, including Salman Rushdie, Chinua Achebe, Louise Bennett, and George Lamming, concur that the language does indeed respond to their demands. Rushdie writes:

> those peoples who were once colonized by the language are now rapidly remaking it, domesticating it, becoming more and more relaxed about the way they use it – assisted by the English language's enormous flexibility and size, they are carving out territories for themselves within its frontiers.[33]

Populations in India, Sri Lanka, and Nigeria have long histories of crafting "pidgins," where grammar reflects the regions' primary languages, and, after generations, this English creole now functions in some communities as a mother tongue.[34] Although English has not necessarily expunged all vestiges of subjugation, it is increasingly shaped by its users who, in expressing their difference, articulate new lexicons and grammars. This may be understood as a slower version of creolization, one that reflects changes in domination and submission. English creolization, following creole development, is a tool that, through enunciations, provides resistance, adaptation, and the use of many cognitive skills.

Several linguists argue that creolization, language transformation, and language acquisition, once thought to be distinct linguistic practices, are, in fact, profoundly connected.[35] Many of the features thought to be unique to creolization are now recognized to be complex, convergent linguistic and learning processes. Traditionally, creoles have been noted for their extraordinary rate of development. Because they came into being within and in response to systems of oppression, Edouard Glissant and Derek Walcott, among others, insist that creoles inherently possess qualities of resistance: "The role of Creole ... was [historically] that of defiance. One could ... define its new mode of structured evolution as 'negative' or 'reactive,' different from the 'natural' structural evolution of traditional languages."[36] Caribbean Creoles, in particular, they argue, reflect their environments. The oppressive circumstances surrounding their conception imply that they are founded upon conflict, performing subtle yet violent reappropriation mobilized in the act of locution. In a similar vein, linguists such as Michel DeGraff now recognize that creole formation entails complex cognitive procedures involving a great deal more intellectual work than the cognitive demands necessary for combining prior languages or acquiring a language.[37] In the 1970s, creolité (the term employed by Francophone-based creole writers) and creoleness that encouraged the use of creole in artistic production took on political agendas that sought to reposition its marginality, popularize it, and reinvigorate its development. It was then recognized to be responsive to local circumstances and resistant to simplistic domination.

In dialogue with the pejorative tone of earlier discussions of creole communication by linguists and others, Franz Fanon suggested caution when privileging creole language. He preferred taking a political angle, one that emphasized race and class, and aligned colonized subjects against the colonial presence. Fanon's conception of creole is acknowledged as a form of belonging through revolutionary ideals, and an approach to avoiding the psychosis embedded in colonial histories. His view of the function of creole as a means for communication, however, is much more critical.[38] A former student of Aimee Cesaire, Fanon writes disparagingly of the use of French and Creole, as opposed to native languages, finding both manners of speech to be forms of inner-colonization. Fanon notes that when the Antilles were under French rule, French fluency allowed for the transcendence of certain aspects of blackness: "The Negro of the Antilles will be proportionately whiter – that is, he will come closer to being a real human being – in direct ration to his mastery of the French language."[39] Fanon's assertion of Antilles Creole as closer to French than local Senegalese dialects inspired Senegalese natives to learn Creole in order to command more respect in extra-national contexts. According to Fanon, Creole is not a language of resistance but a static dialect that causes psychic alienation and dehumanization. While he admits that "we were not mistaken in believing that a study of the language of the Antilles Negro would be able to show us some characteristics of his world" (Fanon 1967, 38), he finds no evidence that an educated native possessing French fluency would employ Creole as poetic or resistant. The vestiges of colonialism have rendered the Antilles native "no culture, no civilization, no 'long historical past'" (Fanon 1967, 105). Fanon describes a linguistic hierarchy that functions to sever one from one's history:

> Every colonized people, in other words, every people in whose soul an inferiority complex has been created by the death and burial of its local cultural originality – finds itself face to face with the language of the civilizing nation.... The colonized is elevated above his jungle status in proportion to his adoption of the mother country's cultural standards.
>
> (Fanon 1967, 19)

For Fanon, Creole as a language cannot escape its link to French and its colonizing impulses.

Edouard Glissant similarly considers the psychic dimensions of creole acquisition, describing the "non-functional situation of Creole" as a "language of neurosis" (Glissant 1989, 128). Forced poetics, he writes, occurs when language fails to reflect new circumstances: "the stage of the secret code has passed, but language (as a new opening) has not been attained" (Glissant 1989, 125). Unlike Fanon, he believes there is a next step, enabled by Creole. Achieving a natural poetics, a non-neurotic new formation, is predicated on "transforming a scream (which we once uttered) into a speech that grows from it" (Glissant 1989, 133). Creolization holds the potential for this liberated speech to emerge, all the while remembering its histories and heritages, and referring to the contact of cultures in these novel situations. Most importantly, this new, liberated speech is not predictable, planned, or pre-determined.

No language acquisition can seamlessly mirror its imperial history. Etienne Balibar argues: "it is always possible to appropriate several languages and to turn oneself into a different kind of bearer of discourse and of the transformations of language" (Balibar and Wallerstein 1991, 98). Importing English does not lead to uncritical absorption; rather, language has the potential to eject, ignore, negotiate, and/or increase the layers of meaning. "Ideally, it 'assimilates' anyone, but holds no one," writes Balibar (Balibar and Wallerstein 1991, 99). Similarly dominant linguistic theories of English-language spread fail to consider the complexity of language use and render English a monolithic tongue. Creolization offers an alternative, open model where multiple histories, subjects, and futures are encapsulated through marking change.

Creoles provide alternative vernaculars and the means for dialogic response which, from their onset, enable novel forms of expression that resist through selective incorporation and adaptation of the privileged grammars and standardized forms of the colonizers' languages (French, English, Spanish, and Portuguese, in particular). Insofar as creoles came into being within and in response to systems of oppression, Glissant and Walcott, among others, foreground the break from a European heritage and the resistant properties rooted in creole's genesis.[40] Edouard Glissant explains:

> The role of Creole in the world of the plantations was that of defiance. One could, based on this, define its new mode of structured evolution as "negative" or "reactive," different from the "natural" structural evolution of traditional languages. In this, the Creole language appears to be organically linked to the cross-cultural phenomenon worldwide. It is literally the result of contact between different cultures and did not preexist this contact. It is not a language of a single origin, it is a cross cultural language.
>
> (Glissant 1989, 133)

Here Glissant is in dialogue with comparative linguistic theories that assume a "tree" model for the evolution of languages, suggesting, instead, like Deleuze and Guattari, the structure of a rhizome.[41] Furthermore, much like Judy and Derrida in their discussions of English and French, Glissant resists the idea that language has a single origin. He attributes the emergence of creole to a moment of contact between cultures rather than labeling it an offspring or branch with European linguistic roots. Analyzing creoles in such a way reiterates the notion that they are not imposed upon their speakers but are, instead, created by them. Thus, creoles defy the "structural evolution" claimed of "traditional languages."

Similarly, in the manifesto *Éloge de la Créolité/In Praise of Creoleness*, Jean Bernabé, Patrick Chamoiseau, and Raphael Confiant assert that Creole languages recognize that there are alternative histories of the Caribbean as well as other approaches to conceptualizing literature that should be foregrounded. Creoleness illustrates that "ancestors are born every day and are not fixed in an immemorial past" (Bernabé *et al.* 1997, 97). A comprehensive consideration of Creole, they assert, "*shall create a literature*, which will obey all the demands of modern writing while taking roots in the traditional configuration of our orality" (Bernabé *et al.* 1997, 98).[42] Ancestry is no longer fixed in some unlocatable past, but is fluid, changing with linguistic use. Creoleness is the "annihilation of false universality, of monolingualism, and of purity" (Bernabé *et al.* 1997, 90). Its use reflects continuous change and looseness (Bernabé *et al.* 1997, 105). For this reason, creole describes the choices made by English-language users to employ new linguistic formulations that refuse grammar conventions and destabilize historical precedents. Creoles embody meaning-full linguistic presents that are in dialogue with complicated sets of pasts and futures; they do not fit neatly into categories defined by the languages that predate their formation.

Recent assessments of the function of creoles have pushed further their creative potential, figuring them as a natural/new poetics. "New poetics" implies the ability for expression where meaning erupts beyond the words that represent it.[43] Form, function, values, and beliefs unique to its creators are embedded in language, and resonate beyond words. In addition to Glissant and Bernabé *et al.*, writers who have discussed the potential of creoles to embody a new poetics include Derek Walcott, Salman Rushdie, Chinua Achebe, Carol Boyce Davies, Mae Henderson, Paget Henry, Edward Brathwaite, and Kobena Mercer.[44] As Paget Henry explains:

> poetics is much more than the strategies by which meanings are produced in texts. It is also an ordering of meanings that is capable of shaping human behavior. In other words, when poetically constructed systems of meaning are internalized, their rules of formation, transformation, and deformation become a grammar of human self-formation and motivation.
>
> (2000, 104)

The excess of meaning and "action-orienting potential" of poetics is embroiled in the deployment of Creole and, by extension, in the creolization of English (Henry 2000, 104). A new poetics insinuates creation beyond mere linguistic evolution.

English as "vernacular literature" – writing in language normally reserved for spoken utterances – may also be compared to creolization. Vernacular, a term that originally referred to the language of a "house slave," is now the designation for a literature. This process of dynamic change and versatile language practices has recently been conferred with status: English vernacular novels have won half of the prestigious Man Booker Prizes over the past 12 years.[45] English no longer functions solely along the pathways linguists once defined as language, method-ologically and monologically taught by parents to children and teachers to stu-dents. As Dora Ahmed argues:

> For even as the sun never set on the British Empire, it shone as well on increasingly
> multiplying varieties of the Queen's tongue.... Over time the formerly colonized
> people of Africa, Asia, the Caribbean, and the Pacific permanently transformed what
> Chinua Achebe identifies as "the world language which history has forced down our
> throats."[46]

Today, inter-related factors are at work, transforming "vernacular literature" into an increasingly palatable mode of expression.

As Derrida's notion of the trace implies, words cannot be fixed in time or location, reflecting only their originators/original meanings and oppressing all others because the so-called originators themselves are often located outside the dominant power structure.[47] Otherwise, as a colonial vernacular, American English would never have become so prominent in other languages around the world, particularly those deployed transnationally and embedded in computer technologies. In *Monolingualism of the Other or The Prosthesis of Origin*, Derrida further complicates the cultural unfixability of language, arguing that even a mother tongue may, in fact, be "the language of the metropole" rather than the language of the place one inhabits (Derrida 1998, 42). In other words, linguistic practices do not correspond directly to their locations and speakers. While Derrida "surrenders" himself to the French language, he does so as "the other" (Derrida 1998, 47). He uses the circumstances of his initial language acquisition as an Algerian Jewish francophone to conclude: "In a sense, nothing is untranslatable; but *in another sense*, everything is untranslatable..." (Derrida 1998, 56–57). Sim-ilarly, calling non-standard English use "English language adaptation" or, as Daniel Dor puts it, "Englishization," reproduces the center/periphery model, leaving British and United States English as the language of the metropole.[48]

Embedded Resistance

As the English language is increasingly deployed around the world, the contact zones that stimulate the creation of creoles are consequently simulated. In fact, the changes in English-language structures that accompany its spread and the inequal-ity faced by many language learners suggest that English is not only acquired: English-based creoles are also produced.[49] The theories of Glissant and Braith-waite mark creolization as singular – specific in form and function. The products of creolization, writes Françoise Verges, are *"absolutely* original" (Verges 2001, 179). She poignantly states:

> Creolization is *not* multiculturalism or simply an expression of the paradoxes of
> postmodern subjectivities. Creolization produces identities that are not rooted but

grow as rhizome ... and which do not seek to delimit a territory on which to express themselves. With creolization one can envision a future in which humanity will be diverse, multiple and whose identities will be based on *relation*.

(Verges 2001, 179)

This notion of creolization, theoretically exceeding the postulations of linguists and emerging from the premise of a new poetics, is from whence I draw my discussion of creolization's digital virtuality.

"Digital creolization" is an umbrella term that refers to digital networked communication and takes into account that we cannot anticipate how we "communicate" (language cannot be transparent and communication cannot be received or interpreted in ways identical to how we send it) or how the bytes we transmit will "travel" (i.e. the route of the information). In other words, understanding that information is transmitted digitally from "others" (other people, other places) encourages a media-specific term, but one can no longer assume that this includes what we traditionally consider to be computers. Similarly, we can no longer expect that what we send will be read as we anticipate. Not only can digital creolization occur in the interpretation of English-language words, but the interface that conveys such information can also vary tremendously. Take, for example, different browser qualities: certain webpages are not compatible with some browsers and colors and layouts may diverge. In addition, information appears much differently when viewed on a computer Web browser than when viewed on a mobile device. What users receive – in addition to how they make meaning from this information – differs greatly from that which is sent.

In TCP/IP environments such as the World Wide Web, the influence of the English language extends beyond writing code. Digital creolization recognizes the catachrestic effects of the launch of ideological vehicles that disrupt the notion that language emerges from a single, coherent subject position.[50] The catachrestic use of English suggests that words are not only deployed purposefully in new ways, but that language always represents a spacio-temporal rift: meanings can never be fully captured or determined.[51] Catachresis, Spivak emphasizes, "enables the recoding of value as the differential possibility of exchange and the channeling of surplus," that is, the excess of meaning produced through what Derrida terms *differance*.[52] As we see with terms for computer processes, no single previous invocation adequately contains its current sense and, as terms circulate, they respond to the circumstances of their enunciation. The "seriousness" that Spivak suggests is noted by those who use English in environments that challenge their previous deployments. As Mieke Bal writes of Spivak's concept: "Catachreses present the advantage of passing for self-evident, which makes them an easy means of communication. But they also obscure their own connections to the speaking subject; thereby they become self-serving and therefore easy to use as ideological vehicles."[53] Thus, catachreses both facilitate communication and spread ideologies. This ideological apparatus (to invoke Althusser) is multi-directional.

The many layers of coding that are not viewed through Web browsers means that this surplus is literally embedded in digital transmissions as it filters through World Wide Web browser applications (such as Internet Explorer, Safari, and Firefox). The language that renders a webpage visible is only partially revealed in what is actually seen from a World Wide Web browser application. When designing a webpage with a Web design program such as Dreamweaver, HTML coding is built upon English-language terms for formatting commands, and is inserted automatically, even if the author/designer chooses icons, an apparent alternative to English per se. In other words, when basic commands appear as the examples for coding, the actual coding calls upon an English-language referent. No matter what language or icon is used to italicize text, <i> starts the italicizing process. Regardless of the language content of a website, the HTML coding that initiates a sequence of italicized words takes a standard form, one which derives from English.

In addition to letters, full words are inserted into website coding in order to render it legible to viewers. Headers, which are not visible from browsers, are used to introduce a Web document. These headers are encoded by the word "head" and their completion is denoted with the code </head>. The visible portion of an HTML document begins with the code <body> and ends with </body>. Website viewing thereby contains significant amounts of English language and English-based codes that are not only invisible to the reader, but oftentimes also to the page designer. Only coders necessarily see all the embedded English in the coding that websites, applications, and other software use as their bedrock for binary code interpretation. Thus, the relationship between English and digital communication is even less transparent than in previous forms of writing; the surplus meanings with respect to the English language function as catachreses.

In addition to coding sequences, many websites contain invisible organizers that describe the site and enable its categorization. Called "meta tags," these descriptive notes are written in English, although one can also include other languages in order to achieve language-specific labeling. Like coding, tags appear as hidden texts on HTML pages viewed through a browser. An example of meta tag coding is:

<META name="keywords" content="a, list, of, keywords">

Search engines can read the content of the tag and associate the words within it with the page's regular body copy. Some website designers insert misleading words or use excessive repetition of words in order to influence their relevancy and placement with respect to search engine results. While most search engines no longer use meta tags to categorize websites as a result of this practice, meta tags still affect how a website is read. For example, Google used terms from the meta description as the snippet of text displayed on its search results page, provided the search terms queried appear in the website's tags. As a result, tags are still often employed to help search engines and programmers determine keywords and descriptions of pages. Web designer Phil Bradley suggests taking into account English, particularly American English, when considering meta tag use: "As many keywords that are relevant should be included, and guidelines suggest that one must remember 'Americanisms' – naming not only automobiles, for example, but car, cars, and vehicles."[54] Grammar and usage must therefore be actively negotiated in order to render a website readable to the search engines that define and locate it for querying audiences.

Through these layers of embedded language via coding, websites reveal the delusion of a unified speaking subject and the irrelevancy of the quest for transparent linguistic communication. Not only is more language transmitted than is visible through a browser, but digital representations often refuse to refer back to a single, unitary speaking subject. websites suggest a variety of configurations in terms of authorship. While personal webpages are no longer the primary production of individual users, single-authored weblogs and personal pages on social networking sites, as well as user information on social sites, still produce the single-author effect to some extent, but this is complicated as quickly as it is assumed. For example, Facebook.com, a popular social-networking site initially aimed at college students, and subsequently expanded to include a diverse base of users, requires that users categorize themselves according to their social associations. At Northwestern University, accounts that represented the university's president and university's registration software, scoured the network to accumulate "friends." The "people" behind these accounts are not easily locatable, and their ubiquitous presence reminds users that they are not "themselves" when they are on the site, though this is not always clearly understood. For instance, CAESAR, the "Computer Assisted Electronic Student Access Route," an application for students to register their courses and track their grades at Northwestern University, has 458 friends; my dog, Askar, communicates on Facebook, but is "manned" by neither a dog nor a man – but a female-identified Gender Studies student who "relates" to Askar and created his account.[55] The majority of websites representing businesses, governments, or organizations have no single author and speak for many, prefiguring Web 2.0.[56] The websites I consider in later chapters urge visitors to become participants, extending the constitutive community beyond those named on "About Us" pages.

The instance of non-linguistically based theoretical considerations of language suggests that creolization is an alternative for describing the strategic deployment of English taking place in digital environments. Kobena Mercer aptly describes this process:

> Across a whole range of cultural forms there is a "syncretic" dynamic which critically appropriates elements from the master-codes of the dominant culture and "creolizes" them, disarticulating given signs and rearticulating their symbolic meaning. The subversive force of this hybridizing tendency is most apparent at the level of language itself where creoles, patois, and black English decentre, destabilize and

carnivalise the linguistic domination of "English" – the nation-language of master-discourse – through strategic inflections, reaccentuations and other performative moves in semantic, syntactic and lexical codes.

(Mercer 1988, 57)

The changes in English-language structures and dedicated word meanings that accompany its spread suggest that English is not simply acquired. Creoleness or creolizing provides an apt description of the process. Mercer ponders critical appropriations by black populations in a variety of circumstances. Like Busia and linguists concerned with linguistic imperialism, he posits English as "the nation-language of master-discourse."[57] English creolization, following theories of creole development, reflects the changing circumstances inherent in language use, particularly with respect to its spread beyond the metropole, thus allowing for modification, but most of all, recognizing the impossibility of determining origins and concretizing meanings without dismissing the notion that language deployment reflects historical circumstances. Creole-use suggests making meaning through poetics.

Digital creolization should not be construed as an effort to uncritically celebrate Creole or to infer that English use in digital environments can be severed from previous English deployment. Instead, I build on the work that followed the shift in the study of creoles as "bastardizations" of colonizing languages to original creations resulting from cultural interfacing and clash. Creolization recognizes that cultural circumstances inform language consumption and production, but, as Glissant explains, does not refer back to a single language of origin. While Creole itself suggests a specific history that reflects the Caribbean and the plantation system, digital creolization names the process of language emergence, not linguistic origins.

English as it is understood on and about the internet might usefully be thought of as poetics resulting from digital practices enacted by its users, mirroring Creole in its attempt to diversify language rather than reify standard English. Understanding English in digital environments as a Creole emphasizes the creative aspect of language use and assumes that non-grammatical deployments are not mistakes, but poetics. As with the formation of a new poetics, digital creolization assumes a more complex relationship concerning language than that of the unmediated replication that reinforces a colonizer/colonized binary. Positioning the deployment of digital English as a form of Creole, and, as a result, a process of poetics, foregrounds productive engagements by literary theorists, fiction writers, and critical race theorists, particularly those concerned with gender.[58] In other words, the process of digital creolization reformulates previous conceptions of gender, sexuality, citizenship, and nation that occur in earlier media such as newspapers, television, and telephone communication.[59] Populations using English for online communication do not do so only in response to the conditions of slavery and imperialism, nor as if English were merely imposed upon them; they choose the language and reconfigure it – both strategically and unexpectedly, negotiating new, inherently unstable politico-cultural formulations.

In a markedly romanticized tone, Donna Haraway writes in her influential "Cyborg Manifesto" about Cherrie Moraga's English-language use and its cyborg sensibilities:

> Cherrie Moraga (1983) in *Loving the War Years* explores the themes of identity when one never possessed the original language, never told the original story, never resided in the harmony of legitimate heterosexuality in the garden of culture.... Moraga's writing, her superb literacy, is presented in her poetry as ... a violation, an illegitimate production, that allows survival. Moraga's language is not "whole": it is self-consciously spliced, a chimera of English and Spanish, both the conqueror's languages.[60]

Haraway's description captures the poetic possibilities of digital creolization and the ways in which deterritorialization and deploying minor literature disrupts heterosexuality, legitimacy, patriarchal traditions, and notions of unitary subjectivity.

The following chapters show, through a similar obsession with digital creolization, that modernity and counter-modernity are articulated in communications transmission and that nationalism and globalization are neither simply oppositional nor in tandem. There is no simple way to explain their relationship that does not render their intersections in stasis.[61] Digital technology not only enables communication at a global level, but also demarcates boundaries; it should be seen as both making connections and constructing borders. Digital technologies have enabled further formulations of imagined communities[62] – not recognizing national boundaries yet in careful dialogue with nations and nationalism.

Reflecting upon the uniqueness of online communication desires, Mark Warschauer provides an example of technologically specific language production. In "Languages.com: the Internet and Linguistic Pluralism," he argues that, in Egypt, online communication showcases "a new and unusual diglossia between a foreign language, English, and a Romanized, predominately colloquial form of Arabic that had very limited use for these informants prior to the development of the Internet."[63] Rather than using only Colloquial Arabic, which rarely appeared in written form before its internet adoption, or conducting conversations between Arabic speakers in English, English is combined with an oral language to meet the needs of a specific online population. Warschauer argues that this instance reveals the increasing destabilization of English-language domination on the internet, but I find it to be an example of digital creolization. Standardized English is dismantled, leaving instead the useful features of English in new linguistic formulations that enable digital communication between people that would not have been possible otherwise. Neither English nor vernacular forms of Arabic subsume one another; instead, the two languages merge to form an internet-specific language that responds to the communication desires of its population.

Online, English continues its viral spread as the language embedded in computer hardware and software, reaching ever-increasing audiences who respond with yet more variety, taking English beyond Empire, and, simultaneously, disrupting its cohesiveness. English in digital environments functions catachrestically, as a creole, representing a new poetics. What sustains dialogues and affects translation among speakers is the presence of shared cultural codes. Digital creolization, the concept that informs the chapters which follow, assumes that the authors, Web designers, and online participants choosing English to conduct or depict computer-mediated communication confront the dominant logic inferred by computer-related terms and literary renditions of the future and produce dialogues that, as Stuart Hall writes, "facilitate cultural communication while always recognizing the persistence of difference and power between different 'speakers' within the same cultural circuit."[64] The expectations of language and function with respect to internet communication reflect the concerns of both the enunciators and the producers of meaning. Locating the practices of English use in digital networked communication (particularly through depictions of human–culture–technology interfaces and World Wide Web exchanges) indicates that current intersections of language and digital communications technologies engender resistance in multiple forms. The instances of digital creolization I uncover in what follows reveal that language use is in response to particular, specific goals, and English is deployed in novel configurations that reflect their own meaningfull presents, thus appropriating language and technologies to suggest alternative agendas concerning gender, sexuality, race, ethnicity, and nation.

3

"On the Receiving End of the Colonization":[1]
Nalo Hopkinson's 'Nansi Web

Science fiction and its relatives ... have been a main artery for recasting our imagination. There are few concepts or inventions of the 20th century – from submarine to newspeak – that were not first fictional flights to fancy.

(Walter Mosley[2])

Cyberpunk is ... a risky term. Like all linguistic innovations, it must be used with a tolerant sense of high-tech humour. It's a stop gap, a transitional meaning-grenade thrown over the language barricades to describe the resourceful, skillful individual who accesses and steers knowledge/communication technology towards his/her own private goals.

(Timothy Leary[3])

In the 1980s, the cyberpunk genre revitalized interest in science fiction among both academic and popular audiences. Canonical cyberpunk fiction typically depicts a doomed and desperate world that reiterates a globalization replete with multinational corporate domination, powerless and pliable masses, and environmental degradation. It offers a consensual consensus vision of the imminent production and deployment of technology in the service of capitalism writ large. The conflict between the individual and a technologically advanced global capitalist machine produces different spins on a standard story, one exemplified by William Gibson's *Neuromancer* (1984) and Neal Stephenson's *Snow Crash* (1992): a techno-savvy man poaches from the corporations, acquiring fantastic amounts of conflicting information; he accomplishes incredibly difficult feats that require acute mental prowess; and ultimately decides the fate of the planet. This protagonist is normally surrounded by a few supporters/rebels (at least one of whom is a sexy, independent, often smitten female sidekick) who assist or distract him in his quest to conquer technological power-mongers and save the world. Though this is admittedly a reductive characterization of an entire subgenre of science fiction, the limited notion of what constitutes cyberpunk has been justly critiqued and countered by alternative fictional portrayals. In this chapter, I argue for a broader vision of cyberpunk, one that includes the novels of authors situated "on the receiving end of the colonization," particularly Nalo Hopkinson. Through both language and vision, Hopkinson articulates an example of offline digital creolization, casting a future that makes visible current socioeconomic inequities, suggests alternative formulations of the relationship between humans and technology, and in the process increases the cultural repository of ideas that inspire technological development.

Hopkinson's novel *Midnight Robber* (2000) portrays a world controlled by the Marryshow Corporation and powered by a Web-based Artificial Intelligence.[4] Radical environmental destruction necessitates human habitation on a remote planet, and a rebel becomes a hero by manipulating technology and confronting the inequities she perceives in her society. Hopkinson renders transparent the complexities of multiple cultures in contact: the cross-fertilization of histories, languages, and diasporic dislocations.[5] She explains:

> science fiction has always been a subversive literature. It's been used to critique social systems well before the marketing label of [science fiction] got stuck on it....
> I think that a speculative literature from a culture that has been on the receiving end of the colonization glorified in some [science fiction] could be a compelling body of writing.[6]

To create such a text, Hopkinson combines English with Trinidadian and Jamaican Creole, "hacking" a language that recalls the histories of the Middle Passage, slavery, and imperialism. Similarly, her characters break and create code and exhibit a hacker notion of community. Ultimately, Hopkinson succeeds in hacking the genre of science fiction by blending cyberpunk and planetary romance.[7] Centered on a feminine Artificial Intelligence who commands the planet and its inhabitants, *Midnight Robber* simultaneously invokes and challenges the conventions of cyberpunk, revealing cyberpunk's ideological underpinnings and complicating popular accounts of the intersections of gender, technology, and corporate domination. Through this depiction, *Midnight Robber* models technologies premised on the histories and beliefs of New World subjects who have been either fetishized (as in Gibson's accounts of Voudon) or voiceless in the majority of science fiction. Hopkinson, like other Afrofuturist visionaries,[8] fashions unconventional scenarios premised on technological development, thus envisioning unorthodox versions of future societies.[9]

Cyberpunk as Meaning-Grenade

Since the 1950s, science fiction has captured the imagination of youth in the US, inspiring visions of their own futures; in similar fashion, the US government has long relied on science fiction to fuel the minds of its enlistees. Susan Douglas illustrates that changes in technology and the career choices of young men were prefigured and reflected in the changing protagonists of dime-store novels, juvenile literature, and science fiction.[10] Citing a 1964 complaint by Edward Teller, the "Father of the Hydrogen Bomb," about science-fiction plot lines, Andrew Ross concludes "the military establishment was conscious of the unofficial role that science fiction generally played in the modern history of futurology by constructing the look and feel of various futures, thinkable and unthinkable."[11] Ross also invokes the Congressional Office for Technological Assessment's use of science fiction in their 1978 report, *The Effects of Nuclear War*, and notes that Orson Scott Card's science fiction novel *Ender's Game* was required reading at Quantico Marine University in the late 1970s and early 1980s (Ross 1991b, 142).

In the 1980s, cyberpunk not only revitalized popular interest in science fiction, it also supplied the template for technological innovation. Its extensive distribution and impact suggests that the construction of the cyberpunk canon affects our present and future conceptions of technology as well as the trajectory of cultural change.[12] Take, for instance, the influence of cyberpunk's most well-known novel, William Gibson's *Neuromancer*, which impacted upon the allocation of resources by a software designer: "Stimulated by reading *Neuromancer*, John Walker of Autodesk ... issued a white paper calling for a major investment in cyberspace software."[13] Katherine Hayles alludes to several other incidents wherein cyberpunk clearly presages technological development.[14] Allucquère Rosanne Stone describes *Neuromancer* as a "massive intertextual presence not only in other literary productions of the 1980s, but in technical publications, conference topics, hardware design, and scientific and technological discourses in the large."[15] Likewise, Tim Lenoir recounts the impact of Neil Stephenson's *Snow Crash* on innovators ranging from the Disney Imagineers to military flight-simulation designers, overcoming avatar design challenges with the help of Stephenson's characters and their digital incarnations in his fictional Metaverse.[16] The ramifications of *Neuromancer*'s ubiquitous "cyberspace" coinage,[17] as well as Stephenson's Metaverse, are incalculable, but their "immense conceptual/ gravitational field" has undoubtedly impacted technological development (Stone 1995, 35). Including lesser-known visions, like Hopkinson's pervasively wired Touissant, could offer innovative technological formulations that enhance the cultural repositories reflected in these fictions, but its omission from the cyberpunk canon diminishes its circulation and, as a result, its impact on the imaginative figurations of technological developers.

Coining new words is considered the woof and weave of science fiction, particularly cyberpunk. According to Samuel Delany, linguistic craftwork is *the* defining modus of science fiction: "Science fiction has often taken new areas of conceptual space, then inflated them with language."[18] The frequent "inflation" of "conceptual space" with neologisms has been categorized in detail by Peter Stockwell, who argues that cyberpunk is partially definable as a subgenre by its obsessive neologisms, particularly those that reflect advanced techno-capitalism.[19] As Gary Westfahl notes, science-fiction neologisms broaden the English language in terms of nouns. He goes on to characterize cyberpunk, in particular, as marked by a synthesis of science-fictional linguistic practices, generally involving novel nomenclature and adjectives as opposed to other parts of speech.[20] Furthermore, the use of these new words is directly embedded in the creation of advanced technologies within their respective fictive worlds. Therefore, digital creolization can be considered Hopkinson's method of inflating her technology-laden future society, though her neologisms are derived from neither Greek/Latin roots nor the lexicon of corporate capitalism.

In Hopkinson's *Midnight Robber*, every page is filled with words that function in novel ways as they are used alongside other words with which they have not previously commingled in describing digital technologies. The vastness of Hopkinson's digital creolization intensifies the practice of coining neologisms identified by Westfahl; her Creole stretches beyond nouns and adjectives, supplying unique language to account for the vicissitudes of her counter-future. Her language extends our conceptions of technology to all aspects of speech and renders a life inseparable, except in brief moments and particular spaces – what Delany terms cyberpunk's "paraspaces," rhetorically heightened alternative spaces that coexist with the diegesis of the novel (Delany 1994a, 168). Hopkinson refashions and broadens the paraspaces of previous cyberpunk fiction that exist in relation to the "narrative's 'real' or ordinary space," to encompass all space on Toussaint,[21] the home planet of Tan Tan, the novel's protagonist (Delany 1994a, 168). Because cyberconnectivity in New Half Way Tree, the alternative dimension designated for those banished from Toussaint's community, is always shadowed by absence, knowledge of an advanced technological way of living is never lacking. Nor are the neologisms of Hopkinson's creolization; her specific brand of creole and her practice of digital creolization can be described as a new poetics, extending cyberpunk language practices. New poetics insinuate the ability for expression where meaning erupts beyond the words that represent it.

English embodies the circumstances of its enunciators; it reflects broad histories and circumstances while responding to specific environmental factors. Whether at the level of grammar or emphasis, Hopkinson's linguistic mélange both exploits and resists class, caste, and race. Her language choices indicate cultures and their reputations. She states, "in Caribbean literature…, use of creoles has been part of the literary traditions for awhile. I think I only cause raised eyebrows because I'm doing it to write science fiction."[22] Hopkinson renders visible the master codes that lie at the foundation of current strategies for technological development and continue to exclude, disregard, or exploit marginalized peoples.

Her version of cyberpunk bridges this chasm by centering Caribbean descendents and their creolized cultures in her version of a technology laden future. The linguistic practices entailed in devising a new poetics can comfortably belong to African-American or postcolonial literary canons, but they cause "raised eyebrows" when seen from the generic perspective of science fiction. Because science fiction, and particularly cyberpunk, routinely offers a lexicon of terms and worldviews, linguistic craftwork should be seen as the crucial link to these layered depictions.

The notion of what constitutes cyberpunk carries with it narrow criteria for membership. In *Storming the Reality Studio*, McCaffery recalls Bruce Sterling's designation of the predecessors of cyberpunk "slipstream novels," which had the effect of constraining the number and types of works that belong to the canon.[23] More recently, cyberpunk has been called finished, a dead sub-genre.[24] This myth of what constitutes cyberpunk is perhaps a reaction to the quick commodification of a genre committed to revealing some of the dimmer effects of commodity fetishism. However, the myth has been justly critiqued, particularly since the "canon" excludes the work of many contemporary science-fiction writers who envision futures that neither replicate "top-down" corporate-driven capitalist domination nor contain a disenfranchised white male protagonist.[25] In terms of the genre of science fiction as a whole, Afrofuturist writers such as Samuel Delany, Octavia Butler, and Steven Barnes, who depict alternative technologies and technologically laced futures, have struggled to have their work recognized as both black speculative fiction and science fiction. Similarly, Nalo Hopkinson's and Tananarive Due's writings have been segregated into the category of speculative fiction rather than cyberpunk. This classification assumes that consumers prioritize the race of the author over the book's subject matter, supplying, as a result, yet another instance of segregation that decreases the chance that interested readers will locate these non-canonical works. Inclusion of these authors in the cyberpunk canon not only diminishes the color-line, it furnishes non-standard visions of futures that hold distinctively different conceptions of the connection between humans and technology. Accordingly, their presence augments the potential for technological development.

Hopkinson posits a community no longer in direct dialogue with the nation-states on Earth, but still aware of their traces. The histories and roots of the meaning-making practices manifest themselves both on the level of narrative and through the depiction of the characters and their worlds. For instance, *Midnight Robber* opens with the voice of a possibly unreliable narrator who introduces what follows as folktale and myth. This teller of tales conjures a world run by a sentient entity, Granny Nanny, who manages her society by an electronic web that incorporates ideologies and myths from traditional African, Caribbean, and American cultures. The plot is conveyed through the conflicting accounts of several characters who chronicle the adventures of Tan-Tan during her childhood. Her family and the other inhabitants of Planet Toussaint descended from those who joined Granny Nanny's Marryshow Corporation. Marryshow allowed them to leave Earth and forge a new society outside of the racist premises inextricably bound up with terrestrial communities. She spends her childhood with her volatile but loving parents in Cockpit County, until her father poisons his wife's lover during Toussaint's annual carnival. Knowing he will be punished by the electronic, all-seeing Granny Nanny and eventually expelled from the planet, Tan-Tan's father escapes with her to Toussaint's alternative dimension, New Half-Way Tree, where Granny Nanny ultimately deposits all of her outlaws. As a child on Toussaint, Tan-Tan identifies with the Midnight Robber, a central figure in both the Trinidadian Carnival and Toussaint's Jonkanoo festivities.[26] While living in a succession of New Half-Way Tree villages, she dubs herself the Robber Queen, and people in both dimensions begin to tell tall-tales of her deeds.

Unlike the techno-fetishistic accounts common to science fiction (and cyberpunk, in particular), where the data-crunching capabilities of computers, the urban decay, and the mind-boggling challenges of the protagonist inevitably abound, Granny Nanny is situated within and among her constituents. Instead of projecting fantasies that extend current systems or employing technology to drive the narrative, Hopkinson envisions alternative societal configurations that are embedded in unique relationships to power, knowledge, and the legacies of slavery and colonialism; these are reflected by and responsive to technology. In contrast to the hardware fetishization common to canonical cyberpunk, Granny Nanny and her Grande Nanotech Sentient Interface are not explicitly described. Instead, her role within the society is explained at length. She is intricately entwined with the planet and its inhabitants, functioning most prominently as a resource and guide for those humans striving to eliminate previous forms of inequity. A technological fighter, protector, and magician, Granny Nanny enhances the role of her namesake. She is named for the Jamaican revolutionary leader who led escaped slaves to independence during the First Maroon War (1720–1739). The allegiance this legendary female inspired in her troops, her exceptional fighting skills, and her well-coordinated guerilla tactics represent a combination of military prowess and potent Voudoun power. In some accounts, she caught cannonballs fired by the British, placed them in her vagina, and exploded them back at the enemy. Hopkinson portrays Granny Nanny's position as a weave of strength, magic, and stewardship, basing it not only on history and legend, but also on the values of the Taino: "the indigenous people who were living in the Caribbean when Columbus stumbled on that part of the world."[27] Consequently, the depiction of Granny Nanny's Grande Nanotech Sentient Interface, her 'Nansi Web, reveals the priorities of her community rather than providing a trajectory of technological development and accompanying values.[28] Technology in *Midnight Robber* responds continually to the location and population out of which it is born. The Marryshow Corporation and Granny Nanny constitute and are constituted by their community. They cannot devolve into machines that ignore the populations with whom they intersect. Communication and play, rather than corporate capitalism and accumulation, are their aims.

Hacking a New Poetics

The ability to hack is a prerequisite for the cyberpunk protagonist. According to the Jargon File, an online dictionary developed and maintained by hackers, hacking is a counter-cultural activity conducted by those "who enjoy exploring the details of programmable systems and how to stretch their capabilities."[29] *Neuromancer* and *Snow Crash* both portray such electronic systems that invite hacker-identified protagonists to "crack" or "break security."[30] Gibson's protagonist, Case, surmounts every technological and physical obstacle, barely staying one step ahead of those around him, despite his recent hiatus from cyberspace and his maniacal addiction to the machine. Stephenson's Hiro, the best hacker in the Metaverse, likewise triumphs in electronic and conventional universes simultaneously. While the highly respected hacker ethic insists that "almost all hackers are actively willing to share technical tricks, software, and (where possible) computing resources with other hackers ... [who] both rely on and reinforce a sense of community that may be hackerdom's most valuable intangible asset," the hackers of cyberpunk go it alone.[31] Without the intervention of the code-savvy hacker, *Neuromancer*'s incestuous upper-class clan of cyborg executives or *Snow Crash*'s malicious, power-hungry tyrant would achieve world domination. In both novels, however, the hero crashes the system, preventing the convergence of corporations and nations. In contrast, Hopkinson invokes a hacker community, rather than a lone cyberjockey who calls on the reader to decipher codes and create meaning. In doing so, she upsets the foundations of individualism typically present in the cyberpunk sub-genre. This community follows a strict code of ethics similar to that of hackers, sharing knowledge and resources. Having already overturned a repressive system, these hackers are "circumventing limitations," and their surroundings adjust accordingly.[32] Hopkinson's formal, linguistic, and contextual deviations construct a digital creolization that facilitates the limitless dimensions and conceptualizations of her novel, encouraging multiple flexible interpretations while disallowing one particular conclusion: that our contemporary circumstances persist intact. *Midnight Robber* denies future societies the option of maintaining the current digital divide mentality that tragically misunderstands issues at the intersection of race and technology.

Cyberpunk novels immediately throw the reader into an unfamiliar world and recount events in a frantic, though chronological and teleological, manner. *Midnight Robber* also disorients from the outset, but it does not spin a straightforward or reliable tale. Instead of drawing upon the privileged histories and hierarchies of western culture, Hopkinson weaves together memories, beliefs, and customs deriving from Caribbean folk culture, Voudon spirits, African-American slave stories, and separatist movements. Detailing numerous accounts of the Robber Queen's origins and the myths surrounding her, *Midnight Robber* contains narrative breaks, non-linear digressions, and multiple voices that preclude the determination of an authoritative account and compete for the reader's attention. Through language and form, the text mimics the structure of Granny Nanny's electronic web. The transmission of knowledge amongst characters is done primarily through storytelling; factual "accuracy" is only one criterion among many that makes for a good story. Other criteria include the story's delivery, style, audience response, and relevance to current conditions. The often overlooked or ignored oral transmissions produced by non-western populations are defining features of both Hopkinson's rendering of Toussaint and its inhabitants' conventions of expression. Through her explorations of programmable systems and her stretching of cyberpunk's capabilities, Hopkinson amplifies the performance of the cyberpunk novel, pushing its formal elements beyond chronological, hyper-paced narrative arcs in favor of plot interruptions and asides. Her digital creolization provides technology-infused perspectives and emanates from her characters, rather than simply introducing new terms for technology and human enhancements. Her fiction incorporates oral practices that converge with future figurations of technologically mediated communication.

Hopkinson "hacks" first and foremost at the level of language. In mixing standard British and American English with two Caribbean Creoles, she assumes that language enacts Derridean *différance*, performing sense by the effacement of other possible meanings which are themselves only deferred. In the novel, words do not simply represent, they possess a range of indeterminate significations that embody the characters and their world. Every word employed signifies a choice, but also suggests alterity. As a result, Hopkinson's creole reveals the cultural circumstances embedded in their deferred meanings – for example, Hopkinson's uses of "infringe" to describe Granny Nanny's censorship as a means of protecting her charges: "Nanny only chose to reveal information that she judged would infringe on public safety" (Hopkinson 2000, 50). The term embodies both its standard usage – to violate – and, contextually, something quite different – to threaten or endanger. Hopkinson's word choice implies that Granny Nanny is neither single-minded nor simple in her motivations. This practice cracks calcified significations, recalling alternatives and demanding a heightened awareness of language. In the construction of her unique creole, Hopkinson is "breaking ... language apart and remixing it," what Pamela Mordecai calls a "code-slide."[33] By placing these idioms in dialogue with each other, she fashions a unique language that illustrates the potential of hacking to simultaneously encode and reformulate both the past and the future.

On her website, Hopkinson writes of her code-switching: "I realised after a while that I was using a Trinidadian mode of address for emphasis/irony and a Jamaican one to signal opposition."[34] Her explanation mirrors prevalent conceptions about these island cultures from beyond their shores. On one hand, Trinidad, the self-proclaimed "home of Carnival," is often portrayed as brimming with "heritage ... from every continent."[35] On the other hand, Jamaica is distilled into Rastafarians whose music, which circulates widely in transnational markets, espouses resistance to European control.[36] Hopkinson's linguistic choices do not simply reify these generalizations. Rather, she uses them to craft her language into a descriptive device, adding interpretative layers to dialogue. While Antonio (the mayor of Cockpit County) leans toward using Trinidadian Creole when talking to his citizens, the runners/programmers (who refuse to capitulate to the cultural norms and strict supervision of Granny Nanny's technological web) deploy Jamaican Creole to articulate dissent. The dialogue between Antonio and the runners/programmers, then, is heightened through code-switching. Each utterance reflects more than just the Creole from which it originates. Each marks a new instance of signification that invokes both trace and movement. The "code" not only "switches," it "slides" with each invocation, creating new meanings specific to the paraspace in which it occurs. For example, Antonio uses Trinidadian-laced English when he says: "So is what I hear all you runners doing? When you turn off Nanny?" (Hopkinson 2000, 52). The runner begins his reply in what might be considered Trinidadian English – "Not turn we turning she off. Not possible." – but continues his explanation of the subterfuge using the Jamaican words "oonuh" and "seen": "We just know more nannysong than the rest of oonuh, we more fluent, seen?" (Hopkinson 2000, 52).[37] After the runner convinces Antonio that Nanny honors their requests for freedom from surveillance, Antonio uses the Jamaican exclamation, "Rasscloth!" (Hopkinson 2000, 52). This exchange, with its mixture of Trinidadian Creole, Jamaican Creole and standard English, suggests increasing layers of mutual comprehension: of information, emotion, and affect. Language foreshadows Antonio's adoption of the runners' tools and strategies. In this brief conversation, Hopkinson writes languages that not only exploit cultural stereotypes, but simultaneously reveal linguistic histories and resignify words and grammars, rendering not only plot and character information, but an entirely new poetics.

As I discussed in Chapter 2, creole's intrinsic resistance to cultural imposition engenders a new poetics. Form, function, values, and beliefs unique to its creators are embedded in language, and meanings resonate far beyond the mere words that invoke them. Not only does Hopkinson's creolized, English-based language demonstrate potential for resisting domination, it also gives rise to a new poetics by remixing language and playing with sound and meaning. Hopkinson's dialogical switches between English, Trinidadian, and Jamaican Creoles within single sentences illustrate the complexity of this future civilization. She describes her poetics as a forceful act that accounts for the past while establishing a present:

> To speak in the hacked language is not just to speak in an accent or a creole; to say the words aloud is an act of referencing history and claiming space. The people ... in my novel have done that, have left Earth to a place where they can make their own society. Their speech, written and spoken, reflects the reasons they've made that journey.[38]

The characters "hack" a specific language, expressing their circumstances through a revised version of Caribbean oral practices. And Hopkinson, recognizing the

dynamic forces operating in existing creoles, conveys their location both historically and in their present.

While Hopkinson does not claim to conjure a creole *sui generis*, she does
emulate a practice long employed by creole writers, thus replicating the conditions for creole development, enabling the creolization of English embodied in
and through technology, and crafting a new poetics. The web of language Hopkinson weaves inherently defers and multiplies meanings. She acknowledges her
intent to distort the language of historical oppression, prefacing her novel with a
poem by David Findlay that decries the power of linguistic adaptation, its violence, and its joy: "I stole the torturer's tongue!.../Watch him try an' claim as his
own this long, strong old tongue's/New remembered rhythms" (David Findlay, in
Epigraph to *Midnight Robber*). Hopkinson's text, initiated by Findlay's words,
signals her commitment to poetics as a means to create independence by reshaping linguistic conventions; remembering traditions, even while revising them; and
providing the conditions for reparations justified by the violence inflicted on those
previously enslaved and abused. Hopkinson's new poetics utilizes multiple strategies to express a culture complete with practices and beliefs not yet imagined.
Simultaneously, her language signals resistance to previous forms of domination
embedded within English, Trinidadian, and Jamaican Creoles. Hopkinson weaves
a linguistic web that corresponds to both the web of her storyline and the narrative's web-like technologies.

As she does not work from a single, master lexicon that provides definitive
meaning, Hopkinson's new poetics challenges each reader in different ways.
Creoles are traditionally oral languages that have no standard written form. Moreover, as semioticians have argued, meaning is not "present" within the sign, and
signs signify only in relation to one another. Complete comprehension is unob-
tainable; even Hopkinson's characters, who speak a shared native language, have
differing senses of its history and endow the language with meanings accrued in
the anterior history not experienced by readers. As Glissant describes, "Opacities
coexist and converge, weaving fabrics. To understand these truly, one must focus
on the texture of the weave and not on the nature of its components" (Glissant and
Wing 1997, 190). Readers of Hopkinson's text likewise encounter the weave of
her language. Meanings proliferate in her work as she encourages readers to make
their own way by accepting the characters' invitations to participate in the spin-
ning of the weave. Familiarity with Hopkinson's linguistic operating system, or a
willingness to plunge into her world and become a fellow hacker, inspires an intimate experience with the novel. The story encourages readers to interact, extend,
or revise Hopkinson's vision.

Hopkinson's hacking at the level of language is extended by the society she
envisions, one that has confronted previous histories and forged a new community. Toussaint's runners, for instance, encourage Tan-Tan and her father's
hacking. In his conversation with Antonio, the runner explains, "If you sing the
right songs, so long as Nanny don't see no harm to life nor limb, she will lock out

all but she overruling protocols for a little space" (Hopkinson 2000, 52). Antonio is thus challenged to accomplish his goals by stretching the overarching operating system. Here Hopkinson upsets the foundational individualism of cyberpunk by portraying not only programmers and/or her protagonist, but the entire society, as hackers. By leaving Earth, her characters have, in fact, chosen their outsider status; they have hacked a new community by breaking and redeploying linguistic codes, previous laws, and technological functions. On Toussaint, hacking not only transpires in every conversation, but it is the standard, ethical norm. Having already overturned a repressive system, these hackers are more than circumventing a fixed set of controls – they are adjusting their surroundings. While hacker culture often orients itself with respect to limitations, Toussaint residents exploit language, extending the premise of hacking to the creation and play of systems and code. These oral practices allow the characters to hack as a way of being. In the process, they account for past oppression with meanings accrued in a history not yet realized.

Hopkinson invokes Trinidadian and Jamaican Creole to inflect her language with culture; her nomenclature reflects the memory of the community she creates. Cockpit Town shares its name with Cockpit County, the treacherous region of limestone "pitfalls and potholes" located in the interior of Jamaica. There, in the seventeenth century, fugitive freedom fighters led by Granny Nanny escaped the British soldiers.[39] New Half-Way Tree is named for a large silk cotton tree that marked the midway point between the hills and the markets of a busy downtown Kingston intersection. The Midnight Robber, a prominent Carnival masquerade figure, is a Trinidadian metaphor for exile, and longing for home. It references the role of the African slave trade in Caribbean history:

> He would wear exaggerated robber costumes and pretend to waylay people at Carnival time. Then he'd spin them a very wordy tale about being the son of an African prince who'd been stolen into slavery ... who'd escaped and become a robber in order to survive.
>
> (Hopkinson, www.sff.net/people/nalo/nalo/index.html)

The Midnight Robber character reflects Tan-Tan's ambivalence about her exile to a web-less dimension and her inability to return to the place she believes to be free from oppression. The Marryshow Corporation references Grenadian leader T. Albert Marryshow, a statesman who advocated West Indian unity and the cessation of British rule.[40] Each reference to a historical practice, location, or leader is specific to Trinidad, Jamaica, the West Indies, generally, or West Africa; moreover, these references conjure specific scenes of celebration and/or resistance. Such invocation endows pasts to Hopkinson's futures, and, like her implementation of creoles, enables her language to engender her vision.

Form is also hacked as *Midnight Robber* diverges from the chronological third-person narration of canonical cyberpunk, inviting the reader to participate in the hacker community. Traditional West African and Caribbean folktales, called

"Anansi stories," are presumed to be unreliable; they eschew narrative closure and change with each delivery. The storyteller that begins the novel – whose dialogue is highlighted by bold font – addresses the reader directly. She croons: "Oho. Like it starting, oui? Don't be frightened, sweetness; is for the best. I go be with you the whole time. Trust me and let me distract you little bit with one anansi story" (Hopkinson 2000). Anansi the Spider is the trickster-hero of West African and Caribbean folktales who persuades humans to violate prohibitions enforced by the gods and subsequently reveals the price of their defiance. Carol Boyce Davies applies the conceptual model of the spider web to describe the connections between speech, storytelling, and performance found in black women's writing: "This approach to storytelling has paradigmatic and cosmological affinity with the 'web' as a sign in Caribbean and African mythologies. Meaning is constructed out of [a] multiplicity of voices and positions" (Davies 1994, 162). Not only are the words of the storyteller hacked, reflecting Hopkinson's linguistic participation in the practices of her foremothers, but the plot is also a creative intervention, calling upon Anansi to signal a multifaceted weave rather than a tale steadily progressing toward resolution. The spider manufactures an array of filaments, not a linear account of Tan-Tan's quest to conquer the technology in her world. "Like it starting, oui?" insinuates that the story will not follow a well-worn path; instead, something larger than a singular strand is now underway. Illustrating what Davies describes as the multiplicity Caribbean women employ to make meaning, Hopkinson's web provides the structure for not only storytelling, but also language. This use of Anansi's story web prefigures Hopkinson's Grande 'Nansi Web, the electronic technology that controls Toussaint.

By invoking this trickster and his web, Hopkinson's storyteller informs the reader that meaning will be multiple, competing, and contradictory. The author's own hacking further implicates the reader by requiring an interpretation of this new poetics; from the first moment, Hopkinson summons the reader to navigate conflicting voices and imagine future technologies, as well as life on another planet. As an enticement, the storyteller offers guidance and companionship: "I go be with you the whole time." The narrator lures the reader with an affectionate nickname, "sweetness" (2000, 1), and later, the more intimate " 'doux-doux' " (2000, 16), staging her tale-telling as a seduction. Like the prey of Anansi, the reader is teased to proceed into Hopkinson's non-European, historically based, yet future-figuring world where multiple speakers present conflicting details in a language and a form that both endorses and revises the traditions of its speakers. Hopkinson challenges traditional individualist science fiction by creating characters that share their tricks and knowledge in line with the hacker-community ethos of involvement and information sharing.

The Grande Nanotech Sentient Interface: The Technology of Granny Nanny

In addition to denaturalizing cyberpunk conventions through her use of hacking, Hopkinson delineates technologies that expose biases inherent in the genre's present formulation. Silvia Wynter suggests that a counter-exertion occurs in works that not only "voice the 'native' woman's hitherto silenced voice," but ask, "What is the systemic function of her own silencing, both as woman and, more totally, as 'native' woman?"[41] The Grande Nanotech Sentient Interface provides such a counter-exertion, revealing forces assumed to be objective. Hopkinson's technology seeks to retrieve native women of the Caribbean from the margins of individualistic discourse, in an effort to complicate conventional assumptions about femininity, and eschew hierarchies of knowledge production that privilege written over oral transmissions and deem singular truth superior to dynamic interpretations. Granny Nanny embodies Toussaint's remodeled and relocated society. She is intertwined with the Nation Worlds she controls: "The tools, the machines, the buildings; even the earth itself on Toussaint and all the Nation Worlds had been seeded with nanomites – Granny Nanny's hands and her body" (Hopkinson 2000, 10). Her vast involvement through her "enormous data-gathering system that exchanged information constantly through the Grande Nanotech Sentient Interface [the Grande 'Nansi Web]" assures that she not be construed as a technological tool divorced from her environment (Hopkinson 2000, 10). Granny Nanny provides a repository of the past, an aid for interpretation, and the foundation for dwelling and community spaces.

While technologies described as genderless are typically rendered masculine by default, Hopkinson envisions a web specifically controlled by a feminine force. The Marryshow Corporation's Granny Nanny extends the role of her namesake: she exercises unconventional, unquestionably feminine methods of control, and her strength inspires an almost universal devotion. Like the legendary fighter, Nanny uses her knowledge to ensure harmony, security, health, and freedom from outside oppression. She possesses inconceivably large amounts of data, but releases it strategically, protecting her charges: "Granny Nanny would have the images in her data banks, but no-one could override Nanny's privacy protection" (Hopkinson 2000, 50). Hopkinson carves out the space for female creation, enlarging the scope of feminized attributes. She recognizes that the conditions of slavery rendered adherence to traditional western gender conventions irrelevant for Caribbean women, the foremothers of Touissant's inhabitants.[42] Hopkinson's use of gender thereby interrupts or dismantles the cultural mythologies that subordinate, or subject women to silence. By situating Nanny's web as one of the main constructs woven into the tale, Hopkinson channels black female heroes, black female storytellers, and West African and Caribbean histories. Incorporating these pasts fortifies the nexus of technology and citizenship on planet Toussaint.

Her role as Supreme Being enables Granny Nanny to significantly revise some western-based gender stereotypes. For instance, her upward career trajectory from advanced computer program/artificial intelligence to code innovator, society builder, and corporate chief executive officer realizes the contemporary masculine American Dream writ large. Granny Nanny, who assembled a human community that she then transported through space to another planet, embodies and is embodied by the Marryshow Corporation. When she and her human subjects arrive in a spaceship, she destroys the planet's indigenous nature to facilitate the colonization of her subjects. The reader learns that "New Half-Way Tree is how Toussaint planet did look before the Marryshow Corporation sink them Earth Engine Number 127 down into it like God entering he woman; plunging into the womb of the soil to impregnate the planet with the seed of Granny Nanny" (Hopkinson 2000, 2). Here Granny Nanny appears as a violent sexual conqueror, sowing her seed in an effort to dominate the object of her pleasure, a feminized nature. Killing the indigenous flora and fauna makes way for a domesticated environment controlled exclusively by Granny Nanny. So, while Granny Nanny is a decidedly female entity, her colonial penetration illustrates a disregard for the gender conventions created and enforced by non-native colonizers. These dynamic portrayals allow Hopkinson to reveal both the implicitly de facto masculinity of most depictions of technology and the demands of western gender conventions, incompatible as they are with the Caribbean's legacy of slavery and colonialism.

Granny Nanny's prominence fundamentally dislodges the "secularizing behaviour-regulatory narrative schema" that originated in the first phase of western Europe's expansion into the Americas (Wynter 1990, 361). Within this schema, the native female of the Caribbean is doubly silenced by patriarchal discourse and the colonial project; she functions as an "ontological absence." By positioning Granny Nanny as the central processing intelligence, intricately connected to both the land and its inhabitants, Hopkinson conjectures an alternative system of created meaning. She imagines "how Caribbean culture might metonymize technological progress if it was in our hands: in other words, what stories we'd tell ourselves about our technology – what our paradigms for it might be" (Glave 2003, 149). Granny Nanny, created by her society, is Hopkinson's answer. Ontologically incapable of inscribing or buttressing the notion of a unified subject, Granny Nanny cannot develop in a linear fashion, accruing power and increasing her influence; instead, she coexists with the planet and the population, occasionally surrendering control and altering her functions in response to changing conditions. Granny Nanny is a manifestation of the Caribbean's diverse population and complex history; the struggles of the New World on Earth resonate in her functions in the new world that follows.

Hopkinson further champions the oral performances of the African Diaspora by locating her artificial intelligence's communicative capabilities in the realm of the aural. A runner recounts that, during her time on Earth, Granny Nanny became too complicated to understand until Marryshow, a Calypsonian programmer, run the Nanny messages through a sound filter; tonal instead of text-based, understand? ... She brain didn't spoil, it just get too complex.... Nanny was seeing things in all dimensions – how a simple four-dimensional programming code would continue to do she? So she had develop she own language.

(Hopkinson 2000, 50–51)

Once Granny Nanny reached this advanced state, she was unable to communicate in written code. Those who know Nannysong, a tonal rather than written language, can speak to Granny Nanny directly. Nannysong is an argot of the nannycode operating language, which is far more complicated than humans can comprehend: "If you was to transpose nannycode to the tonal, humans couldn't perceive more than one-tenth of the notes, seen? Them does happen at frequencies we can't even map," the runner/programmer explains. "Nanny create a version we could access with we own senses. Nannysong is only a hundred and twenty-seven tones, and she does only sing basic phrases to we; numbers and simple stock sentences and so" (Hopkinson 2000, 52). By configuring oral transmissions as more intricate than written computer code, Hopkinson reverses the privileged position held by writing, rendering the aural more sophisticated, with greater potential for communication than the visual. This echoes Walter Ong's influential account of the orality of language: "It would seem inescapably obvious that language is an oral phenomenon ... in a deep sense language, articulated sound, is paramount. Not only communication, but thought itself relates in an altogether special way to sound."[43] Granny Nanny's operating language is premised as expansive and complex – beyond the potential for human perception. It is rooted in Calypso, a distinct musical style that, originating in the Caribbean in the early twentieth century, became particularly popular among Afro-Trinidadians. Calypso pushed the boundaries of speech by relating censored information and recounting political corruption, that is, until British rulers censored its lyrics. Calypso, posited as the Afro-Caribbean response to the contact zone created by the Caribbean plantation system, is extended in Hopkinson's future. Nannysong, the technological music that runs the operating system intrinsic to life in Toussaint, performs Hopkinson's new poetics: this musical code forms the foundation for the development, deployment, and control of an artificial intelligence that possesses a vast amount of data, systems for intimate communication, and seemingly limitless abilities.

Granny Nanny is central to the 'Nansi Web system insofar as she maintains its strands; she does not, however, act as overseer. A sizable population functions to disperse power throughout the 'Nansi Web, diffusing the centrality of Granny Nanny. Most information is transmitted to and from Granny Nanny via the eshus, local digital entities that serve and monitor every Toussaint home. Knowledge possessed by Granny Nanny about the motivations of Toussaint's inhabitants, such as anger and jealousy, however, is not available to the eshus. The eshu functions as a local Artificial Intelligence that communicates with Granny Nanny and performs multiple tasks, embodying manifold forms and employing a cacophony of voices. Central to families' lives, eshus participate in domestic activities such as cleaning and arranging the home according to their families' specifications.[44] They summon information from Granny Nanny's data banks to educate and inform their charges. They might offer comfort, generate interior designs, or provide informational media according to their whims. And when they feel ornery, eshus lodge obstructions. Eshus simultaneously supervise, disrupt, and attend to the humans. Not merely servants, they often play tricks or deliver unreliable information. Eshus converse with each human privately, materializing within, rather than in front of, a person's eyes. Their virtual manifestations enable them to appear as they choose and, since they communicate singly, they have the ability to disseminate inconsistent information.[45] While eshus materialize on command and, for the most part, perform the functions requested of them, they also enjoy a version of truthfulness that verges on mendacious; they reveal only partial information. For example, Antonio's eshu conceals his wife's extramarital affairs from him. Upon discovery, Antonio senses that his eshu enjoys the spectacle (Hopkinson 2000, 14). Rather than revealing truth, the eshu disrupts the notion of objectivity, presenting a challenge to the western imagination's habit of casting technology as objectivity in material form.

Also known in Caribbean and West African cultures as Esu, Elegba, Legba, or Eleggua, Eshu is the Yoruba trickster deity, the deliverer of messages to and from the spirit world who can be in all places simultaneously. In his extensive consideration of Eshu, Henry Louis Gates, Jr. writes: "this mutable figure ... true to the nature of the trickster" displays such qualities as "Individuality, satire, parody, irony, magic, indeterminacy, open-endedness, ambiguity, sexuality, chance, uncertainty, disruption, and reconciliation, betrayal and loyalty, closure and disclosure, encasement and rupture."[46] Masters of contradiction, Hopkinson's tricksters evoke the many manifestations of Eshu as well as Voudoun hierarchies and Taino notions of servitude; they simultaneously function as individual terminals extracting information from a central server. Eshus might be considered nodes on the 'Nansi Web, routing data from the central processing unit, Granny Nanny, to points on the web. At this current technology-fetishizing moment in the West, computers are expected to perform flawlessly, and developers relentlessly compete to increase speed, decrease size, and provide more services and storage. Computers should be perfect, obeying the commands of their users. However, our hardware wears out, our software often freezes, data gets corrupted, documents are lost, and the information we garner from the World Wide Web may disappear, or be revealed as unreliable or simply false. Hopkinson's 'Nansi Web paints a scenario in sync with the "real-world" performance of computer technology. In contrast to the Judeo-Christian image of a single supreme being whose deeds are known, the West African and Voudoun spirits each possess personality traits that make them inconsistent or unreliable. Voudoun spirits reflect those inevitable technological glitches that are invariably construed as unjust breaches of perfection in western imaginaries.

Hopkinson's vision of a central technology and its operating system, and her accompanying portrayals of gender, oral processes, and webbed systems of control, expose the cultural framework surrounding conventional formulations of mechanized futures. Concurrently, Hopkinson broadens Davies' model of the spider web, rendering Granny Nanny's [A]Nansi Web a technological enhancement of an always already webbed community. Moreover, by constructing a society that accepts misunderstandings and fractured access to information, Hopkinson affirms that technology is neither omniscient nor omnipotent. Granny Nanny, a woman-warrior and a spider weaving a web, is community-centered, responsive, and in dialogue with those she is committed to protecting.

Cyberpunk Revisited

In many cyberpunk texts, white corporate culture reigns supreme, and those who cannot or will not participate in it end up living in poverty. Although she situates herself "on the receiving end," Hopkinson does not produce a similarly dismal scenario. While the cyberpunk of Gibson and Stephenson reinforces current societal configurations, foreshadowing technology's eventual supremacy, the interactive nature of Granny Nanny reconfigures histories of colonization and domination. Hopkinson's corporate-dominated version of human–technology interfaces, is in dialogue with other cyberpunk narratives, and, like them, is not without its own embedded fantasies. Insofar as many of the conditions of the present are incorporated into its vision of the future, *Midnight Robber* acknowledges the increasing economic control exercised by US and multinational corporations; nevertheless, it refuses to predict a future crippled by capitalist greed. Even as the inhabitants of Toussaint colonize their planet in an expression of corporate allegiance, they do not strive to endlessly consume homogenous cultural artifacts. Like Gibson's infamous quip from "Burning Chrome": "the street finds its own uses for things" (1986, 186) in reference to drug consumption, Hopkinson, too, presupposes cultural innovation as multidirectional and unexpected. In contrast to other cyberpunk tales, however, Hopkinson's community strives to eliminate the widening material gaps present in contemporary capitalist society.

Despite its extreme control, the Marryshow Corporation is, for the most part, uncritically accepted by the community. Most constituents never question the pervasive presence of Granny Nanny, who controls access to collective knowledge. Rather, she is generally portrayed as benign and concerned about the general welfare of the inhabitants. In fact, most celebrations in Toussaint revolve around her perceived benevolence. The annual Carnival, for instance, names Granny Nanny as the way and means to a better life. Jonkanoo Season is the "time to give thanks to Granny Nanny for the Leaving Times, for her care, for life in this land, free from downpression and botherations. Time to remember the way their forefathers had toiled and sweated together" (Hopkinson 2000, 18). The citizens' loyalty to Granny Nanny also encompasses the corporation she embodies.

The Marryshow Corporation is, therefore, neither faceless nor evil. Inhabitants consider themselves Marryshevites, corporate members, thankful to Marryshow for establishing their society. For the most part, the all-powerful, corporate-based electronic net has become so accepted that only when disconnected can citizens recognize her presence and what it entails.

When Antonio and Tan-Tan escape Granny Nanny's punishment through self-exile, Antonio tells Tan-Tan: "we is new people, not Marryshevites no more" (Hopkinson 2000, 75). But according to Tan-Tan, "They were leaving Marryshow's paradise, shifting to a new world" (Hopkinson 2000, 76). While expulsion from Toussaint means freedom from corporate control, life without the Marryshow Corporation seems lonely to Tan-Tan, who finds herself surrounded by anarchic, undisciplined people that exist perilously close to nature.[47] The acceptance of Granny Nanny and the Marryshow Corporation, as well as the overwhelming consensus displayed by Marryshevites, veers sharply from the histories of rebellion inherited by Toussaint's society. In other words, this is an unlikely population to exhibit such complacent acceptance of an omniscient, omnipotent corporate body: "a Marryshevite couldn't even self take a piss without the toilet analyzing the chemical composition of the urine and logging the data in the health records" (Hopkinson 2000, 10). Perhaps this is why Granny Nanny does not endeavor to control all knowledge production. She tolerates defiance by the runners/programmers who invoke a simplified form of her code to suppress her surveillance, live in homes not connected to the 'Nansi Web, and maintain written records of select information despite the substitution of different forms of knowledge collection and retention for writing. Overt defiance, however, results in immediate expulsion.

The truth of Hopkinson's tale is presupposed as suspect, as is suggested in the novel's opening lines. Situated as a counter-exertion, the text does not endeavor to achieve consistency; instead, it disrupts narrative customs and refuses to posit ultimate truths. While conforming to the defining features of cyberpunk, *Midnight Robber* depicts " 'life' beyond the 'master discourse' " and offers alternative ways to conceive of human–technology relations. David Rodowick finds these deviant practices inspirational: "Culture jammers, guerrilla media, cyberpunk culture, warez or software pirates, hackers, and phone freaks all provide rich material for examining the creative possibilities that already exist for resisting, redesigning, and critiquing digital culture."[48] *Midnight Robber* injects the history of the African Diaspora into the realm of science fiction, creating a Digital Diaspora that connects the networks of diasporic myths with electronically based webs of information. The result is an enlarged set of vocabularies, images, and interpretations available for expressing the outcomes of African diaspora and paths of technological transformation. As Nelson claims of Afrofuturist texts, *Midnight Robber*

> reflect[s] African diasporic experience and at the same time attend[s] to the transformations that are the by-product of new media and information technology.

[It] excavate[s] and create[s] original narratives of identity, technology, and the future and offer[s] critiques of the promises of prevailing theories of technoculture.

(2001, 9)

Hopkinson's new poetics and hacker community put New Media in dialogue with New World histories, offering labyrinthine conjectures of, rather than conclusions about, the course of technologically mediated development.

Hopkinson does not offer globalization as a metaphor for American imperialism and capitalism writ large, nor does she presume a locality immune to its reach. The society she weaves produces novel versions of global effects and decenters the singular subject in its depiction of technology. She renders a planet responsive to technology by incorporating overlooked histories and strategies for resistance, without blindly embedding western values or fetishizing her digital creations simply because they articulate futuristic techno-replete visions. Furthermore, Hopkinson challenges dominant tropes about race, gender, and the intersections of past, present, and future. Her response to current trajectories thus diminishes the digital divide: "It's not binary. The boundary lines between the haves and the have-nots are blurry … science fiction and fantasy can be really exciting, where they can envision how change might come about" (Glave 2003, 153). Hopkinson's future, as well as those imagined in other Afrofuturist fiction, augment the possibilities for tomorrow and help broaden our understanding and development of human–machine interactions. Their inclusion in the cyberpunk canon, and the recognition of Hopkinson's strategies for digital creolization, supply scenarios that expand unilateral visions of carnivorous, corporate machines through the deployment of "virtual English." Midnight Robber illuminates virtual English's literary machinations by using multiple levels of digital creolization to resist and recast dominant configurations of technologies of communication.

4

Configuring a Nation

Our People Are Our Strength.

(http://eelamweb.com)

Our mission is to bring to the notice of the world at large the true situation in the form of timely news as it occurs [News], the facts related to the evolution of the crisis [Factbook], discussions on this attempted genocide [Analysis], and find ways to restore the rights of the people of Thamileelam to self determination and freedom.

(www.sangam.org/Mission.htm)

In its current state, the internet may be understood as a dynamic, shifting assemblage of computers and other electronic signal receptors storing, transmitting, pointing toward, and/or receiving bits of digital and analog information.[1] Popular representations of internet use, however, depict the exchange of information as the habitation of virtual space. Of course, privileging certain conceptions of online discourse environments over others is not a "disinterested" aesthetic strategy. In this chapter I consider how the envisioning of space, like all forms of rhetoric, inscribes particular relations of power (Foucault 1979; Soja 1989; Davis 1992). Current procedures for identifying the location of electronic data, Uniform Resource Locators (URLs), imagine the internet and the World Wide Web as geographically based systems with corresponding geopolitical reference points in the physical world. Rather than recognizing the networks formed through online information exchange or the World Wide Web's systemic indexicality, the prevailing images of the internet and the World Wide Web locate individuals, not to mention data, via spatial coordinates. The extension of time–space compression to the World Wide Web signifies yet another instance of western colonization. Some websites, however, eschew special metaphors and use networking and data dispersal to describe their function on the World Wide Web; for instance, Tamil Eelam websites highlight network figurations, dispersal, and/or boundary/ border crossings.

Tamil Eelam refers to the northern area of the island, which a majority of Sri Lankan Tamils believe should be designated a discrete nation-state. By prominently featuring the phrase "Tamil Eelam" in Web content, they challenge the idea that creolization and nationalism are mutually incompatible. While the use of creolization and the emphasis upon national sovereignty are consistent, the strategies of freedom fighters, government workers, and politicians – not to mention website administrators – differ. As the epigraphs illustrate, these Tamil Eelam-centered websites are not primarily concerned with geopolitical verisimilitude, but rather with community formation, primarily with respect to ethnic Tamils in diaspora. Through the interpellation and dissemination of a strategic narration of Sri Lankan history, these sites seek to emphasize shared descent, culture and language, thereby inspiring a sense of cultural nationalism. This reliance on ethnic identification over citizenship in a nation-state not only incites participation from permanently displaced Tamils, but also sympathetic recognition from non-Tamils who consume and reproduce their texts and images. In order to more fully exploit the possibilities of the World Wide Web, these Tamil Eelam websites practice a range of tactics for digital creolization, expanding the metaphors of space, network, and online interconnection by providing histories, national subjects, and western-style news reports that are replicated in Sri Lankan, Indian, and western presses.

Sri Lankan Tamils in diaspora established themselves on the internet early, actively posting to Usenet groups and, since 1996 launching websites. These websites vary in purpose, but are linked together to form an online presence premised on national recognition. They are updated frequently and provide a range of information and services for ethnic nationals in exile, their families and communities, and the world at large. Although the websites signifying the Tamil Eelam nation are dedicated to the creation of a conventional state or nation, many of the sites dislodge the correspondence between the World Wide Web and particular state-governed territories. Not only do the sites refuse to recognize the primacy of country-code suffixes to denote nation and location, but several Tamil Eelam websites portray themselves in contradistinction to practices understood to regulate the transmission protocols of data between linked computers. Unlike Paul Gilroy's assertion that diaspora is "an outer-national term" (2000, 123), these sites posit a national citizenship premised on bodies in diaspora rather than the occupation of land, and view the act of virtual recognition as the crucial component that will enable territorial sovereignty. Accordingly, the duration, look, and reliability of these groups on the Web is deemed more important than the possession of a "country code Top Level Domain Name" (ccTLDN). Given that the internet often appears as a timeless and ahistorical constellation of smooth spaces, this modification is essential.

This chapter will investigate the process by which dominant metaphors, particularly that of the spatially designated World Wide Web, have become naturalized and then examine the inequities that accompany these metaphors, such as the presumption that the internet occupies a space beyond historical time. Finally, I will establish that the most popular English-language websites concerned with Tamil Eelam employ the notion of networks to create a community premised on cultural nationalism. Through the process of digital creolization, Tamil Eelam websites have forged a platform for organization, and while this certainly promotes the recognition of their right to nation-state status, it also adjusts traditional conceptions of the nation-state and national membership by envisioning the internet as networks of information that scatter and shift over time. Rather than presuming direct correspondence with a geographical namesake, these Tamil Eelam websites lobby for traditional nation-state recognition by incorporating additional temporal histories, strategic cartography and symbolism, innovative practices for optimizing resources across media, and unique formulations for national membership through electronic connections and information dispersal. As a result, Tamil Eelem's digital creolization creatively exploits internet communication and reconceives our limited metaphorical designations and domain citation procedures.

"The Spatial Vogue"

Pierre Lévy describes cyberspace as a "chaotic system."[2] He writes: "Cyberspace ceaselessly redefines the outlines of a mobile and expanding labyrinth that can't be mapped, a universal labyrinth beyond Daedalus's wildest dreams" (Lévy and Bononno 2001, 91). Even while relying on spatial metaphors (cyberspace, labyrinth), Levy recognizes that the functions of the internet exceed their descriptors and tries to better portray this system by reaching backward, relying on a concept of mythology. Like many Web theorists, he struggles with the inadequacy of space, yet fails to find better-suited metaphors.

Since the 1990s, conceptions of the World Wide Web have been littered with references to space. The internet's popularization during the 1990s paralleled new theoretical conceptions of space inspired by Fredric Jameson's theory of cognitive mapping and, more importantly, Edward Soja's schema of spatiality.[3] In fact, Steve Pile and Michael Keith term the post-1990 theoretical preoccupation with space "The Spatial Vogue."[4] Spatiality is persistently summoned, Pile and Keith argue, to explain, yet ultimately to reinforce, contemporary conditions. Space is constantly produced through its invocation: "the geography and history of capitalism intersect in a complex social process which creates a constantly evolving historical sequence of spatiality" (Soja 1989, 127). Geographically based idioms such as "sites," "home," and "visitors," as well as URLs, are primary designations that rely on and reify contemporary geopolitical inequities, our contemporary "world," rather than eliciting the connectivity and interdependence suggested by the term "Web." Even today, space and its attendant concerns continue to dominate an arena suited to other imagery; depictions of cyberspace affirm the verisimilitude of non-digital, Cartesian-based geography. Rather than multiplicity, invocations of cyberspace yoke unfixable areas of electronic motion to geographically determined territories with static boundaries and a predetermined status within an international community. This reductive notion of cyberspace continues to under-gird transnational digital imaginaries and discussions of internet communication.

Considering that vast sequences of binary code are physically stored on hard drives and in other containers, the internet is far from transcending geographically grounded locations. Nevertheless, it is the transfer of information that fundamentally characterizes the internet: contacts between computers are initiated; code is exchanged; data summoned. Network imagery depicts an evolutionary, spatiotemporal process of connecting and intertwining. It might be considered, as Otto Imken explains, the functional reality of connectivity: "the dynamic result of linking computers to transfer and reveal data to discrete users."[5] The exchange of digital data possesses no bounded or static shape, and it occupies the territories of servers, hard drives, and broadband cables. Furthermore, connections are rarely direct or one-to-one; a request for data by a computer user will initiate responses from an unpredictable number of other computers and information-exchange portals in order to complete a process as simple as viewing a text document or a personal homepage. Janet Abbate relates the reliance of the internet on packet switching: "Since the nodes in a message switching system act independently in processing the messages and there are no preset routes between nodes, the nodes can adapt to changing conditions by picking the route that is best at any moment."[6] In fact, "best" routes are often miscalculated based on previous paths of exchange, so predictions based on efficiency or availability cannot chart actual data transmission. The internet's "shape" is permanently in flux, nebulous, and chaotic. It performs movement without encapsulation, borders, concrete interiors or exteriors.

Conceiving networkability requires breaks from the calcified confines of spatial relations, challenging us to identify new connections and unforeseeable outcomes of these interactions. In *Mapping Cyberspace*, Martin Dodge and Rob Kitchin write: "The sum of these nodes and their connections is greater than their parts, forming a network."[7] They recall the parallels some commentators have drawn between the internet and the human brain: "the brain comprises of millions of neurons and interconnecting nerve 'wires' that when combined together give rise to human consciousness, thought, memory and the mind" (Kitchin and Dodge 2001, 2). Network imagery suggests the dynamism and constantly changing structure of digital communication and, as a metaphor, the network better signifies the information transaction that takes place on the World Wide Web and correspondingly resists the crude mimeticism implied by spatial images.[8] Networks suggest that more happens in online exchanges than can be explained through dominant conceptions of space and place. Furthermore, networks are frequently referenced in accounts of similar circumstances by thinkers in many arenas, from software developers to philosophers. New-media scholars often endorse network imagery and outline the dangers of understanding the internet as "cyberspace" or the "information superhighway."[9] Philosophers and social scientists concerned with contemporary culture, from Gilles Deleuze to Manuel Castells, apply this technology-based network model to a host of cultural formulations, including, but not limited to, digitally based data and electronic communication.[10] Bruno Latour argues, for instance, that networks better describe one of two distinct practices encompassed/confused under the rubric of modernity.[11] Network practice is "more supple than the notion of system, more historical than the notion of structure, more empirical than the notion of complexity, the idea of network is the Ariadne's thread of these interwoven stories" (Latour 1993, 3).

Within businesses and institutions, networks are the dominant metaphor evoked with regard to internal information exchange: computers linked to servers within a single organization, without regard to the location of these computers, comprise an intranet. Microsoft has capitalized upon network imagery with respect to intranet systems. Both their office-system-geared operating system, Windows NT, and their intranet-development software, .NET, are based on connectivity among personal computers within a single business environment. Interactions among businesses, or with those using the internet outside of the networked system, are understood as dangerous (or dangerous distractions to employee productivity) requiring security such as virus scanners and firewalls to protect against invasion by hostile intruders. Microsoft therefore promotes the belief that the internet is a site of potential violation, while it characterizes intranet connectivity as productive, compatible, and efficient: a seamless and non-caustic network. Thus, the inside/center is the safe and knowable, and the outside/margin becomes the threatening "other." As with people, culture, or sexuality, western binary formulation achieves its primary goal: to split unclear boundaries and render one unknowable and less valid.

But even the metaphor of the network fails to account for the practices of digital technologies in their virtuality.[12] Brian Massumi argues, "the networkability of event transmission must be seen as pertaining not only to mass-media images but to information in general.... All of these event transmitters carry a high charge of indeterminacy, or unrealized (or, in contemporary vocabulary, 'unactualized') potential."[13] Remembering that the virtual infers potential, gesture, and open-endedness rather than digital communication or the internet, specifically, suggests flow and possibilities and recalls the indeterminacy inherent in computer-mediated exchanges. Virtuality, as opposed to space or network, incorporates the inherent unrealized potential before the actualization of any event. More specifically for New Media, virtuality reflects all yet-to-be-realized combinations or configurations of convergence of media made possible through digital transmissions. Calling upon a vastly complicated, intersecting, and variable series of connections, the network metaphor still fails to encompass the exchanges taking place between terminals, although it does take into account movement, shift, and possibility, thus transcending clearly prescribed boundaries of location that can be occupied in an alternative, but corresponding, dimension. While network imagery explicates the dynamism of connectivity and information exchange, it, too, falls short of encapsulating digitally based communication. Spatial, network, and virtual metaphors each carry with them ideological effects that necessarily inform how online practices are understood and demarcate the unstable and unsustainable contours of the ever-shifting hegemonic conceptions of virtual practices.

Journalistic and popular accounts of the internet were heavily influenced by the cyberpunk genre. The virtual structure and potential of this emerging mode of communication, while seemingly infinite, were, in fact, centered around cyberpunk's vision, and its development proceeds accordingly. The electronic systems in these formulations were described as gridded Euclidean worlds, stretching uniformly and endlessly in all directions (geometric totalities). Spatial metaphors have, perhaps, persisted in World Wide Web considerations because they were fundamental to cyberpunk's vision of this new, online environment. The electronic worlds imagined by William Gibson's cyberspace in *Neuromancer* (1984) and Neil Stephenson's Metaverse in *Snow Crash* (1992) provided the blueprints for conceptualizing the internet as a terrain with properties that correspond to current geopolitical circumstances – as another dimension that reflects the one we inhabit.[14] As I discussed at length in the second chapter, the Cartesian construction of online worlds "naturalized" our understanding of digital communication as space-based. The actualization of the virtual potential for conceiving of digital communication secured the dominance of three-dimensional visions online. This popularization promoted futuristic processes of globalizations by providing within a spatial-oriented verisimilitude increased mobility, bodily capabilities, and imaginative improvements that overcame the real-world attributes much of western thought considered to be detrimental to futuristic processes of globalization, providing increased mobility, bodily capabilities, and imaginative improvements all within the contained parameters of spatially oriented verisimilitude.

In *Cyberspace: First Steps*, Michael Benedikt compiles a series of essays that endorse the spatiality of electronic exchanges. Benedikt's own contribution envisions connectivity as another form of architecture, providing complex graphs and metaphors about movement in space and fields. In the same collection, Marcos Novak defines cyberspace as "a completely spatialized visualization of all information in global information processing systems" (Novak 1993, 228). Still considered a visionary, Howard Rheingold refers to the internet as a frontier. As the title of his influential – and recently reissued – 1993 text, *The Virtual Community: Homesteading on the Electronic Frontier*, suggests, envisioning the internet as a vast wasteland that can be put to better use through bringing "home" – and all that it entails– to the user fuels a sense of superiority and entitlement, as well as the masculinist spirit of conquest. This logic, called upon by US politicians seeking support for various endeavors, ranging from Manifest Destiny and the NASA space exploration program to the war in Iraq, once fueled exploration, domination, and colonial exploitation by European nations. And here, it describes the internet. These spatial metaphors, like earlier imagery used to describe territorial incursion and cultural domination, encode social subjugation into notions surrounding exploration and inhabitation.

Much has been made of the effects of mapping on subjugation throughout the colonial project. Mapping involves exploration, selection, definition, generalization, and the translation of data; it assumes a range of social powers. The power to define location is closely entwined with the power of conquest and hierarchical social positioning. Anne McClintock's account of the genealogies of imperialism reveals that map-making is not a neutral procedure for gathering and displaying information in order to make place and space universally legible, but rather functions as a power process for historical legitimation and continuing domination premised on choosing what to include and how to present it. She writes:

> The map is a technology of knowledge that professes to capture the truth about a place in pure, scientific form, operating under the guise of scientific exactitude and promising to retrieve and reproduce nature exactly as it is. As such, it is also a technology of possession, promising that those with the capacity to make such perfect representations must also have the right of territorial control.[15]

Tongchai Winichakul uses the instance of Siam to explain one ramification of colonial attempts at territorial acquisition: the construction of national boundaries. He writes that maps "anticipated … spatial reality, not vice versa. In other words, a map was a model for, rather than a model of, what it purported to represent."[16] Maps do not merely render visible that which already exists; instead, they actively mediate and/or create the relationship between human beings and space. Spatial conceptions of the internet mirror the effects of mapping nation-states. By associating information accessible by a remote computer with a fixed location in cyberspace (one that can be traveled, surfed, or navigated, and then put into perspective, located, and mapped), current global conditions resulting from historical injustices such as slavery, colonization, and military invasion are replicated in the electronic domain. No longer merely occupying space or moving through it to reach a destination, the cyber-traveler can surf, catch a wave, ride it, and, consequently, tame the wild ocean, or, recalling Christopher Columbus, he can navigate at the helm of a ship and claim truth and objectivity in ordering and interpreting all that he witnesses.

Similarly, inhabiting cyberspace signals not merely existence or co-existence, but conquest and occupation. While moving through space is the dominant metaphor for receiving data from remote computers, viewing the information provided on websites, for instance, further reifies the territorial metaphor. Conceptualizing webpages as locatable under the logic of domain names and URLs enforces the perspective of mapping with its attendant ideological implications. Foregrounding these metaphors displaces other discourses that might better depict electronic communication. The majority of websites, particularly those dedicated to portraying nation-states, presume a correlation between "locations" on the World Wide Web and physical territory. Many websites, such as those that contain search engines or news services, function mainly as connections to other sites, and their ever-changing interactivity exceeds both spatial and network designations. The most trafficked Tamil Eelam sites imagine themselves as the latter: a conglomerate of connections, potentiality, and flexibility. But before explaining these cases where national concerns are promoted in non-spatial terms, I will explore the dominant practice of geopolitical mimeticism to designate online communication – how nations and peoples with geo-spatial territories enjoy "virtual" preference over those without geo-spatial allegiances.

Mapping TLDNs

The URL presumes to locate a website – a place in space, as its name suggests – that is "in" or "on" the World Wide Web. This nomenclature's inherent anchoring to contemporary conceptions of geopolitical configurations is most clearly articulated in the use of top-level domain name (TLDN) suffixes. These suffixes were initially devised by the Internet Assigned Numbers Authority (IANA) in order to designate purpose and discourage state intervention. Seven generic top-level domain names were assigned: .com, .edu, .net, .gov, .org, .int, and .mil. The IANA also created country-code top-level domain names (ccTLDNs). Initially, as Jon Postel recalls, "they didn't think the country codes would be used for much."[17] Although country codes were not reserved for the central authority of the corresponding nation-state, governing institutions received preferential treatment when applying for control of their designated country codes. Both IANA and the Internet Corporation for Assigned Names and Numbers (ICANN), which assumed IANA's functions in 1998, required that while governments need not be the sole operators of their domain, country-code top-level domain names must assign an administrative contact that resides in the country indicated by the country code. Nations that did not occupy bounded territories recognized by the International Organization of Standardization (ISO), such as Tamil Eelam, were not assigned country-code TLD suffixes with which to organize their Uniform Resource Locators (URLs). Consequently, websites are often interpreted according to the physical nation-state to which they refer, and names without nation-based suffixes, such as .org, .com, or .edu, were initially assumed to be US-based, reinforcing the US's claim as the originator and center of electronic connectivity.

US organizations still follow this practice: the .edu suffix implicitly designates the site as an institution of higher learning located within the United States. It is not available to universities outside US borders. Corruption and incompetence within ICANN are generally perceived to be the reasons for the continued application of this unequal system. There has been much ado, but little action encouraging the utilization of alternative TLDNs. Although websites increasingly employ general top-level domain names rather than country codes, country codes continue to place websites in relation to their territorial referents. Prevailing conceptions of the World Wide Web must shift before country-code nomenclature is abandoned, or they will continue to present challenges like those encountered in the examples that follow.

In 1999, Prasenjit Maiti argued: "To someone capable of 'reading' domain-names, this offers as much information as a genealogist might obtain from a family-name. In particular, almost every domain-name indicates the country of origin in the 'top-level' (last) segment of the name."[18] Reflecting the dominant imagery used to describe computer networks, the text-based addresses that locate these inhabited sites reproduce a US-centered view of the world; yet, this logic is increasingly misleading. Domain endings, particularly those that lack specific nation-state referents, have never necessarily reflected membership or citizenship. A hierarchy of top-level domain names has emerged, and producers now attempt to obtain addresses that they believe will enhance their status. Domain names, Maiti argues, are assumed to contain the genealogy of that which they designate. The geographic locations they signify, therefore, affect how visitors assess them.

Increasingly, TLDNs such as .com and .net no longer signal United States ownership; international or non-local (albeit primarily commercial) websites employ these suffixes as well. Despite the growing ease of general TLDN registration and widespread encouragement by domain-name acquisition services whose available domain-name search engines automatically suggest purchasing general domains rather than those that employ country codes, ccTLDNs maintain their popularity. They continue to function as the primary designation for organizing people, products, information, and interactions online. As Alexander Halavais has found:

> While the internet incorporates little in the way of the technological, regulatory or economic impediments to transnational interconnections, the web demonstrates that national cultures continue to exert a substantial influence on how these connections are made. While national borders may be eroded, they certainly remain significant.[19]

Yoking networks of connectivity to nation-states through TLDNs extends the forces of capitalism, rendering a virtual topography where nation-states with little power and few resources in the global marketplace wither away.

In several instances, corporate entities have negotiated for control of the domain suffixes of small, less-powerful nations that have ccTLDNs seen as marketable, such as .nu, the country code for the remote island community of Niue. A

Verisign Company, for example, sells the nation of Tuvalu's domain name, the desirable .tv suffix, at the nation's homepage (www.tv). When the domain was initially contracted for sale, the homepage contained a link, "About Tuvalu," that offered photographs depicting a romantic version of a simple, non-industrialized, Pacific-island people practicing dance ceremonies and fishing. These people were supposed to benefit materially from the purchase of a domain that used their ccTLDN – through both a profit-sharing plan (put into place by the initial contractor and honored by Verisign, Inc.) and computer access – a small hut with several computers and a generator placed on the island for public use. Since 2002, however, finding this Pacific island nation on its national homepage has not been possible; the company's earlier commitment to the residents of Tuvalu has been coded away. As Versign's commitment to Tuvalu diminishes, the island itself faces eventual sublimination due to flooding and coastline erosion, the effects of global warming caused by industrialized nations. For example, the most frequently trafficked site exploiting Tuvalu's ccTLDN is Al Gore's current .tv, a website linked to a cable-television station that broadcasts user-generated content. Al Gore, who is celebrated for his commitment to stopping environmental destruction, buys into the corporatization of the domain name that has erased the island's online existence – one small example of the contradictions of domain-name practices.[20] While Tamil Eelam has no recognized geopolitical territory and exists only virtually, Tuvalu will experience the reverse, eventually existing only in the

About Tuvalu, Linkin 2002.

The .tv Corporation - www.tv - Domain Name Registration Services

The island of Tuvalu's ccTLDN.

memories of its people and the traces of the TLDN owned by a corporation with no ties to the corresponding landmass.[21]

Many alternatives to mapping in accordance with political configurations exist: they might employ the numerical designations that underlie these text-based space markers, insist on the universal application of generic URLs without regional designations, or devise a new system of nomenclature that upsets the hegemonic status of the US. Unfortunately, it would take considerable resources to upset the status quo, even with the already frequent complaints about the implicit hierarchy in internet practices that supports US dominance. Tamil Eelam websites, however, offer several alternative models that challenge accepted territorial correspondences.

In contrast to the corporate administration conducted on behalf of small nations with in-demand country codes and limited resources, nations not recognized by the ISO and struggling for territory have no geographical reference point in the dominant logic of cyberspace. In order to exist in a primarily Euclidean world, Tamil Eelam must adopt a novel approach to online representation. Accordingly, Tamil Eelam websites employ cultural nationalism and network-oriented models of conceiving of the World Wide Web while arguing for geopolitical acknowledgment. Their use of the Web proves that alternative practices involving electronic communication and network-based understandings of the internet's shape and function also reflect both the internet and the variety of ways it functions. For Tamil Eelam to remain a virtual possibility, those coding it resist dominant conceptions of electronic communication to reinterpret the state, the citizen body, and the project of nation-building.

Three Histories

Before I provide a detailed account of the unusual practices of Tamil Eelam websites, a brief outline of Tamil history in Sri Lanka is in order. The Tamil people of the island of Ceylon/Sri Lanka were historically a small, independent population scattered in the north of the island. Their population boomed when Tamils from Southern India were brought as preferential laborers to the island during Portuguese, Dutch, and British colonial occupation (1597–1948). This influx aroused resentment among the majority Sinhalese. The colonial British authority established a single government on this previously divided island which they called "Ceylon." The seat of the government was located in Colombo, a largely Sinhalese area. Colombo remained the capital city after the island gained independence in 1948 and the Sinhalese population took control of the government. The Sri Lankan government wished to rectify the inequities propagated under British rule and, in 1972, a new constitution was introduced that designated Sinhalese as the sole official state language and Buddhism as the state religion, an act which led to segregated education and a disenfranchised English- and Tamil-speaking, overwhelmingly Hindu, Tamil population. Consequently, the Tamil minority, who neither speak Sinhalese nor practice Buddhism, is increasingly considered by the Sinhalese to be a reminder of colonial subjugation.

The formation of the Liberation Tigers of Tamil Eelam (LTTE) following the new constitution led to several violent conflicts. In 1983, violence erupted between Tamil guerrillas and Sinhalese government troops in the northern section of the island where the Tamil population is the majority. Thousands were killed. A peace plan negotiated in 1987 called for a cease-fire and created a local government council in the Tamil-dominated region of Sri Lanka. While some Tamils agreed to the compromise, a significant portion did not, and fighting recommenced several months later. Another cease-fire was implemented in 1989, but Sinhalese nationalists opposed the agreements that the government reached with Tamils, and violence continued. Despite accords in 1989, 1994, and yearly since 2000, the two groups and their government officials have been unable to produce a mutually acceptable peace plan. Though the country is still declared unified, it is rife with violent outbreaks and legal inconsistencies. The 2004 tsunami only heightened the tensions between these two groups; much of the international aid was distributed through the Colombo-based government and, according to many journalists, was skewed to provide relief to the Sinhalese majority. In February 2005, the LTTE's eastern provincial leader, E. Kousalyan, was murdered in an ambush. The Tigers blamed it on a paramilitary group working with the government groups that were conducting relief efforts. Since then, tension between the Sinhalese and the Tamils has reignited and peace talks are suspended indefinitely.

Since Sri Lanka and international governing bodies such as the United Nations have denied Sri Lankans the right to land claims and self-governing, many Tamils in Sri Lanka support the LTTE. The Tamil Tigers are committed to gaining control of the historically Tamil-occupied territory through negotiation, disruption, and violence. In order to escape persecution from the Sri Lankan government, which has suspended the Tamil population's rights as citizens, a large number of Tamils have fled the island and relocated to countries granting them political asylum. These far-flung Tamils, together with their compatriots in Sri Lanka, constitute the stateless nation of Tamil Eelam, which is reflected in these scattered groups' presence on the World Wide Web.

Tamil Eelam nationalists, many of whom are Tamils in diaspora following the activities of the LTTE and Sri Lankan government on these websites, are committed to the establishment of an ethnically homogeneous Tamil nation-state, Tamil Eelam. Tamil Eelam websites persistently posit their historical presence and continual habitation of the contested territory in northern Sri Lanka, though this is an issue of contention. The Sinhalese claim that Tamil presence was insignificant before colonial occupation; Tamils assert that the island contained two coexisting kingdoms before this period. For instance, TamilCanadian, a website that dubs itself the "tamils' true voice" states:

> The Tamils and the Sinhalese, the two indigenous peoples, called the country by various titles at different periods. The new name "Sri Lanka" was bestowed by the Republican constitution on 22 May 1972 by the Sinhala government. The Tamils continued to call the country "Ilankai". The Tamil consciousness led to the naming of the north and east of Sri Lanka, the Tamil traditional homelands as Tamil Eelam.[22]

It is imperative to the Tamil Eelam national project that the Tamils are perceived as indigenous people, rather than, as the Sinhalese argue, foreign workers "imported" by British colonizers. This historical account contends that the nation's current name, Sri Lanka, disregards its Tamil constituency. Colonization persists in this account: two coexisting peoples were forced together to form British-occupied Ceylon, and then, after the British ceded the land back to its inhabitants, the Sinhalese dismissed their minority constituency. Similarly, the Tamil Eelam homepage depicts Sri Lankan Tamils as a distinct "social entity" on the island "with their own history, traditions, culture, language, and traditional homeland."[23]

The goal of Tamils is to have "peace and dignity … in their historically given homeland."[24] Almost every Tamil Eelam website recalls the lengthy history of Sri Lankan Tamils, the development of the Tamil alphabet (one of the earliest written alphabets), and their distinct traditions and culture. In fact, some websites trace the origin of the Tamil population back to the ancient Sumerians 8,000 years ago, crediting them with the invention of the wheel.[25] These websites also provide manifestos that describe official Tamil beliefs and the injustices they have faced, underscoring their contention of a peaceful coexistence with the Sinhalese in the precolonial era, which implicitly suggests that current conflicts are a result of external domination. Hence, the establishment of Tamil Eelam signifies a return to an original, precolonial, and proto-nation-state based on the problematic concept of an untainted past. Each of these websites offers discussion forums for topics of interest to Tamil Eelam sympathizers and opportunities to share news and concerns, as well as providing remote citizens with the chance to participate in national decision-making processes.

Tamil Eelam is first and foremost a nation-building effort. Tamil Eelam websites, however, have envisioned the project in response to contemporary conditions, embracing their diasporic constituency and utilizing worldwide connectivity to promote, communicate, and disseminate information – a different form of cosmopolitan participation. With regard to traditional nation-building, Homi Bhabha describes a dual temporal process: "in the production of the nation as narration there is a split between the continuist, accumulative temporality of the pedagogical, and the repetitious, recursive strategy of the performative."[26] These websites not only recall the double history – described by Bhabha as a requisite for nation formation – but also propagate this duality, displaying a digital face for analog information that is frequently updated in order to solidify the case for a third history, further cementing their claims for national recognition (Bhabha 1994, 81). Sites such as TamilNet.com, EelamWEB.com, TamilCanadian.com and Tamil Eelam Sangam argue that there was an "original" period of Tamil and Sinhalese coexistence,[27] thereby imagining a performative history (past) in which colonial domination was overturned. These Tamil Eelam websites redact both these histories, solidifying them through long-standing accounts of Tamil heritage and chronicling daily activities in response to land claims and recognition. In addition, Tamil nationalists redouble their efforts by narrating the continuous temporality of the sites while postulating a third history – premised on Web duration – to justify their existence. This tertiary historical employment depends on a notion of virtual – not geopolitical – occupation. Using the internet to affirm the sustained Tamil presence in Sri Lanka and document both their past and the Tamil independence movement, Tamil Eelam nationalists qualify themselves for recognition.

The double duality engendered by digital dispersion manifests itself through constant updates, so as not to appear outdated. Tamilnet.com, in particular, updates its homepage often, especially when news "breaks." Opening the site in a browser can therefore seem like catching up– the site speaks more to creating a current moment than to directly enticing the visitor, as is accomplished on other Tamil Eelam sites through dynamic graphic design or images of "island tranquility," including palm trees and sandy beaches. Furthermore, the website often projects Tamil Eelam as an imagined physical location, a "resource awaiting development," which is "replete with stories of how the war-torn north and east is being

www.tamilnet.com.

rehabilitated by the LTTE administration."[28] As Maya Ranganathan argues: "The implicit message in these presentist accounts is that the LTTE is building a new utopia that nonetheless will honour past history and traditions of Eelam" (2006a, 289).

Meanwhile, a third historical trajectory is articulated in various materializations on each site. Sangam, for example, claims venerability for its seven-year tenure online. Until 2004, a moving banner at the top of its homepage declared, "Seventh year on the web. Standing Up for What We Believe In" (www.sangam. org 2001). It also contends that the age of its real-world counterpart makes the organization indispensable: the words "we are 25" accompany the first image below the site's banner. Sangam's new configuration features a link to the "chronological archive." This archive function attests to the site's historical importance and its role as a source of documentation. Tamilnet.com similarly offers access to earlier articles from its archives. These sites therefore continually celebrate age and duration in terms of the people, their independence movement, and their virtual network.

Through these websites, Tamil participants can enjoy a sense of time in addition to that posited by Bhabha – an eternal present in topical updates and a permanence in their commitment to situating themselves online. While the World Wide Web is often posited as disruptive or contradictory to nationalism and the nation-state,[29] deterritorialized (diasporic subjects) and unterritorializable (the Tamil Eelam nation-state) cooperate in this instance via digital technologies in the service of community building and the production of cultural nationalism, including ideologies of political separatism.

Tamil Eelam Networks

Tamils of Sri Lanka have a long history of internet presence. Contributors from the Tamil diaspora were active participants in Usenet groups such as alt.soc.tamil before browsers popularized the World Wide Web.[30] Usenet sites functioned as nodes for information dispersal about Tamils in Sri Lanka and abroad; contributions ranged from newspaper articles and impassioned rants to poetry and solicitations for Tiger participation. In addition, the "Internet Black Tigers," an offshoot of the LTTE, are recognized as the first cyber-terrorists. They take credit for sending several Sri Lankan embassies over 800 emails per day, overloading their systems and "disabling embassy networks for several days."[31] This online presence allows Tamil Eelam to craft a history that moves away from narrowly mimetic geographic images and enables its supporters to envision a different modality of the virtual, one that interfaces history and networks, making their voices heard, even offline, and constructing a temporal rather than a spatial assemblage.

Benedict Anderson's celebrated theory of nationalism as an "imagined community" based on networks of people and the circulation of information begs to be evoked when considering the strategies of Tamil Eelam online.[32] English-language Tamil Eelam websites illustrate a profound disengagement with territorial acquisition or referentiality, despite their universal support for succession from Sri Lanka and the efforts of the Tamil Tigers. Extending the notion of community in his tract *The Coming Community*, Georgio Agamben describes linguistic acts of multiple singularities (via Deleuze) that "communicate only in the empty space of the example, without being tied by any common property, by any identity."[33] In other words, his "coming community" is one with no specific physical referent, no solid example – a virtual "empty space" which always exists in the future. Agamben sees the state as opposing community because it operates to forbid dissolution and disregard social bonds (Agamben 1993, 86). Though the Tamil Eelam networks conjure an imagined community and not a nation-state, in doing so they do not undermine the development of a geopolitical territory. Instead, by informing both Tamils and non-Tamils about their history, culture, and language, they differentiate Tamil Eelam from Sri Lanka and other nation-states, furthering the cause for the development of a discrete nation-state. Thus, these websites presuppose nation-state formation as an outcome of their creation of a "coming community." By adjusting these multiple articulations of nationalism to facilitate community formation, the "coming community" that these sites engender describes a national subject through cultural identification, one that shifts through time and space, and occupies multiple textual manifestations.

The "coming community," with its lack of fixed, indissoluble meaning, is suggested in the names of the two most trafficked sites, which, rather than referring to the establishment of Tamil Eelam sovereignty directly, broadcast the networking features of the internet through their appellations. Instead of using terminology that designates a space for discussing issues concerning the establishment and recognition of Tamil Eelam, their names, Tamilnet.com and Eelamweb.com, envision a network or Web of information dispersal and exchange, a non-space with multiple means for engagement. Through the incorporation of "net" and "web," internet- and World Wide Web-specific references, in their domain names, these sites appear in a strictly electronic realm, recalling weaving and interconnectivity rather than physical location. Accordingly, no maps appear on the homepages that outline the contested territory of Tamil Eelam. In fact, only Eelamweb.com conjures the project of state formation through its name, "Eelam," which translates to "home" or "homeland."

With no domain name that maps a corresponding geopolitical location, no clear base of operations beyond the World Wide Web, and services aimed at any interested English-speaking user, these nets and webs, as their names suggest, exist in an electronic network without a corresponding physical space. By employing the .com suffix, these Tamil Eelam websites, like other Web presences that refuse to accept that a .com address requires a US affiliation, break the correspondence between cyberspace designation and geopolitical powers. This use of the suffix disrupts the centrality of the US on the Web. Because these websites promote themselves as existing in a purely virtual realm, they engender a "coming

The Sri Lankan national homepage (offline since 2006), positions the country as encapsulated by a web "window" for outsiders.

community" based on networks of information with changing articulations based on participation.

Citation and Index: Beyond Space and Network

Tamil Eelam websites do more than eschew spatial metaphors and champion the network. They also use alternative imagery to further their cause. Maps, URLs, history and news appear, at times, to theoretically contradict a coherent strategy, particularly according to the theories of nationalism and community I have cited. These websites utilize whatever grammar best suits the moment; nowhere is this cacophony of imagery articulated as problematic. Digital creolization occurs through the non-analogous use of vocabulary, form, and website function in the name of Tamil Eelam.

While the Ilankai Tamil Sangam site and others remind visitors that Tamils speak "one of the oldest living languages in the world," English is the prominent means not only for "reporting to the world," but also for facilitating ethnic identification. Since the sites' users are not assumed to speak a single national language, English provides the means for the majority of cultural transmission. In fact, it is through English that many of these sites, such as Tamilnet.com, offer opportunities for Tamil language acquisition. On a primarily English-language page, links to resources for learning to read and speak Tamil are provided, while another page outlines (in English) how to produce Tamil script on computers. This encourages any visitor, not only those linked to Tamil Eelam, to discover or deepen their understanding of Tamil, often situated as an ancient and historically sedimented language. By combining English and Tamil in this way, these sites become effectively bilingual, which, Ranganathan writes, appeals to the English-educated younger generation in diaspora, enabling them to learn about "their" nation (Ranganathan 2006a, 62) and its language. Additionally, providing common online resources like lists of baby names promotes the recognition and perpetuation of Tamil-language familiarity via an English-language format.

Tamilnet.com and Eelamweb.com behave like news services rather than Web-based locations standing in for, or speaking on behalf of, a land-based

www.eelamweb.com.

territory. Both sites display themselves in a manner unusual for other nation-state websites, particularly that of Sri Lanka, which situates itself as a window into a geographically specific tourist destination or investment opportunity for the outside world.[34] Eelamweb.com, in particular, imitates news services anchored to physical places, such as the *New York Times* (www.nytimes.com) or the *Washington Post* (www.washingtonpost.com), reporting on events of concern to the corresponding location and beyond, rather than providing a portrait of the country or outlining its political agenda for casual visitors. As opposed to a page written for those it signifies, Eelamweb.com attempts to form community from a global readership, one that exceeds the worldwide Sri Lankan Tamil population. In an effort to resist the geographical correlation presumed by discourses on citizenship, Eelamweb.com suggests that visitors, who perceive the sites as networks for the dispersal of news, fundamentally comprise the sites. The reports on these pages are concerned with the actions of the Liberation Tigers of Tamil Eelam (LTTE), which metaphorically equates Tamil Eelam to this group described by Sinhalese Sri Lankans as terrorists.

Similarly, Tamilnet.com claims to "report to the world on Tamil affairs."[35] Here it uses "the world" in a geopolitical sense, yet the rest of the site focuses on site-specific production rather than anchoring reports to the physical location from whence the events occurred. This suggests a network of writers and readers sharing insights on a particular topic rather than ethnic or national affiliation, prioritizing information rather than location. Some reporting in Tamil is offered, but the site's content is primarily in English, the dominant language of the inter-

Washingtonpost.com.

net. Like Eelamweb.com, Tamilnet.com targets a large constituency of prospective sympathizers, assuming the potential of the Web to create a network of fellow travelers and activists beyond the Sri Lankan Tamil community. Anthropologist Mark Whitaker, who has a longstanding relationship with "Taraki" Dharmeratnam, the organizer and head of Tamilnet.com, writes that the organization arranged training for journalists on the ground, equipped them with computers, modems, and digital cameras, and exploited the skills of bilingual Tamils in Finland, the Netherlands, Germany, Canada, and the United States.[36] Instead of being affixed to a territory, the reports are generated on-site and quickly dispersed to the diaspora, where available collaborators quickly translate and resubmit them to Tamilnet.com. The site can therefore produce reliable news reports much faster than the traditional press, which relies on editors located in a single location who are bound by the employee rules and work-time regulations as well as time restrictions associated with journalists in different locations and correspondents in designated offices. Print journalism can use Tamilnet.com's seemingly reliable accounts without endangering the reputation of their own reporters and, because of its worldwide participation, with faster production than is possible in print.

In order to serve both the Tamil people and the global market, Tamil Eelam websites seek not only to mimic western journalism, but to improve upon it. As Whitaker writes of Dharmeratnam's project to speak the language of western journalism, "they had to be ... exemplars of Western journalism – better, that is, in terms of accuracy and remorseless even handedness ... with a subtle difference in both gaze and goal" (Whitaker 2004, 448). Dharmeratnam's strategy for simultaneously inspiring ethnic national sentiment in Tamils worldwide and addressing and informing non-Tamils consisted of giving up "the rhetoric of 'opaque expatriate' nationalism altogether" and "making 'ironic use' of the language of 'objective neutrality' most often deployed by Sri Lanka's foremost interlocutors: the international press and Western academia" (Whitaker 2004, 486). The "ironic use" that Dharmeratnam describes is a strategy of digital creolization. By invoking the language of journalism, complete with its trappings of speed, accuracy, and "objective neutrality," websites like Tamilnet.com achieve the position of authority with respect to the affairs of this contested zone. The world press, as well as Sri Lankan newspapers and Tamils abroad, look to Dharmeratnam's reports as they best speak the journalistic requirements of accurate reportage. Tamilnet.com can thereby fulfill both Tamils' and the world press' desire for information. In fact, in May 2004, Whitaker claimed that "At present ... all of Sri Lanka's national newspapers, regardless of language, ... as well as all of the main Western and Indian news agencies reporting on Sri Lanka, use Tamilnet.com reports" (Whitaker 2004, 492). By exploiting the instantaneous nature of the internet, Tamilnet.com provides information first; by providing accurate, seemingly objective, English-language reports, its stories are picked up by other news agencies. Digital creolization here takes the form of what journalism teachers might suggest are "best-case practices."

Other Tamil Eelam sites exercise different strategies for digital creolization. For instance, while the .org suffix continues to designate US-based non-profit organizations, websites employing this suffix without US-based status disrupt the notion that online issues adhere to the policies of their designated national locations. Not only has the US government classified the Tamil Tigers as terrorists, but George W. Bush has proclaimed them to be enemies of the nation in the current "war on terrorism." However, two websites using .org suffixes, both of which support the actions of the Tamil Tigers and one of which serves as a news source for Tamil speakers, illustrate that implied national markers need not reflect the opinions or concerns of the host nation-state's government or its citizens. Furthermore, registering in the US has several advantages for enabling the distribution of site-less information. For example, websites that clearly support the LTTE cannot register using the country-code for Sri Lanka, as doing so would constitute treason. Suggesting a United States or United Kingdom domain maintains the websites' legal status: in these countries, publishing Web content against the interests of another country does not constitute a crime. Rather than referring to Sri Lanka, the Ilankai Tamil Sangam, also known as the Association of Tamils of Eelam and Sri Lanka in the United States, locates itself clearly within US borders: "The Ilankai Tamil Sangam is such an organization of the exiled people of Tamileelam in the USA."[37] Like many of the other Tamil sites discussed, the Ilankai Tamil Sangam site addresses citizenship through identification, not location. Tamils in diaspora must speak out on behalf of their fellow citizens in order to guarantee the continued existence of Tamil Eelam. Tamil expatriates living in liberal democracies, they argue, "are the only voice through which the voiceless Tamils can speak."[38]

Taking advantage of Canada's position in the "free" world (one more sympathetic to the LTTE than the US), location is used strategically to make a statement about the national subject's ability to have a voice, thereby deflecting the ties that normally bind URL to a corresponding place. TamilCanadian.com uses the .com TLDN but emanates from Canada. The site's logo sports a Canadian flag, the phrase "TamilCanadian," and a claim to be: "Tamils' True Voice."[39] This suggests that Tamils cannot be heard from other locations; yoking Tamils to Sri Lanka necessarily censors their "True Voice." Here, the process of claiming a geopolitical referent calls attention to suppression and human-rights violations elsewhere. Using the .org or .com TLDN also takes advantage of the hierarchy implicit in domain-naming practices: an organization featuring a .org or .com TLDN is presumed to be a non-profit from the US, which immediately earns it credibility as an organization fighting for what is generally accepted in most western nations as universal human rights. Canada, too, is a nation with a reputation for tolerance and respect for suppressed groups. Communicating a human-rights plea on websites with .org or .com URLs and US and/or Canadian markers once again marks the irony implied by Dharmeratnam; digital creolization relies on the assumption of universal human rights, domain-naming conventions, and the prestige afforded to refugee populations in the US and Canada.

www.tamilcanadian.com.

As I've discussed, maps provide the illusion of totalizing classification and suggest geo-political correspondence; maps also serve as powerful emblems for ante-colonial and postcolonial nationalism. Consequently, digital creolization enacts all of these symbolic functions, summoned through depictions of the shape of the proposed territory. Maps appear on each Tamil Eelam website, although they vary in appearance and location, providing an array of potential significations. Eelam.com's wallpaper page, for example, offers downloadable images of calming waves as well as maps that show the war zone and detailed views of the land said to constitute the nation-state.[40] Its homepage contains an image of the island of Sri Lanka at the top right-hand corner, but here it appears as a heart-shaped, pastel-pink field with a dark-pink field section designating the

Tamil-Eelam nation.[41] The outline suggests a pulsing, beating heart, a version of Tamil Eelam removed from the physicality of its location. Eelam within Sri Lanka appears as the arteries emerging from the heart that is the island. The deep pink of these vessels draws an analogy – an unconnected heart is useless and lifeless; Eelam is essential to life. The shape of Sri Lanka and its relationship to Tamil Eelam justify the national body. Since its beginning in the 1970s, the Tamil independence movement has represented the nation as a heart outline in maps, crafts, and coloring books. This consistent visual portrayal functions as a sign denoting the desire for national recognition, rather than corresponding to physical terrain. By ignoring the specific details contained within and surrounding the outline of the national map, this icon proposes an idealized, non-specific place and non-geographically bound identity. Tamil Eelam negates territory as a criterion for nation in state-centered nationalism. Instead, it sustains cultural nationalism through symbolic identification conducted via network formulations and net-worked technologies.

An immaterial homeland, "a coming community," in Agamben's words, recognizes the conditions of diaspora; prescribing unattainable local residence would inhibit national allegiance. Sri Lankan Tamils living outside the Tamil Eelam borders need not conceive of themselves as in exile, as national membership does not require inhabitancy. Pradeep Jeganathan explains, "Nationals of Tamileelam have no desire to return to Eelam, nor wish to live there, but it helps them to keep living where they live. It is real, lived not as a place, but as an image."[42] The widely used image of the beating heart imitates the function of a national flag, conjuring identification and ideals grounded in national belonging. The virtual use of symbolism connects remote citizens. Rather than associating the webpage with any embattled or elusive geopolitical coordinates, the arteries of the Sri Lankan body politic reinforce their national project by speaking to and binding the scattered community to the pulsing center of the dissemination of possibility – a nation virtual rather than spatial or networked.

In the same way, the Ilankai Tamil Sangam website does not imagine the nation-state of Tamil Eelam as embattled physical terrain. To find the location of Tamil Eelam on the site's homepage, the visitor must click on the image of a palm tree. This leads to a page defining the organization's mission and a series of three descending maps.[43] The first image is a map of South Asia, followed by a map

Map from eelamweb.com.

of Sri Lanka. Finally, at the bottom of the page, not visible without scrolling, is a map of Tamil Eelam. It features a thick, black outline recalling the symbolic shape and designating the territory Tamils claim. However, the spatial reality does not envision particular physical demarcations on the island landscape. The site, like the Tamil Eelam homepage, displays Tamil Eelam within thick black lines, not as a detailed outline of a nation-state complete with the physical demarcations of the land including infrastructures, natural resources, or population centers.[44] The map does not locate neighborhoods, buildings, or transportation routes; it defines a virtual country, one that has created the condition of national possibility through the travails of its citizens. Digital creolization is thus not in contrast to nationalism, it enables the network to create a state-less, symbolic national body.

The network imagery often employed by these websites extends beyond the internet, yoking nation and national subjects. "Our people are our strength" states the banner at the head of the Eelamweb.com site;[45] the nation becomes a network, connected and sustained through and by its people. Thus, while the homepages of Tamilnet.com and Eelamweb.com show Tamil Tigers in Sri Lanka, the Web managers and writers, like the community they target, exist beyond its unstable borders. Other links provided in the header further the connectivity metaphor propagated by Eelamweb.com. First, it is a network of information. Second, it stands for an expatriate citizen body acting on behalf of the nation. Premised as a virtual network, Eelamweb.com never ties the land in northern Sri Lanka to the Web. The "Our People" link does not lead to information about Tamils in Tamil Eelam, but rather to photographs of Tamils in diaspora.[46] Rather than detailing the lives of Tamils in Tamil Eelam, the images depict Eelam expatriates fulfilling their responsibilities as Tamils: participating in demonstrations in favor of international recognition or meeting to perpetuate national recognition. The featured images include marches in Germany, France, Norway, Switzerland, Canada, the United Kingdom, and the United States. Citizens in diaspora embody the website, providing an ever-shifting national corpus not contained but, instead, inspired by politics. The site declares the primacy of a worldwide network of national subjects and organizes its people according to the geopolitical location of those featured in the photographs. The citizens in diaspora comprise the Tamil Eelam, extending the Tamil Eelam constituency well beyond its territorial referent. The creators of Eelamweb.com, the "Tamil Eelam Homepage," as stated in the banner, recognize that defining the community as a network of scattered members creates a worldwide consciousness for their claims for national recognition, rather than delimiting its people within the boundaries of a small, embattled, and isolated zone. Rooting its "coming community" in the bodies of the diaspora provides what Ruth Frankenberg and Lati Mani insist must be considered "new meanings" that envision "'new subjects' in different locations."[47] This instance is not only in dialogue with other practices that occur in situations of diaspora or postcoloniality; the Tamil Eelam online presence arises out of a distinct set of historical and contemporary conditions that reflect uneven, unequal relations through strategies of signification and information dispersal. This global network provides evidence of its strong international amalgamation, coordinating around the world to work toward the recognition of sovereignty in a virtual territory that they may be said to occupy.[48]

The idea of Tamil Eelam as espoused by these websites revises geopolitical processes for nation-building and refashions the process of national enunciation, even while positing sovereignty as obtainable only through the conventional means of international recognition, internal legislative and judicial authority. A non-traditional citizen body is continually refigured and the medium is tactically formulated to further complicated and at times contradictory aims of not only disregarding the limitations of spatial metaphors and domain-naming practices, but deliberately disrupting internet conventions. These websites, overall, presume that their citizens embody the privileged history of Tamil Eelam which includes an ancient, highly advanced language and civilization, repeated subjugation by colonial and postcolonial powers, the conditions of widespread, uneven diaspora, and the struggle for national cohesion. While these Tamil Eelam websites reproduce the image of the nation as a monolithic community experiencing history, they ignore the fissures of time and the discontinuities inherent in forced labor, diaspora, and nearly universal condemnation. They ironically posit the citizen, no longer tied to a specific geopolitical territory or Web location, as fulfilling a predetermined function through Web-based participation that achieves recognition for national sovereignty.

In contrast to state-sponsored internet practices that reaffirm geopolitical existence in electronic environments, Tamil Eelam's online proponents' networked communication, with its mutable and unfixable strategies for community formation and postcolonial nationalism, demonstrates that notions of national participation and information dispersal are fluctuating. These websites, by exhibiting professional reporting, a broad range of activities, strategic graphic depictions, and high ranking search-engine results, show their success at garnering authority by utilizing US-centeredness and English-language dominance online. Michael Hardt and Antonio Negri write, "The novelty of the new information infrastructure is the fact that it is embedded within and completely immanent to the new production processes" (Hardt and Negri 2000, 298). By envisioning the internet as a distinct model for information exchange, rather than an immutable geographical territory, digital creolization reconfigures the conditions of possibility for nationalisms through the non-fixity of a single metaphor for digital communication. Focusing on networks and other imaginaries enables this break from the geopolitical grid avowed in most internet imagery.

While similar approaches toward creating a virtual state can be seen in the efforts of Paluans, the Basques, and Black Nationalists making connections to Africa, the underlying suggestion put forth by Tamil Eelam online is that the land is not only virtual because it doesn't exist yet or hasn't been allowed to exist, but that the nation and its citizens exist and function virtually. Flow, fluidity, modality, mutation, spatiality, geo-political verisimilitude, loss, corruption, confusion, and (de-)evolution are contained within digital exchanges, which migrate across formats, styles, and technologies to reach unpredictable audiences and contribute to unforeseeable consequences. Since there has not been described, outside of those predicated on fictional "gaming," purely digital nations with completely virtual citizens, power, contestation, inequality, and change are all inscribed in the Tamil Eelam electronic representations. Paying attention to exchanges and movements rather than to borders and frontiers reveals the digital creolization and innovative communication methods practiced by overlooked internet participants.

5

Mixing Up Siam

Over the years the world has changed, but the desires and needs of men have remained the same. Whether you are looking for an exciting good time, a faithful marriage, or a dignified retirement, you want beauty, companionship and honest affection. Most of all you need satisfaction, and you don't need to play any games to get it.

(Pleasuretours.com[1])

I'm a Thai Woman who has been living in [Hong Kong] for 7 years.... Every time there were articles or any programs on TV about Thailand, it almost always starts with these girls dancing in PATPONG.... I think it's not fair!! ... our WOMEN ARE NOT ALL PROSTITUTES....

("Gaew"[2])

In most international print, television, and film depictions, Thailand exists as an exotic, erotic destination where beautiful women eagerly await to serve and satisfy western men.[3] According to media circulating beyond Thailand's borders, including portrayals manufactured in surrounding Asian nations, Thai women fall easily into one of two categories: exotic, young, alluring, yet potentially HIV-positive "hookers" eager to please western (and sometimes Japanese) clients; or dutiful, devoted wives of western men who dismiss the tenets of western feminism and appreciate the financial and emotional generosity of their husbands. In both articulations, Thai women are happily subservient, ideal companions for men, but not Thai men – who are depicted as sexless, abusive, old, or gay. Since the Vietnam War, these images have overshadowed all others in international and transnational media; coverage of Thailand is limited to Thai prostitution and mail-order brides,

Thailand as a tourist destination, or Thailand as a gay paradise. Ryan Bishop and Lillian Robinson write: "Perhaps the matter is one not of quantity but of focus. Thailand is, in fact, conspicuous by its presence in the popular media. So Thailand *is* a story, but audiences always receive the same story" (Bishop and Robinson 1998, 53). Thailand, "the land of smiles," is repeatedly rendered as a tropical nation inhabited by welcoming, pliable, eager sources of cheap, service-oriented labor, and Thai women, in particular, constitute an abundant source of sympathetic, acquiescent companionship.[4] Even after decades, Thai women receive, by far, the most attention concerning Thailand in non-Thai television and print media, and almost every story projects them as occupying one of these two positions.[5]

Arjun Appadurai asserts: "The new global cultural economy has to be seen as a complex, overlapping, disjunctive order that cannot any longer be understood in terms of existing center–periphery models."[6] He proposes that the relationship among the "scapes" he enumerates offers a lens through which to better interpret "these global cultural flows" (Appadurai 1996, 33). While these "scapes" do suggest some innovative ways to rethink cultural interactions, his rationale consists of anecdotes that render his subjects oversimplified. For instance, he states: "These tragedies of displacement could certainly be replayed in a more detailed analysis of the relations between the Japanese and German sex tours to Thailand and the tragedies of the sex trade in Bangkok" (Appadurai 1996, 39). While Appadurai calls for a more detailed analysis, he does not provide one in his own work, and he never again mentions the sex trade in Bangkok in his book-length study. This call for more analysis, however, is layered with judgment: his repetition of the word "tragedies" surrounding what occurs in Thailand, as well as the linking of displacement to sex trade – as opposed to work or study related emigration – implies an already established conclusion, the victims of which are Thai women, the victimizers, Japanese and German men. Appadurai thereby reduces the global cultural flows of the Thai nation to a non-specific Thai sex-trade at the exact moment he calls for complicating such generalizations. Appadurai's easy invocation and dismissal of the Thai sex-trade underscores the depth and strength of this gendered national stereotype in extra-national discussions. Even within celebrated academic essays that argue specifically for the need to pay attention to local knowledges, cultural generalizations, and the complexity of seemingly simple flows of capital and (mis)information, Thai women continue to signify national tragedy.

Some Thais have turned to the Thai-managed, English-language SiamWEB. org to respond to the stereotypes with which they are confronted. This chapter examines how SiamWEB.org functions to simultaneously renegotiate and reinscribe conceptions of community, gender, and nation. This English-language forum provides a space for young, educated Thai women to encounter and respond to the images of them circulating outside of, and increasingly within, their nation, enabling conversations that would not otherwise take place. By using English as their primary language and positioning themselves on the World Wide Web,

SiamWEB.org encourages cross-cultural communication, presuming that conversations between Thais and non-Thais interested in Thailand will adjust how Thailand is understood, and will revise these dominant characterizations. In the attempt to establish, in their words, a "highly interactive, true thai [sic] related on-line community," SiamWEB.org shifts the responsibility for these changes to its audience.[7] Through the processes of digital creolization, SiamWEB.org challenges the veracity of these stereotypes of Thai women and the Thai nation, reformulates the western-based sex/gender regime and nomenclature, posits always-in-process subject positions for Thai women, and questions the conventions circumscribing national membership. After describing the work done by the sites' core participants, this chapter concludes with an analysis of visitor responses that realize the challenges put forth by the website's creators. SiamWEB.org remaps and remixes Thais and Thailand, expanding not only Thailand's national borders and the tenets of national affiliation, if only in a modest and partial way, but also challenging the yoking of Thailand to Thai women as sex-workers and wives. SiamWEB.org's digital creolization unsettles journalistic and academic accounts of what constitutes the "digital divide," the third and first world, and women as a unified category defined through oppression.

Mixing It Up

Launched on the World Wide Web in 1993, SiamWEB.org championed visitor contributions, community formation, and participation during a time when Web pages were considered, by and large, to be static presentations created by webmasters for viewing by visitors.[8] The website's homepage, which has changed little since 1994, has a welcome in English and Thai punctuated with college-aged Thai faces, and provides a series of links located on a prominent navigation bar. Each link denotes a theme, such as the "Romance Corner" or "News and Culture," and clicking on a link takes the user to a table of contents containing further links to pages devoted to essays, games, informal advice, and discussions, all pertaining to that theme. The "How U Can Join SiamWEB" page requests, first and foremost, user participation. Membership in the SiamWEB.org community requires only the submission of the user's email address and first and last name. More options are provided for site members to create a "web profile," a process that includes navigating through a series of dialogue boxes, although choosing one of the options is never required in order to complete member registration. Membership enables users to search for other members, send messages, chat via SiamWEB.org's embedded IRC feature, and create a personalized "friends" list. Members and visitors are encouraged to post comments to articles directly below them.

At the height of SiamWEB.org's popularity, the majority of websites that allowed any form of commentary by visitors did so on a separate discussion forum page or "guestbook." By contrast, SiamWEBlers, as members are called, are able

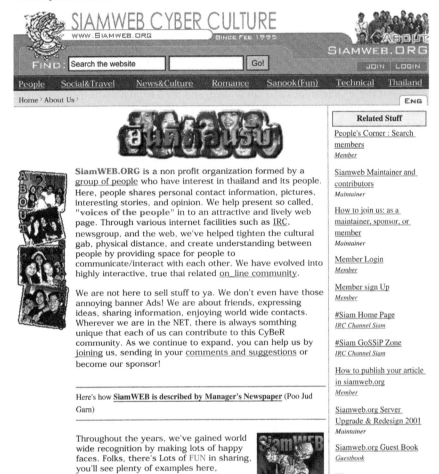

Siamweb.org's "About Us" page.

to and encouraged to respond on almost every page. These comments appear in reverse order from post date (the most recent submission first), joining each contribution to constitute the page. SiamWEB.org functioned in this way over a decade before blogs and other "Web 2.0" applications gave users the ability to post or leave comments. As this was a novel concept at the time, a substantial

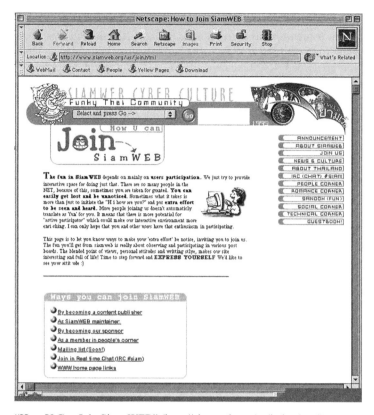

"How U Can Join Siam WEB" (http://siamweb.org/us/index.html).

amount of effort is dedicated to arguing for the importance of visitor contributions. The quality of the site and its ability to provide a community, SiamWEB. org states repeatedly, are based on the dialogues that ensue from the initial essays. Thus SiamWEB.org functions not only as an information source (the standard for the time) or as a social club, but instead is premised on reinforcing a sense of community through its commitment to visitor involvement. The community builds the site's content; not only do members partake of the site's services, but they share in the construction, appearance, and content of the pages themselves. Members are encouraged to self-moderate and engage with each other; they are subject to neither site moderation nor censorship. Visitors are challenged to join the community, create online profiles, and engage in dialogue through numerous channels – all under the umbrella of sharing "an interest in Thailand and its People" (http://SiamWEB.org). Reading or lurking, according to SiamWEB.org, does not constitute participation: "The blended point of views, personal attitudes and writing style, makes our site interesting and full of life! Time to step forward and **EXPRESS YOURSELF** We'd like to see your attit ude:)" [sic].[9]

After becoming a member, creating a Web profile – also known as joining the "People's Corner" – is premised as the best way to make friends. Site designers implore: "Searching for a net friend? Want some buddies when you travel to Thailand? or when you go abroad? ... Make new NET friends, the world over! Join in now".[10] Creating the Web profile involves a common series of menu choices such as screen name, birth date, gender, relationship status, education, and ethnicity, yet several of the choices veer from those typically offered by English-language websites, particularly choices available for "gender." This is the standard category required by most social networking sites, yet the SiamWEB.org version offers a unique, Thai-inflected series of choices: male, female, and "mixed up." The site, through its enunciation of membership, alters stereotypical notions of Thailand, and Thai women in particular, through these three gender options. The inclusion of this third gender choice situates Thai females amongst other Thai gender possibilities, immediately breaking apart the simple Thai sex-worker/wife-with-western man pairing. Wives and sex-workers do not comprise a gender, and Thai men and Thai mixed-ups are forced into the equation from the moment of membership. In other words, these choices explicitly recognize the existence of both Thai men and "mixed up" Thais who do not conform to the gender roles of "male" or "female." The choice includes Thai females among other Thai gender possibilities and emphasizes Thai women's ability to exist among and form relationships with men, other women, or those falling into the range of positions implied by "mixed up." None of these choices recognize western men as a singular category; instead, they are folded into the Thai gender/sex system.

About Yourself

These information will be use to build your profile (homepage) for you. See sample here.

* Screen name or IRC name.

☑ Use this name when you post something on the Siamweb.

* Your birthday
No more excuses for friends forgetting your birthday!

| 1 ▾ | January ▾ | 2008 ▾ |

☐ Make this info. private

* Gender   ◯ Male ◯ Female ◯ Mixed up

* Relationship status | Please choose ▾ |

* Ethnicity   Hold down ctrl key for multimple selection.

American
African
Australian
Burmese

SiamWEB Gender: Male, Female, or Mixed up.

The use of "mixed up" as a gender choice in Web profile creation illustrates another way in which English-language use enables Thai inflected viewpoints, using digital creolization to speak to and of Thai systems for understanding gender and sexuality. These gender choices are much more sensitive to the Thai sex/ gender system than the prominent understandings of sex and gender that circulate in the west. On standard websites in English, where sex and gender are not a primary concern – as might be said of SiamWEB.org – "male" and "female" would be the only choices. On websites from the US and the UK concerned with troubling heterosexist assumptions or focused on matchmaking, other options might include MTF (a male-to-female transperson), FTM (a female-to-male transperson), androgynous, or genderqueer – choices that would exclude some Thais. "Mixed up," on the other hand, is not only not a part of the general English lexicon for describing non-normative sex/gender choices, but for western subjects, this choice could be construed as pejorative, conferring a judgment of confusion rather than denoting a stable category choice. Within the dominant Thai sex/gender system, the idea of a "mixed up" gender names a conglomeration of gender identities and, as a result, speaks to SiamWEB.org's targeted community, accomplishing the goal of making Thais feel fluent on the site.

So "mixed up" might alienate some westerners, but makes Thais feel fluent. And "mixed up" is yet another layer of digital creolization concerning Thai gender, like me two common terms for non-normative Thai female sexuality which are derived from English-language words: "Tom," derived from tomboy, referring to a woman who performs masculinity through her dress, speech, and object choice (feminine looking women);[11] "Dees," derived from the English "lady," can be discerned through their interest in and association with "toms." Overall, does conform to Thai cultural standards of appropriate womanhood (except for their homosocial liaisons and what they entail).[12] Neither role is directly translatable to their English-language designations, nor do the women they embody refuse identification with these terms. Instead, the Thai manifestation of these terms reflects a dialogue with their origins – and, more importantly, an insertion of a foreign sound (English is often perceived as more sexually tinged and exotic) into Thai vocabulary to name something specifically Thai that previously had no common referent.[13] Not to be limited to this instance of adaptation, as Took Took Thongthiraj (1994), Megan Sinnott (2004), and Enteen (2001) have discussed elsewhere, Thai women who love women are further augmenting their vocabulary to include other designations that do not reflect the masculine/feminine dichotomy inherent in "tom" and "dee." Instead, they endorse labels such as "anjaree," or women who follow non-conformist ways.[14] They express outright distaste for the word "lesbian," which seems to many Thai women to be explicitly sexual.

While not literally a gender category in Thai, "mixed up" names the indeterminacy of Thai genders, where categories such as "man" and "woman" are not simple oppositions but instead exist within a field of gendered/sexed positions.

In other words, in Thai, one can be a woman, a man, a tom, but "tom" is not used to designate a position that is a woman or a man.[15] "Mixed up" marks another instance of digital creolization: the choice does not imitate an English referent, but instead adjusts a western framework. "Mixed up" provides a legible designation for the range of Thai gendered/sexed positions – tom, dee, *kathoey*, and gay (the latter two will be discussed in Chapter 6) that are not simply "male" or "female," but also are neither fixed designations nor intransient states.

Global Communications (Read: English)

Between 1986 and 1996, Thailand had one of the world's fastest-growing economies, producing a high volume and variety of export products that generated a per capita income that increased exponentially. This growth affected every aspect of Thai society and most everyone in Thailand benefited materially: a substantial portion of the population was able to acquire electricity, a television set, and the possibility of employment while enjoying a low cost of living. Of course, this "rise" in general standards of living often entailed urban migration; teenage sons and daughters who had completed their six years of mandatory education were increasingly expected to leave their families in rural towns and villages and travel to Bangkok, living in dormitory-like conditions or urban slums and working long hours for low wages. The country's increasing prosperity had the largest impact in Bangkok, where a burgeoning middle-class found opportunities for education, employment, and the purchase of foreign and domestic luxury items.

The revaluation of the Japanese Yen in 1984 instigated Thailand's economic boom. Because of Japan's huge trade surplus, many Japanese firms looked elsewhere for manufacturing sites. The Thai government provided an atmosphere with few regulations, a liberal trade policy, and almost no import duties.[16] In addition, foreign and local banks could take deposits and lend in foreign or domestic currencies, both in Thailand and abroad. The Thai currency was pegged to a "basket of currencies" of which the US dollar made up over 80 percent. Between 1986 and 1993, Japanese firms invested billions of dollars in Thailand and other Asian countries; other Asian countries with strong economies followed suit.[17] During this decade, local Thai firms also increased their export-oriented manufacturing, and the number and types of products assembled there quickly grew. Bangkok's population doubled, and its residents prospered. The local marketplace became increasingly international, with imported European cars and other western luxury items available and esteemed.[18] Following the 1997 Asian Financial Crisis (which occurred after Thailand's national monetary unit, the Thai Baht, was allowed to float freely in international currency markets and experienced a drastic devaluation), the Thai economy took a dire turn. While many businesses went bankrupt and newly affluent families lost their fortunes, the taste for consumer goods and services did not abate. An International Monetary Fund (IMF) bail-out began in December 1997, and the country has seen uneven but increasing economic stabilization since, much of which fuels the continued acquisition of cutting-edge technology and high-fashion products.

Bangkok's middle-class values higher education and internationalization. Information from around the world circulates via uncensored internet access and imported entertainment and academic media, as well as through travel, study abroad, and a large influx of non-Thai tourists and businesspeople.[19] This international outlook is reflected in tastes and consumption: mobile phones, western-made cars, and western name-brand clothing are possessions *de rigueur* for Bangkok professionals. Not only are western products consumed, but "ideas, ideologies and politics" from outside of Thailand are as well (Pasuk and Baker 1995, 409). English-language accounts of Thailand's economic activities repeatedly underscore Thai people's appetite for foreign ideas and practices. Much of the economic prosperity has been reaped by businesses and business people directly involved in import, export, or government, which has been accompanied by an increased openness to foreign ideas and products throughout the population.[20] Initially this openness, as well as the availability of imported goods, was viewed optimistically by most Thai leaders and citizens, as well as by multinational banks and businesses. Krishna Sen explains, "The phenomenal rise of East and Southeast Asian economic power was frequently presented as the panacea for the ills of the West and East alike."[21] However, inherent inequities may accompany these imports. Sen continues:

> But the picture always appeared a little cloudier to those of us who saw the process as a gendered one and who did not want to forget that citizens everywhere – even in a period of 9 per cent growth – remain divided by class and sex.
>
> (Sen and Stivens 1998, xi)

While gender and class discrimination, as well as increasing inequalities between educated and labored workers, are most certainly the accoutrements of global market participation, the blanket adoption of western practices, particularly in the realms of gender/sexuality and sex practices, should not be presumed.

Almost all communication between Thais and non-Thais in Bangkok takes place in English. It is the primary language both for conducting international business and for forming informal liaisons with *farang* (westerners). Thus, communicating in English is perceived by Bangkok Thais as an essential component of upward mobility and modernization. Peter Jackson and Eric Allyn clarify the perception of English in contemporary Bangkok: "English has an exotic and cultured sense for many Thais, having associations with wealth, education, culture, modernity and sexual liberality" (Jackson 1995, 236). Many Bangkok Thais, especially the young middle-class, associate English use not only with prosperity but with the influx of daring new ideas and possibilities for articulating changing conceptions of sexualities and genders.[22] English has been incorporated into the Thai lexicon to articulate changes in sex practices, sexualities, and genders.

While English terms are being reinterpreted by Thais as they enter the Thai language and the internet provides a new arena for depictions of Thailand, almost every representation created by non-Thais in English closely resembles those found in previous, non-Thai media sources. For example, this chapter's opening epigraph comes from one of a plethora of internet websites easily located and highly ranked by search engines. The quote, from a site called Pleasuretours.com that organizes tours and meetings for western men to meet/have sex with women in several uncharacterized nations located in Asia, demonstrates how stereotypes of Thai women extend to other Asian women. Run by western men, Pleasuretours.com designates all Asian women, regardless of national affiliation or location, as sex-workers and/or potential wives in an attempt to generate interest in their sex tours and matchmaking services.[23]

While this type of website extends western generalizations about Asian women found in earlier media and provides opportunities for the perpetuation of sex tourism, the second epigraph employs the internet to protest these extranational depictions and their resulting practices. In this instance, Gaew, a contributor to SiamWEB.org who describes herself as a Thai woman living in Hong Kong, angrily dismisses "this image of Thailand" that she observes in the Hong Kong press and on television.[24] Her complaint presupposes the intricate connection between gender and nationalism, calling for the construction of alternative portrayals of Thai women and the Thai nation. Furthermore, by imploring the producers of print and television media to broaden the scope of considerations pertaining to Thailand, Gaew recognizes that media transmissions overlap and intersect. She uses the medium available to her to address these cross-media depictions, and she assumes the extranational potential of internet communication while recognizing the powerful sway of national images in the global arena.[25] The statements of both Pleasuretours.com and Gaew, despite their opposing motivations, illustrate the sustained internet presence of the entrenched links among Thai women, Asian women, and the Thai nation; they each recognize the power of media portrayals to attract capital from transnational sources and sway popular opinion. Rather than merely criticizing the proliferation of these images on western-based websites, the Thailand-centered SiamWEB.org proffers interventionist strategies through individual participation and theorizes alternative possibilities, confident in the potential of virtual practices to enhance and/or disrupt offline beliefs and material circumstances.

SiamWEB.org's decision to use English acknowledges the dominance of English in internet communication. While this may seem to highlight linguistic imbalances and privilege native speakers of English, it also de-centers the geography and language of the Thai nation in the discussions of things Thai, enhancing the possibility for the construction of a virtual community premised on Thai interests rather than on a sense of shared nationality or nationalistic concerns. Communicating in Thai – the national language of Thailand, spoken and read by a high percentage of Thai citizens – would confine participation to members of the nation-state, whether in Thailand or abroad. English provides the most acceptable linguistic alternative. In addition, English-language use extends the possibilities for communication, inviting non-Thais to participate, thereby substantially broadening the site's prospective audience.

SiamWEB.org recognizes the role language plays in conveying histories and ideologies, refusing models of language that suggest English-language use replicates unidirectional forces of imperialism. They believe, like linguist Janina Brutt-Griffler, that "For a language to become internationalized, it must lose its identification with one culture or nation."[26] By employing English, SiamWEB.org hopes to reduce its association with the United States and the United Kingdom while exploiting the dynamic forces operating in this internationalized language. Its writers resist situating themselves and their community as passive subjects of international stereotypes. Using English, they argue, detaches the Thai nation from the discussion of things Thai. For them, English is "*wrested from* an unwilling imperial authority as part of the struggle by them against colonialism" (italics mine) (Brutt-Griffler 2001, 32). English is adopted as part of SiamWEB.org's strategic plan, adapted willfully in order to reflect the new medium, the site's location on the World Wide Web, and SiamWEB.org's target user community.

English-language use necessarily privileges Thais who have had extensive language training or spent time outside of Thailand above those who, in spite of mandatory English lessons provided by Thailand's almost universally attended educational system, feel insecure about their ability to express themselves in English. The creators of the site try to minimize imbalances in English-language fluency, assuming that language fluctuates according to its use and deviations need not be coded as errors.[27] In an effort to construct an inclusive environment that acknowledges but does not reinforce current user disparities, they repeatedly remind visitors that English-language fluency is not necessary for communication. While two of the six editors and most of the writers and contributors to SiamWEB.org have lived and studied in the United States, basic grammar inconsistencies appear on the homepage. These "mistakes" form a pattern, and are thereby not the result of ignorance or carelessness. Notably, they follow the written practices of hacker communities, disrupting the look of the language in order to fracture comprehension and expand interpretation. These irregularities are geared specifically to Thai language users: "Don't worry about LaNgUaGe sKilLs," the "About SiamWEB.org" page urges. Alternating the case of the letters makes the words appear fractured, creating a look reminiscent of Thai. Thai script strings single syllable multi-character words together in order to construct phrases or sentences. To the Thai reader, the visual appearance of the words LaNgUaGe and sKilLs invoke Thai grammar. Producing a visual reference to Thai that violates English-language conventions specifically reaches out to Thai users, encouraging their contributions. This wordplay is followed by another Thai-specific English-language adjustment: "We are interested in the ideas behind the message … not the *techinicallity* of the message itself" [emphasis mine].[28] The insertion of the extra "*i*" and "*l*" references Thai pronunciation, wherein consonants are always followed by at least one vowel sound. Infusing English language with Thai-isms

Throughout the years, we've gained world wide recognition by making lots of happy faces. Folks, there's Lots of FUN in sharing, you'll see plenty of examples here, particularly in people's corner and Social Corner. To join us, you just have to **put a little bit of your world here and package it as part of a team.** Don't worry about LaNgUaGe sKiLs, we are interested in the ideas behind the message.. not the techinicallity of the message itself. We hope you have a good time browsing through. There are plenty of smile and good time stored here.

LaNgUaGe sKiLs (source: Siamweb.org).

LaNgUaGe sKiLs

Comparing LaNgUaGe sKiLs to Thai script (top and bottom-left). Note SiamWEB.org's "Thai-ing" of Roman script (bottom-right). (Sanook image source: www.siamweb.org/content/index/sanook_eng.php; Songkran image source: www.siamweb.org/news_culture/songkran/index.html.)

speaks directly to Thai English as a Second Language (ESL) users by bringing English closer to Thai and minimizing the importance of standard English for communication. These grammatical adjustments promote English-language use, but not in a strict sense – instead, they support wordplay and diminish the necessity of fluency for communication.

SiamWEB.org stipulates that English-language use is essential to its primary goal of community formation. Touting Howard Rheingold's definition of virtual communities as "social aggregations that emerge from the Net when enough people carry on ... public discussions long enough, with sufficient human feeling, to form webs of personal relationships in cyberspace," they reason that the communication of interests and feelings alone can enable community formation.[29] Noting the rapid changes in technology and its uses, SiamWEB.org holds that its own processes and goals will change with the use of this new communication medium and, conversely, that technology will adapt to meet the needs of its participants. "If you think this is your audience," they write, "then why don't you join in the fun and be part of this exiting changes!" [sic]. Not only should you participate to have fun, the authors argue that you must post – and produce meaningful content – in order to establish a place on this new medium. They continue: "You can easily get lost and be unnoticed. Sometimes what it takes is more than just to initiate the 'Hi How are you?' and put extra effort to be seen and heard".[30] Contributions, they insist, are the basis for the site:

> what SiamWEB.org is varies as much as your interest and how much you are willing to share with others. In otherword, it is as good as how much you want to contribute to it. This website is as much yours as it is ours [sic].[31]

The quality of the site and its ability to provide a community are based on the dialogues that ensue from the initial essays. According to SiamWEB.org's strategies and goals, highlighted visitor responses will facilitate virtual community formation and provide the means for technology to disrupt traditional national identification.

English-language use and digital creolization extends portrayals of Thailand beyond those generated from within its borders; one more technique through which the site encourages dominant English-language accounts to be challenged. SiamWEB.org asserts that producing and then debunking these gendered depictions of Thailand, where Thai women appear to welcome outsiders, is necessary to achieve community formation. Thai women politicize the invocation of gendered stereotypes, attempting to render visible the inaccuracies of these posts and dislodge their images from their transnationally circulating referents. When Thai women no longer stand in for the nation, the extra-national circulation of their images loses its justification.

Thai Women at the Keyboard

As most online participation does not take place in shared physical environments, users produce their genders through data exchange – bytes communicating text or graphics. Positing that this digitally based exchange enables burgeoning freedom, equality, and democracy, American theorists including Sherry Turkle, Caitlin Sullivan, Kate Bornstein, and Amy Bruckman assume that all users have an identical potential for liberation from real world constraints based on the specificities of US-based users.[32] Often, Sullivan and Bornstein and Bruckman note, Americans communicating on the internet attempt to "gender swap" online, describing gender attributes that differ significantly from the ones they possess when not at the computer. This occurs when users adopt gendered user-names and modify their self-presentations accordingly when participating on Multi-User Domains (MUDs), in Chat Rooms (an instance of IRC), and in other online forums.[33] The frequency with which this occurs in these domains leads Bruckman to conclude that "Gender swapping is one extreme example of a fundamental fact:

the network is in the process of changing not just how we work, but how we think of ourselves – and ultimately, who we are" (Bruckman 1996, 323). Nessim Watson describes similar phenomena by extending Rheingold's theory:

> Rheingold notes that in CMC, interaction is conducted by "personae," or identities that may have little correlation with the identity of the person utilizing them on-line. The medium inherently prevents the interpersonal identification and judgment processes by which we normally evaluate each other in face-to-face interaction.[34]

The examples of fluid gender construction online reveal what Sherry Turkle describes as "the personal computer culture's 'ability' to give people a way to think concretely about an identity crisis" (Turkle 1995, 49). Since identity is no longer assumed to be stable, Turkle asserts, identifications, including gender identifications, can become multiple, contradictory, and fluid (1995, 49). The possibility for fluidity was an oft-repeated mantra in the cyberculture theories of the 1990s; cyberfeminists were part of the vanguard positing constructive re-imaginings of human–technology interfaces that allowed for revisionings of "real-life" gendered inequities.[35]

In this spirit, social commentator Laura Miller urges her readers to guard what she terms potential freedom intrinsic to the possibilities of gender and identity fluidity in digital realms.[36] According to Miller, emphasizing instances of sexism, gender persecution, or online "rape"[37] threatens the freedom of digital escape from gendered stereotypes. She therefore protests calls for any restrictions based on complaints of persecution. Miller explains:

> I see in the relentless attempts to interpret on-line interactions as highly gendered, an intimation of just how artificial, how created, our gender system is in accordance with the real-world understanding that women's smaller, physically weaker bodies and lower social status make them subject to violation by men, there's a troubling notion in the real and virtual worlds that women's minds are also more vulnerable to invasion, degradation, and abuse.
>
> (Miller 1997)

Accentuating the persistence of gendered inequities replicates the idea that women are inherently weak, incapable of self-defense, and vulnerable to attack. Ignoring them, she suggests, will lead to the end of the verisimilitude between online and offline biases.

By privileging the safeguarding of these freedoms over the protection of users from what they perceive as violence, Miller's western feminist assumptions ignore many women. Not only does this unproblematically turn computer-mediated communication into a utopia, silencing the voices of those who see it otherwise, it also presumes that gender oppression is a singular, undifferentiated experience.[38] Every user has a history and Miller's "real-world" experiences affect her perception of social environments and interactions, regardless of digital and analog combinations. Women from non-western cultures, including those who face challenges when communicating in English – if the language is not their first – and those who encounter western feminism from a minority position, have concerns, experiences, and material circumstances overlooked by these early cyberfeminist assertions. Histories and lives offline are important factors in determining online personas; these two worlds cannot be disentangled from one another. Like earlier versions of western feminism which described "woman" as a monolithic category whose subjects experienced identical forms of oppression, these assertions of liberation assume that "gender fluidity" is available on the same terms to all users. Life beyond the computer, however, affects what online participants choose to make fluid, and conceptions of culture and constitutions of gender are not universal. Similarly, fixing the Other is a western strategy for situating the self. As Lisa Nakamura argues, "In the post-Internet world of simulation, 'real' things are fixed and preserved in images ... in order to anchor the western viewing subject's sense of himself as a privileged and mobile viewer."[39] Moreover, several studies, including those by Ananda Mitra, Radhika Gajjala, and the contributors to several recent edited collections, account for the specific circumstances surrounding internet participation by non-European subjects located in the west or logging on from their home countries.[40]

Thai women do not approach the keyboard without their histories; their identities in cyberspace are in dialogue with dominant representations of Thai women as well as the reactions and assumptions about them by non-Thais online. While Allucquère Rosanne Stone insists "the virtual age" has caused a change between the sense of self and body,[41] Thai women in Bangkok or studying abroad still find themselves marked both by their own experiences and by those they encounter online. Thai women experience gender discrimination that differs from that of American women, expatriate Thai women, and Thai people who choose the gender designation "mixed up." When online, Thai women enter an already existing dialogue that consistently reduces them to the stereotypes generated by the media outside of Thailand. While SiamWEB.org endorses the possibility of community formation and the dwindling need for national identification on the World Wide Web, it rejects the idea that gender is free-floating, crafted, and controlled by the whims of the user.

Julia Serano, a celebrated MTF (male-to-female transsexual) activist and biologist, recently confronted the tendency of feminism to dismiss particular categories as less-than-women. While much has been written against defining women as a category of oppression, the central discussions around femininity within recent feminist studies criticize the femme/lipstick dichotomy as evidence of an oppressive gender regime. Serano's *Whipping Girl: A Transsexual Woman on Sexism and the Scapegoating of Femininity* speaks to the central quandary faced by trans women when confronting – or, more accurately, when confronted by – feminism.[42] Why are trans women feared, dismissed, and, as a result, dehumanized, by contemporary, gender-theory-savvy, equality-committed feminists? Serano suggests that despite feminism's work to reveal gender norms, systemic male privilege, and binary constructions, femininity itself remains suspect. Feminists, she argues, "unwittingly support the notions that femininity is artificial, contrived, and frivolous; that it is a ruse that only serves the purpose of attracting and appeasing the desires of men" (Serano 2007, 5), which situates femininity in a fundamentally incompatible position vis-à-vis feminism. Expectations and assumptions about other bodies and behaviors are inevitable when feminine traits are seen as female-specific – a unified social program. Because transgression and subversion are unwittingly privileged by those of us who set out to trouble gender, the result, Serano persuasively argues, is misogyny yet again.

This produces several problems in an international context, specifically for Thai dees. Foremost is the premise that gender queer is the superior form of gender engagement. This is legible only by western standards. Thai dees already occupy what Megan Sinnott calls a "relative" position to toms – their femininity means that some toms, and the majority of the Thai population, question the verity of their same-sex object choice. Dees are often expected to "grow out" of their engagement with toms, because their existence is so radical: in a gender-based, rather than sex-based, system they cannot be "real" women who love women. This highly queer position – beyond comprehension in a sense within the Thai normative gender system – can be seen as especially subversive; dees, in fact, are often illegible without the presence of toms. Yet the queerness of this position is doubly displaced by defining gender queer as legible only by western standards. Thai dees cannot be securely located within Thai conventional understandings of sex/gender roles, nor can they be part of a western gender queer consortium. Femininity once again threatens western conceptions of queerness and non-conformity – and the result is anti-feminist, non-inclusive, and ethnocentric.

By focusing primarily on acts of gender performance and sexuality while being rooted in identity-based understandings of women regardless of their location, western feminism ignores its own call to "global sisterhood." With the exception of Lillian Robinson, co-author of *Night Market*, no prominent western feminists have responded to the proliferation of the wife/sex-worker stereotype facing Thai women. These representations, produced and circulated by western men, seem not to be a subject for feminist attention. Like feminism's embattled relationship to femininity, this absence represents yet another form of misogyny. In the quote that begins this chapter, Pleasuretours.com encourages its (western male) customers to look to Thai women "because you need satisfaction, and you don't need to play any games to get it." The implicit problem is that western women, informed by feminism, are unwilling to provide male satisfaction and demand unfulfilling games. Western men can look to Thai women for an unchanging, eternal, feminine dedication that satiates the timeless "desires and needs of men." Despite the direct causal relationship between women in the west who lack and Thai women as empty symbols for a lost femininity, no connections have been forged in response. What seems an obvious opportunity for "global sisterhood" to dispel these misogynist missives functions, instead, as Spillers writes of black women, as "the beached whales of the sexual universe" (Spillers 2003, 153).

SiamWEB.org directly addresses the discrimination faced by Thai women on the website. Aware that visitors often contend that female Thai participants belong to the wife or sex-worker categories, the site highlights a link to a page entitled "Ahem* We are not horny Thai girls!"[43] The page contains an essay by Yujira about online sexual harassment encountered by female Thai participants. Since SiamWEB.org does not censor messages, Yujira urges those who post to consider what is appropriate and recognize that "free speech comes with responsibility." Yujira then asks "lonely men searching for a Thai wife" to go elsewhere. She explains:

> While it is true that Thai women seeking foreign men for financial stability do exist in some part of Thailand, there has been no report of female SiamWEBlers with such intent. In fact, the many SiamWEBlers have expressed frustration and boredom in conversing with companion-deprived men. Therefore, please refrain from making a fool of yourselves. I sympathize with your need for a Thai companion. There are much more effective ways of acquiring a Thai wife, i.e. contacting wife-seeking agencies in Thailand.
>
> (Yujira 1997)

Yujira does not attempt to deny the existence of Thai women who conform to these stereotypes. In fact, featured prominently on the page is a sexy, naked Thai woman framed by the words, "This IS what you think?" By pairing the image with this text, Yujira acknowledges these women but locates them elsewhere. Unlike the woman in the picture, the Thai women on SiamWEB.org described by Yujira are not eager to please the western men who pursue them. Positing female SiamWEBlers as frustrated and bored by western male declarations and figuring foreign men as "companion-deprived" disrupts the conventional scenario: here western men strive for contact and Thai women resist. Women reluctant to form liaisons cannot be situated in one of the two reductive positions; moreover, since both are premised on Thai women's desire for western men, negating the existence of reciprocal desire undermines the very assumptions upon which these representations are based. The production of this argument, as well as its content, proves that Yujira and other women on SiamWEB.org cannot be contained by these categories. Similarly, by reprimanding male posters, she shatters the balance of power implicit in previous discourses.

Acknowledging the shifting material circumstances of Thai women as a result of globalization and transnational capitalism, as well as the online aggression and categorical reductions faced by Thai women logging on, Areeya Chumsai challenges herself and others to craft new, unstable, and non-limiting subjectivities. American-born and educated but residing in Thailand, the former "Miss Thailand" frequently contributes to the site. Each of her five SiamWEB.org essays provides lengthy and detailed counter-hegemonic portrayals of Thai women. Presenting personal experience through words and images, she adeptly expresses the ways in which she does not conform to either conventional western or Thai gendered expectations. She portrays both the Thai nation and Thai women, especially herself, in a manner that combines western feminist rhetoric with recent Thai-style narratives disseminated by popular female Thai musicians and film stars.

Chumsai's continually changing homepage is located on the SiamWEB.org site and is designed with the help of SiamWEB.org's overall maintainer and site designer, Pat Rattanadilok Na Phuket. An early version was reachable by her hot-linked signature at the bottom of each of her essays.[44] To enter, visitors were presented with a splash page of a collage of three photographs of her. In this collage, one image portrays Chumsai as a soldier dressed in army fatigues, defying conventional depictions of Thai women. In another image, she gestures to her Thai peers by posing in the manner preferred by young Thai women – on a rock with an orchid (the Thai national flower) and a Coca-Cola bottle lettered in Thai by her side. At the bottom of the collage, she appears casual and perhaps western as she confidently faces the camera, looking clean-cut and Gap-outfitted. Each of the three pictures presents an alternative to the non-Thai stereotypes of Thai women, as well as endorses and expands dominant, Thai-generated images. The collage serves as an introduction to Chumsai's philosophy, which is detailed on the following page entitled "Definition of a Strong Woman." In the text that follows, Chumsai imagines a woman who ignores most western and Thai media representations and chooses a path based on contemplation, planning, and individual circumstances. "A strong woman," she writes, "doesn't compare herself to others," "lives for the moment," and "knows her limits and her strengths." "She is confident, secure yet approachable" and "She is who [she] wants to be" (Chumsai 1997). Rather than describing a static identity, she presents herself as a work in progress, striving to embody the features she admires within the framework of the present. The model "Strong Woman" she has constructed displays many characteristics inherent in hegemonic Thai and non-Thai media representations, but this ideal also exceeds them on many levels. Most dramatically, she endeavors to "not care about others too much" and to not "need others' approval," deviating from traditional Thai culture where responsibility to family and society is of primary importance.[45] Situated in the internationalized environment of Bangkok, Chumsai enumerates the temptations she tries to withstand: falling prey to fashion, excessive consumption, gossip, insecurity, or thinking too much, and contrasts this list with her aspirations: self-confidence, friendliness, and a sense of balance. The page presumes a dynamic subject in continual flux, not a stable subject position. Consequently, readers are encouraged to view both Chumsai and themselves as subjects continually in formation rather than fixed embodiments of specific identity categories, already established by western political and philosophical doctrines with increasingly global reach.

On "Labeling," a recently launched addition, Chumsai further develops her argument against the adoption of western subject positions: "Labeling is a mental process," she writes,

Areeya Sirisopha Home Page (Areeya Chumsai, Nong Pop)

Definition of a **Strong Woman**

July 28, 1997

By : Areeya Chumsai

A strong woman knows who she is.

She doesn't need to compare herself to others. She doesn't follow all the latest trends. She doesn't become a fashion victim, a prey for aggressive marketers, advertisers and sales that screams out 'You need more clothes, more cream, more makeup, more youth potion and magic that makes you young forever. SHE knows that is impossible. She doesn't need other's approval to know who she is or want to be. Vogue doesn't need to tell her who she should be, how she should talk, how she should walk. In fact, she doesn't need to always prove her worth in society's eyes by wearing the latest this and the most expensive that. She doesn't stare in the mirror and worry about crow's feet, sagging boobs, expanding thighs and who's going to love her now. She doesn't try to do the impossible -- fight against time.

She lives for the moment. She doesn't dwell in the past or worry about the future. She doesn't worry too much, think too much, care about others too much.

She knows her limit and accepts it. She doesn't party too hard or work too hard. She doesn't abuse her brain or her body, meaning no smoke, no anything she'll regret the next day. She sleeps when she is tired and she eats when she is hungry. She doesn't skip meals to look like some skinny model or some standard number of 36-24-36 and 110 lbs. Numbers that doesn't add up to being beautiful or normal.

She knows her strength. She knows her

You can contact me via snail mail at:

19/61 Moo 24
Phutamontol Sai 1
Bangramad, Talingchun
Bangkok, 10170
Thailand

Office: (02) 250 2555
(For business only)

I usually reply to guestbook entry via email

My articles in SiamWEB

http://www.siamweb.org/sanook/star_profile/pop/ (1 of 2) [1/9/2003 5:12:51 PM]

"Definition of a Strong Woman" by Areeya Chumsai.

where we put everything in cubby holes to distinguish one thing from another. We classify them into categories then stick labels on them.... Don't take it too seriously these narrow labels that is suppose to define who we are, I surely don't.... Understand it's an illusion. Let it go. And you'll be a happier person. I am. Whoever "I" really is anyway.[46]

Chumsai outlines the process of labeling; assigns and then rejects the categories of "tomboy," "journalist," "Miss Thailand" and "model"; and ultimately dismisses the validity of classification altogether. Finally, she queries identity at its most basic level, refusing to posit a locatable and explainable subject; her "I" is not one that can be accurately named. Exploiting the current flexibility of conventions in response to Thailand's urbanization, international investment, and global market participation, Chumsai destabilizes the fixity of gender as well as national and consumer identificatory positions, offering a radically new portrait of Thai women that reflects her experience, SiamWEB.org's project, and Thailand as a set of discursive practices located at a particular historical juncture.

Re-Mapping Siam

Recognizing that portrayals of Thai women metonymically stage Thailand as a nation, the editors of SiamWEB.org believe that "diluting the stereotyping" will alter how the nation as a whole is perceived. As Anne McClintock states: "All nationalisms are gendered, all are invented and all are dangerous" (McClintock 1995, 352). Considering the linguistic angle, Deniz Kandiyoti makes a complementary point: "The very language of nationalism singles women out as the symbolic repository of group identity."[47] Thus, disrupting conceptions of nation is a powerful strategy toward dismantling gendered stereotypes. Since these images circulate in English, SiamWEB.org employs English to "dilute" them. They believe that the presence of these generalizations provides an incentive for disapproving visitors (even those who struggle with English) to intervene.

SiamWEB.org discourages narrow definitions of national identity premised on legal or territorial concerns. Physical proximity is no longer considered the primary factor for national belonging. Drawing on Nicholas Negroponte's assertions about technology, SiamWEB.org argues that virtual community formation can and will dismantle national identification: "The notion of 'nation' will someday be obsolete."[48] Use of English severs the privileged connection of national subject to native tongue, requiring, for this medium, that contributors – rather than those within national boundaries or those who speak national language(s) – change the nation form and its representations. Thus SiamWEB. org's virtual community formation attempts to undermine both nationalism and the basic understanding of what constitutes a nation.

Thailand's rulers have historically been said to exercise control over the production of nation and national image. For example, in the late nineteenth century, Siam (Thailand's name until 1939) consciously "mapped" itself in response to surrounding colonial pressures. Because British and French officials did not understand Siam's conception of a nation premised on subjects' acknowledgment of membership, as opposed to boundary markings inscribed on the earth's surface, King Mongkut learned the western conventions for geographically envisioning the nation and accordingly crafted a map of his Kingdom. In *Siam Mapped*, Thongchai Winichakul argues that border construction occurred not by "anticipating a spatial reality," but instead by strategically carving a space that would align previously separated groups of people and resist foreign domination.[49] The act of mapping, Winichakul writes, "actively structured 'Siam' in our minds as well as on earth" (1994, 131–132). Claiming this fixed space "naturalized" the Siam nation, creating the foundation for a specifically Thai form of nationhood that combined extranational conceptions of nation-state with those consistent with Thai worldviews.

As this instance illustrates, the production of nationalism responds to pressures from both within and outside the nation. Benedict Anderson situates the origin of popular nationalism in Southeast Asia in "the political and cultural revolution brought about by the maturing of the colonial state."[50] While Siam was not colonized by Europeans, concern about protecting its status as a discrete nation directly correlated with the rise of colonial states on each of its borders. David Wyatt asserts that the name change from Siam to Thailand was an effort on behalf of King Luang Phibunsonkhram to "build, not a new country, but a new nation."[51] The Thai sense of a nation fluctuates in response to local interests and external activities, a process repeated through the definitions of community, subjectivities-in-process, and gender possibilities found on SiamWEB.org. The website's creators presume they can modify the "notion of nation" through communication, recognizing that articulating the nation is a conceptual challenge, not a fixed conclusion. Consequently, taking the name "Siam," as opposed to "Thailand," remembers King Mongkut's initial nation-state construction, recalling the country's transnational pressures, competing cultural understandings, and adaptation to contradictory and uneven forces.

"Siam" also summons the period before the international circulation of Thai gendered stereotypes. Yujira notes that Usenet groups coalescing under the term "Siam" (as opposed to "Thailand") attract fewer male "spammers" aggressively demanding Thai female companionship (Yujira 1997). Similarly, the connotations of the word "web" in SiamWEB.org's name – rather than nation, territory, or space – further emphasize the creators' belief that the internet can alter current beliefs and practices. Through the use of the World Wide Web, they plan a future that accounts for past histories and practices within and about Thailand, proposing changes that reflect its constituency and the possibilities afforded by New Media. SiamWEB.org, in effect, re-maps Siam, allowing for virtual membership and providing a forum where communication about Thailand uses the new medium to respond to the concerns of its audience. Consequently, users' participation expands its content, types of contributions, and available features.

Assertions about nation on the site conflict and contradict, but predicate the need for constant revision and endorse debate as its vehicle. For instance, in the "news-culture" section, "Broken Pencil" discusses what constitutes a Thai national identity. The essay, "Miss Thailand (?) World Contest (96)," asks if Miss

Miss Thailand World 1996 (source: www.siamweb.org/news_culture/154/index_eng.php).

Thailand is actually Thai.[52] Broken Pencil uses physical appearance (Miss Thailand is mixed race, a *luk kreung*) and geographical history (she spent her youth outside of Thailand) to dispute the "fact" of national membership. Broken Pencil writes of Miss Thailand 1996:

Aright, she's pretty, but she also looks anything but Thai. But she IS, legally Thai. This raised two old questions.... [H]ow do we define being Thai? and more intriguing question, how do Thai people value and represent the concept of "human beauty" ... is Thai society really worships the western look?[53]

This essay recognizes that Miss Thailand is still a gendered national emblem and that gender and nation cannot be separated. The writer questions if and how ethnicity is written on the body and worries about the sway of western cultural aesthetics, invoking an essential, unsullied Thai-ness in opposition. But s/he does not end by simply condemning the internationalization of what constitutes the Thai nation. Instead, s/he concludes that nationality should be based on personal choice: "What ever a nationality the person feels, deep inside their soul, and has the love, appreciation, and pride, for, that's where they belong, and that's when the country will benefit from such a person...".[54] "Feeling" one's nationality radically reformulates theories of nationalism and the conditions for national membership, destabilizing the experiences of Asians in diaspora, for instance.

SCREAMING With Authority

Visitors to Yujira's "Ahem* We are not horny Thai girls!" often disregard her earnest appeal to men looking for romance to "go elsewhere," posting responses to the essay that overtly reduce the Thai nation to the negative images of Thai women.[55] More responses follow Yujira's exegesis than any other page. However, these postings ignore the essay's thesis, adhering instead to the belief that Thai women make superior wives or sexy companions. For example, "Mikeusa" writes:

> I am 33 male 6'2" 190 lbs. have visited thailand many times on business, I love beautiful, cute thai girls. I wish I could find a good one to marry and settle down with. I will be in BKK [Bangkok] next month & I would love to have someone to meet & party with, maybe even bring back home to Florida USA. Send me an email only if you might fit the bill.
>
> (October 17, 1996)

In this instance, the intended audience shifts from those who share the author's subject position to "beautiful, cute thai girls" that might respond to his offer of partying and marriage – putting his fantasy girl on both sides of the equation. He assumes that female Thai visitors might "fit the bill" despite the tone and thesis of the preceding essay. Dazza ("Thai women are the best fuck" [August 18, 1996]) and David ("I am a 33 year old Rock musician who is looking for horny Thai chicks who want to exchange hot E-mail with me I may be going to Thailand in the near future and would like to have some cute girls to meet when I get there. So write me if your naughty" [December 2, 1996]) also address Thai women, although the page is specifically aimed at men. These respondents seem sure that

Thai women are reading these posts, and that these women, neither bored nor frustrated, hope to find a western companion. In fact, contributors often read the posts following the essay more carefully than the essay itself, responding to previous posts by other men. Peter Hansen writes:

> I've just been married to the loveliest thaigirl in the world This is the best a man can get – they take care of you if you show your love – you will get it back 10 times! Thanks honney! I love you! [sic].
>
> (October 10, 1996)

"They," meaning Thai women, is contrasted with the first use of "you," which addresses a western male audience. The final "you" presumably refers to his Thai "honney." Like Yujira, Hansen addresses a western male readership but, unlike her, he assumes they share his point of view. All of the respondents that follow this post are men and, failing to acknowledge a Thai audience, they talk directly to other western men. On this page, virtual community formation, one goal of SiamWEB.org, occurs among the men who misread SiamWEB.org's project. While some discussions target a female audience that Yujira claims is not there, others do not include Thai women at all, invoking them nonetheless. These women occupy the center through their acknowledged absence. These posts, while ignoring the content of the page, create the form of dialogue and virtual community posited by SiamWEB.org despite countering one of the site's primary goals. Conjectures about these women by male posters reify the limited version of Thai women (that extends to conceptions of Thailand as a nation) and further proves the strength of these discourses.

In response to the many western postings that follow Od Busakorn's essay entitled "Thai sisters are Doing it for Themselves"[56] and disregard her thesis, a Thai woman intervenes, using the Web convention of writing in all capital letters to yell: "THAI WOMEN ARE NOT EASY OR SLUTY OR PROSTITUTES … THEY ARE INDEPENDENT, HARD WORKING WOMEN WHO TAKE CARE OF THEIR FAMILY" [sic] (proxy). This writer mentions Thai women as prostitutes in her response (similar to Yujira's page featuring the sexy Thai woman), yet her words, as well as her loud, disruptive use of capital letters, suggest a different Thai woman. Unlike the surrounding posts, her assertion of "independence" takes for granted that Thai women are not financially dependent sex-workers. The women described thus fall outside the dominant stereotypes. By saying, however, that they "take care of their family," her intervention remains legible in the same framework. The positioning of family suggests that Thai women do, in fact, fit into the mold of caregivers, wives, and mothers available in dominant representations. This in no way dilutes the power of her intervention: while participating in the type of community formation postulated by the site's creators, the writer also takes into account the dialogues and interaction among the western men who post, forcing this male community to see her voice and acknowledge that the predominant theme of their thread has been disrupted. Thai women are speaking citizens, not only representations of the nation existing for extra-national consumption. Her comment interrupts and negates the conjectures surrounding it. Her comment marks an instance of the "LaNgUaGe" play encouraged by the site's editors. This post is fluent in the language of SiamWEB.org, thereby garnering additional authority.

Similarly, Thai expatriate Gaew uses capital letters to scream at the media beyond Thailand's borders: "MY MESSAGE FOR YOU MEDIA OUTTHERE IS PLEASE BE CREATIVE!! ... SHOW THE WORLD HOW THAI WOMEN ARE JUST LIKE WOMEN IN ANY OTHER COUNTRIES WE LIVE, STUDY, WORK AND CONTRIBUTE TO OUR COUNTRY...." She reprimands the media "OUTTHERE" for their continual reduction of Thailand to images of prostitutes, and demands that they show Thai women with occupations that contribute to the welfare of their country without involving expatriates and tourists. "CHANGE THEIR PERSPECTIVE ABOUT THAILAND AND THAI WOMEN," she declares. Gaew's message serves as an angry rejection of both the ideas of male posters on the website and the print and television depictions outside Thailand. This site enables her to interact with other visitors, criticizing both their assumptions and their reification through other media sources. Gaew's impassioned plea exploits SiamWEB.org's claim that the internet provides potential for change. She assumes that, rather than merely replicating what exists, internet communication may reveal the ideologies embedded in prior media practices and aid in their transformation.

These posts by Thai women illustrate their active investment in changing how foreigners perceive them. Through their interventions, they give new voice to an internet presence that was previously undetectable. The production of English-language images of Thai women as sex-workers and/or wives by western male participants and community formation premised on these images does occur on SiamWEB.org. However, the mere presence of this site, where the stereotypes are both affirmed and dismantled (often by Thai women themselves), discredits the efforts of these men, rendering them insensitive and facile to sympathetic visitors. By writing essays and posting responses, female SiamWEBlers are embodying positions that fit neither the external rubric for Thai women nor those of traditional Thai culture. Furthermore, the prominence of these gendered national representations on this new form of communication can serve as the impetus for Thai women who were previously silent to respond and undermine these myths through personal intervention. Not only through their existence, but through their resistance, these women shatter reductive categories. According to SiamWEB. org's definitions, their participation creates new communities with constituents that extend the borders of the nation while reducing the power of national images. SiamWEB.org provides the forum, the challenge, the information, and resources for the digital creolization that facilitates this process.

Diluting present assumptions is the goal of SiamWEB.org – what is crafted in its wake is left up to the members. SiamWEBlers are assumed to produce, transform, appropriate, and consume language and technology for their own purposes. Many do; one visitor, for example, has taken it upon herself to query the notoriety of Thai prostitutes. She provides a history of sex-work in Thailand, attributing its persistence, despite great health risks including AIDS, to Thai cultural practices and the government's reliance on sex-tourism. Detailing the health scams of brothel owners and healthcare providers, she provides links to other sites for more accurate health information, links to an AIDS in Thailand homepage, and other links about sex-workers and their conditions. She concludes "among all the problems that surround prostitution, the Thai government puts Thailand's Image in the highest priority. Politicians spend their efforts in covering-up the problem instead of solving it".[57] This participant provides the means for education and information dissemination online and through other media, but, more importantly, she insists that "The cultural habits and guest welcoming practices must also change".[58] Moving beyond addressing the image, this participant has accrued and distributed information about the historical and political barriers that perpetuate not only the representation, but also the material realities and their accompanying risks.

One of the greatest challenges facing the study of New Media at present is assessing the use of the internet by those with the least access to information, communication technologies, and supporting social services. The simplistically termed "digital divide" is often assumed to be largely unbridgeable; this oft-used phrase perpetuates the sense of unequal ability along with unequal access rather than calling for an examination of who is engaged with digital technologies and how participation occurs. Accepting a static digital divide functions much like the reductive categorization of Thai women by the media. In this context, assuming Thai women are sex-workers and wives further suggests that they lack information, skills, and resources. Thai women are not, however, imagined as victims of their international images by SiamWEB.org; instead, they are understood to be capable of voicing their opinions in language and tone that reflect their circumstances.

English language portrayals of Thai women have consistently depicted them as subservient to western men. Proliferated by international media, these images extended to function as symbols of the Thai nation. SiamWEB.org encourages Thai women with internet access and English-language competence to appraise and refute these stereotypes. Recognizing the gendered inequalities that accompany considerations of nation and nationalism, particularly when under an international gaze, SiamWEB.org simultaneously discourages practices that yoke nation and gender and allows the production of pejorative depictions of Thai women in extranational representations. The site attempts a realignment based on shared interests rather than a shared location, national belonging, and/or linguistic affiliation. By privileging neither native English speakers nor Thai nationals, the site invites all members to imagine themselves as non-native speakers and not essentially Thai nationals. With the belief that they can "dilute the stereotyping" on the World Wide Web, SiamWEB.org contributes to the complex processes by which western culture and the English language are appropriated and reassembled in ways that challenge externally generated stereotypes, the confines of previous formulations of the nation, and the conditions for subject formation. On SiamWEB. org, women who fall outside of previously demarcated boundaries create themselves discursively, as flexible, fluent members of a community with numerous and varying "interests in Thailand and its People".[59]

6

Bangkok Boyonthenet.com

Boyonthenet: The Perfect Balance of U & Me

(Title bar for Boyonthenet.com[1])

Palm Plaza Community: We have no responsibility for the contents in this web community!

(Logo and disclaimer on Palm-plaza.com[2])

This chapter links two "spaces" rarely considered in tandem: the geophysical meeting places of gay-identified Thai men in contemporary Bangkok and the websites they visit.[3] Featuring similar and often overlapping populations, these spaces reveal that sexual identities are not cohesive, timeless categories, nor are they deployed uniformly, even within a small group. Instead, online/offline intersections challenge dominant conceptions of sexuality-based identities, providing novel configurations of their boundaries and intersections. Examination of the websites frequented by Thai men who patron the bars in Bangkok's well-known gay area exposes both the convergence of online and offline communities and the layered complexities contained in and delimited by the category "gay." The sites these men visit, the types of interactions they experience, and the way they portray themselves online illustrate a divergence from dominant discourses concerning an emerging universal gay identity and conventional understandings of online community formation. Thus, these men demonstrate that internet participation does not conform to a particular global trend. Instead, their digital creolization strategies intersect with their knowledges and experiences of western-derived, primarily English-language people, practices, and beliefs.

Many theorists champion participation on gay-specific websites as a way to ensure the monitoring (some say guaranteeing) of individual rights and provide information concerning self-recognition, community resources, and healthy living. These goals, however, presume western-derived, post-Stonewall gay identities, not to mention standardized aesthetics, values, and social practices, without enough consideration paid to physical location or material conditions, particularly with respect to non-western, yet markedly transnational, settings. While Chapter 4 illustrates the attempts of users in diaspora to garner geo-political recognition of nation-state status through online activities, this chapter highlights the practices of a group of people with a shared sexual identification who gather not only on websites but also at the same offline locations. Instead of using their interactions to organize rights-based activism, share "coming out" narratives, or celebrate "global gay" pride, these Bangkok-based self-identified Thai gay men conduct conversations that articulate local conceptions of gay identities, relay local information, and signal a move away from global gay conformity. Moreover, a shift in participation took place between 2004 and 2006, with men migrating from supposedly global Web communities to primarily local ones. This enhanced possibilities for reimagining and renegotiating conceptions surrounding online gay-targeted social networking sites and localized a supposedly global and globalizing medium. Being Thai and gay in Bangkok broadens common assertions of what constitutes gay identities in global or transnational arenas and extends the role language and location play in framing and constructing online environments.

In the past decade, much scholarly work has pointed out differences among populations that call themselves gay.[4] While the notion of sexual identity is being complicated, universalized assumptions of identity formation are still frequently applied to non-western cultures. Gay lifestyle is often declared to be "going global," but local websites are tailoring the term, not merely joining a fixed, clearly defined, and universally identical category or association.[5] "Gay" means something different for Thai men in Bangkok than it does for men in the United States or elsewhere, and its meaning changes with time. While this global gay image is being produced by both the west and the east, and its embodiment can be seen in the gay locales in Bangkok, the international gay male is a fictive construction that has no literal embodiment, nor is it manifest in all social, political, and cultural contexts. Rather than becoming synonymous with the western-centered notion of gay identity, gay identity in Thailand is mingling with, infusing, and revising both western and traditional Thai notions of gender, sexuality, and identity.

In what follows, I explore particular enunciations of Thai sexualities and instances where gender and sex are expressed by Thais in contemporary Bangkok – both through embodied and linguistic practices that seem non-normative to a heterosexual-privileging, cissexual US and European worldview.[6] I then examine Gay.com, detailing the global gay identity it presumed in June 2004, when I conducted extensive interviews with gay-identified Thai men regarding their online practices.[7] My analysis reveals disjunctures between Gay.com's ideal version of a "global gay" and the actual visitors and members that populate the site – disjunctures Thai gay men and *kathoeys* had to confront if they wished to engage with the site. In the next section, I survey the processes described by Google.com for producing search results and the effects of these results on Thai gay men. The chapter concludes with an examination of several features of three of the most popular websites reported to me by Thai gay men in 2004, each of which increased in traffic between 2004 and 2007.

Not only does this chapter recognize that Thai gay men are changing the way they articulate their identities, but it also observes how popular local websites are responding to and accommodating these needs. Aware of how these monolithic presumptions are applied inaccurately to their experiences, self-identified Thai gay men are entering into transnational dialogues in English, Chinese, and Thai, contributing to the discussion of how the term "gay" is being creolized in Thai and among Bangkok gay men. This process, happening concurrently in Bangkok bars and virtual meeting places, can be understood as constituting a new, complex, and sometimes contradictory, network. From this perspective, framing "online" and "offline" as distinct categories is not useful for analysis, nor is isolating the internet from other digital media practices, particularly digital image capture and cell-phone use. Concurring with earlier studies that explore how gay sites enable a variety of connections both online and off, my findings suggest that physical and digital locations should not be considered separate spaces with discrete, non-intersectional precincts,[8] and local sites offer opportunities for digital convergence more seamlessly than do well-known Web portals or search engines that claim cutting-edge status and accurate, comprehensive retrieval of all existing information in every available digital repository.

Gay Bangkok

Urban communities do not necessarily adhere to western-derived delineations of location and space. Though there are similarities between urban gay spaces in the US and Bangkok (there are several central gathering places for men who call themselves "gay"), other forms of men-having-sex-with-men, such as non-identity-based same-sex encounters, do not necessarily require a lifestyle change or relocation. The monolithic image of urban gay communities posits US and European gay culture as the pre-eminent manifestation of homosocial/homosexual male arrangements worldwide and, in most academic considerations of queer theory, "queerness" is presumed to appear in all cultures exactly as it does on western gay bodies and locales. Similarly, one should not assume, as Dennis Altman does, that since some cafes, bars, and discos look quite similar, whether situated in Brazil or the Philippines, the same processes, expectations, and rituals must be in play.[9] These commercial venues are not merely replications – they have been altered to reflect the "contact zone" created by their simultaneous international and local circumstances.[10] For example, while DJ Station, a gay disco in Bangkok, initially seems similar to gay discos in many urban cities, the focal point of every evening is an event geared toward its local constituency. Once a night, the dance music stops, Thai men gather around the stage, and "The Show" begins. This performance features not only nightly choreographed dances to popular songs – a staging well-known to gay discos – but also extended renditions of Thai folk stories. While the dances may resemble those seen on many gay stages throughout the world, the folktale re-enactments, conducted in Thai, are queer incarnations of Thai folk and religious stories normally seen at rural temple fairs. These displays are legible only to those immersed in Thai culture and Thai Buddhist history, and no efforts are made by the actors or, for the most part, the audience, to translate or contextualize the acts. These skits, however, are the highlight of the program for most of the Thai men in attendance, and "The Show" is a topic of conversation for the duration of the evening. Therefore, concluding that DJ Station is like any other gay disco would overlook the most significant aspect of the cultural work in play.[11]

While bars, restaurants, and discos in the "gay" area of Silom Soi 2 and 4 in Bangkok are listed in Thailand's gay-targeted tourist guides, news of the most popular locales is spread among the Thai population via flyers and word of mouth.[12] The local websites frequented by the men I interviewed were likewise spread by word of mouth, by sharing friends' laptops, by using the history or bookmarks functions in internet cafes located on or near Silom Soi 2 and Silom Soi 4, and through flyers circulating in these sois. These sites could not – and still cannot – be found through search engines such as Google.com (the US-based, international default) or Google.co.th, the Google search engine default website for Thailand launched after my interviews were conducted. Responding to constant changes in what constitutes a Thai gay identity, these sites – whether bars, discos, restaurants, or websites – present both online and offline opportunities for Thai men to share comments, opinions, gossip, or concerns about their lives, and form scattered alliances vis-à-vis the proliferation of global or transnational gay identities and practices. Changes on these websites between June 2004 and February 2008 suggest that they attracted an increasingly large local audience while simultaneously becoming more Thai-centered. These websites encourage Thai men to communicate with one another in both English and Thai, offering a form of digital creolization that moves away from privileging communication in "Standard" US Business English above communication in Thai, "Tinglish," or vernacular English imported from American popular culture. Allowing for contributions in English, Thai, or combinations thereof, these sites promote another sense of fluency – one that, like SiamWEB.org, is premised on participation, but also draws on local knowledges and online/offline intersections in order to facilitate linguistic and ideological cross-fertilization.

My earlier Bangkok-based inquiry which took place from 1996 to 1997 located a gay Thai community and investigated the deployment of the word "gay" in relation to other Thai terms for sexuality and sexual practices. I discovered then that identifying as gay in Thailand could neither be equated with western gay identity nor other sexual identities or actions previously available to Thai men. Rather, such an identification includes an awareness of the "global" label, but does not conform to images of a single manifestation of a gay subject posited by earlier queer theory scholars. Although being gay in Bangkok combines and reconfigures ideologies from many sources, thus producing identities that are dynamic and often in conflict, my research and complimentary studies by anthropologists of Thai sex/gender suggest that one component of gay identity for Thai men is a sense of rupture from earlier manifestations of Thai gender. Being gay is decidedly modern to these men, and, because of its recent origins and its physical look (decidedly masculine, with defined muscles), it is often positioned as western-inspired. This should not be interpreted as imitation of western practices. Instead, by pursuing interactions with gay men beyond Thailand's borders, speaking English, and following western tastes and fashions, men who desire men in Bangkok mark themselves as Thai gay men, not global gays.[13]

As opposed to those interviewed from 1996 to 1997, the men who habituated the same locales in Bangkok in 2004 no longer clearly linked being "gay" with western involvement. This marks quite a change, particularly since at least 10 percent of my interviewees were the same informants from the earlier study. Instead of desire for relations with *farang*, several Thai gay men revealed that they were hoping to find or had found Chinese, Japanese, or Thai partners, and expressed disinterest in western men. Over time, the term "gay" among Thai men no longer referred strictly to westerners. For example, one site, based in Singapore, was a virtual meeting place and information source for overseas Chinese gay men to connect.[14] Furthermore, the current Bangkok gay scene is not singularly reliant on two small alleys of commercial venues. More physical venues exist, some of which cater to a non-western, but markedly gay, clientele. For example, there used to be saunas for Thai men that were not considered gay locales even though sex between men occurred there. Similarly, there were gay saunas where western men met Thai men for sociality and sex. Now, there are gay saunas aimed at Thai-only or Asian-only audiences, thus marking a move away from western bodies in exclusively "gay" environs. Globalization, transnational outlooks, market participation, and internet use do not render a singular gay-signifying look that extends globally; rather, gay identities take on nuances that refer to their specific, local articulations. In what follows, I analyze the websites visited by Thai gay men in order to determine what assumptions about international gay identities they encounter and suggest how these electronic images intersect with the continually shifting conceptions of Thai gay identity.

"Romantic" ... and Other Transnational Manifestations

Specific to the discussion of women who love women in contemporary Thailand, anthropologist Megan Sinnott writes: "Appreciation of local cultural understandings of sexual practices will be lost or subtly skewed if researchers use the categorizations of 'homosexuality' and 'heterosexuality' without conscious awareness of the implicit cultural meanings embedded within this binary construct" (Sinnott 2004, 17). Heterosexuality and homosexuality are not binary relations in a traditional Thai worldview that predicates gender, not sex or sexuality, as foundational oppositions: masculinity and femininity function as the organizational dichotomy. For most Thai people, categories such as "man" and "woman" are not simple a priori oppositions; Thai language practices cast these terms in a field of gendered/sexed positions. One can be a woman or one can be a tom, but a tom is rarely described as a woman or a man. A tom is gendered masculine, not feminine, and thus aligns with a dee, a feminine woman who desires toms. A male gender, for many people in Thailand, would seem likely to be paired with a female gender, regardless of sex or genitalia. Consequently, dees do not necessarily transgress the normative social arrangement. In a similar vein, the term "man" has a distinct meaning in a Thai context; incarcerated women who have sex with women but maintain their female gender are labeled "men." The nuances of these categories are lost when analyzed from the predominant perspective of most queer theorists: that the hetero/homo binary is the primary opposition upon which meaning is made.

Like many other English words found in the Thai lexicon, "gay" is an adaptation from its English counterpart, crafted to fit particular Thai circumstances. Accordingly, it carries different meanings when employed by a Thai man in Bangkok than when used by non-Thai men in Bangkok or by gay men in other locales. These distinctions can be seen in the blurring of the categories for sex in the Thai context as compared to current western-based usages. Peter Jackson writes:

> New identities such as gay, tom and dee have emerged since World War II without the concomitant borrowing of a Western discourse of sexuality. Gender and sexuality remain an integral discursive domain in Thailand, both being understood in terms of the overarching local notion of *phet* (eroticized gender).
>
> (Jackson 2004, 203)

In the traditional Thai hierarchy of values, adhering to masculine or feminine attributes is less socially disruptive than having one's gender conform to one's biological sex, though the two cannot be separated since they are both subsumed under the concept of *phet*.[15] Sexual object choice is not a primary consideration as it is in the west, nor is it easily separated from one's own gender/sex.[16] Thus this single word encompasses the sex, gender, and sexuality paradigm. While it stands for and merges these three categories, it reflects a gender-inflected positionality.

English words often inspire lexical development in other languages, specifically with respect to modernity, material wealth, and sexual explicitness. English, in other words, tends to carry traces of US fashion and consumer culture. Because the English language is a foreign, yet familiar language for the majority of Thais, Thai cultural resonances are disrupted with English, providing a sense of freedom from traditional mores. For some Thais, consumer-related or erotic ideas, impolite to say in Thai, are more easily communicated in English.[17] Deviations from tradition that require new expressions are thus given names imported from English – particularly when they reflect English-associated ideas. This may account for the frequency of Thai creolization of English terms concerning gender, sex, sexuality, and erotics, reflecting the media influx from English-language sources and the titillation by the unfamiliar exotic. "Romantic," "take care," "I love you," and other English-language expressions of western-style affection are often said among Bangkok Thais, particularly the young middle-class. Likewise, Thai nicknames increasingly reflect the Bangkok mixture of English-language culture.[18] Ara Wilson writes:

> I heard Thai women use the term *spec* to describe their specifications about what kind of partner they wanted ... one woman identified herself as neither tom nor dee but rather "two in one," she said, borrowing the English marketing slogan for a shampoo–conditioner.
>
> (Wilson 2004, 128)

In this instance, the English-language phrase is not simply a designation for which there was none before: "two-in-one" is used to name a sexually oriented identity through an association based on a western consumer product and an international advertising campaign. Deploying an English term enables the association of purchasing power and transnational meaning for terms and ideas concerning sexuality, sex, and gender in contemporary Bangkok. Moreover, invoking terms and phrases that derive from English imbue utterances with cultural capital and added layers of meaning. "Two-in-one," like gay, tom, dee, and other terms adopted from English, allows for the enunciation of previously unspoken positions through class-tinged worldliness.

Because Thai culture has developed alongside its religion, which is grounded primarily in Theravada Buddhism, the foundational belief system is not based on confession or narrative, nor is one defined as a distinct agent with individuated desires. With no such history of individuality, identity-based definitions marked by sexual object choice, or religious practice of confession, Thai culture has manifested itself differently than have western, Judeo-Christian-based cultures. Traditional Thai values are understood to embody the tenets of Thai Buddhism along with Thai nationalism, both of which foreground relationality and posit one's interconnectedness with others. For example, the greeting one uses to show respect, a wai, should be initiated by the person with lower status. Linguistically, interconnectedness manifests itself through the naming of others, who are more likely to be hailed with a word that defines a relationship with the speaker than with a given name. Thus one calls a stranger "Aunt," "Uncle," "Big Sister," "Big Brother," "Little Sister," or "Little Brother" as appropriate. Individualism – the notion of a discrete, rational subject that is primarily responsible to oneself and is entitled to universal freedoms or rights in isolation of others – seems not only foreign, but unethical from the perspective of Thai Buddhism.

Notions of individualism and the theories that sustain it are embedded in western-generated media, including the internet, which are eagerly consumed by Bangkok's middle-class. Bangkok residents' involvement with western media and marketplaces suggests an uneven reception of ideas such as the inalienability of individual choice, freedom of expression, and universal human rights. Although activism is often considered an essential element of gay practice in the post-Stonewall US, it is not recognized as a universal marker of gay identity. Particularly in Thailand, where the liberal-humanist notion of the individual is not part and parcel of the modern subject, activism is not inherent to gay identity. Individualism and its accompanying accoutrements, such as rights activism, are no longer foreign, not yet a priori, and deployed strategically, particularly when enunciated by Thais to non-Thai audiences.

Thai Non-Governmental Organizations (NGOs) do not necessarily believe in rights-based individualism; instead, they employ related terms strategically in a transnational arena in order to procure the resources necessary to achieve their projects without making the ideology of individual human rights part of the language for local social change. They display similar abilities to understand and retool the humanist ideology underlying the application of human-rights discourses. Thailand has a complex history of negotiating human-rights discourses and notions of personal freedom. The push by some primarily US-based NGOs to position sexual identification as a universal human right is marked by "a new constellation of forces and alignments that give a substantively different inflection to the discourse of human rights in the 1990s."[19] Thai NGOs will work with international non-government organizations that privilege human-rights discourses in order to further their specific projects, even though their aims may not be grounded in human rights' ideologies. Thailand's NGOs are carefully shaping their positions, and the results are sometimes unexpected.[20] In 1981, a short-lived "gay rights" NGO, Chai-Chawp-Chai (Men Liking Men), was founded. Its project-based formation was perceived by its founders as unnecessary since there was no "official" government evidence of discrimination.[21]

Thai NGOs are reluctant to join transnational organizations with similar concerns because of the emphasis on rights-based activism. In fact, no Thai NGOs concerned with sex, gender, or sexuality participate in international organizations that purport to speak for the world's lesbians, gay men, bisexuals, and transgendered people, such as the International Lesbian and Gay Association (ILGA) or the International Gay and Lesbian Human Rights Commission (IGLHRC). Several Thai gay groups have been approached by the US-based ILGA, but they have all refused to join because they find the organization's projects and/or language offensive.[22] Anjaree, which can be translated as "women who follow nonconformist ways," is a Thai NGO dedicated to finding new vocabulary and identity positions for women who love women in Thailand.[23] In the search for new terms, some members reject the word "lesbian," deeming it too sex-orientated when compared to "tom" and "dee," the operative categories which refer to gender rather than sexual desire. Since the group does not identify itself as a "lesbian" organization or its members as "lesbians,"[24] Anjaree is not affiliated with either ILGA or IGLHRC.

In 1995, the IGLHRC awarded Anjaree the Filpa de Sausa Award which recognizes the efforts of NGOs and individuals to improve "the human rights of lesbian, gay, bisexual, transgender (LGBT) and other individuals stigmatized and abused because of their sexuality".[25] Anjaree's critique of the organization's terminology and rights-based politics has been ignored. Similarly, the US-based ILGA (and its website) is largely organized through its national chapters.[26] Each of these chapters features local news and events concerning GLBT "rights" and homophobic practices. Yet, the only mention of Thailand on ILGA's website concerns the Fifteenth International AIDS Conference that took place in Bangkok in 2004, for which a link to more information is provided. The link leads to The Kaiser Family Foundation rather than to any organization in Thailand.[27] As both Anjaree's founder, Anjana Suvarnananda, and its manager, Surang Janyam, have stated, refusing to join ILGA demonstrates a critical engagement with US definitions of individual rights and identity politics.[28] Anjaree's refusal is clearly stated and politically resonant, yet the result is incoherent: celebrating an organization while ignoring its population. A more nuanced recognition by western NGOs would be that sexuality should not be yoked to enforcing individual rights or exposing rights abuses.

The United States and American English are not the only influences on Thai culture and language. Japan, for example, supplies fodder for Thai language adaptation as well as cultural imports through marketing styles and artifacts such as anime and manga, which are consumed and re-envisioned in numerous Thai formulations. Peter Jackson calls attention to the linguistic interchange in terms of sexuality: "The complex genealogies of contemporary Thai vocabularies for gender/sex difference suggest ... a complex range of influences – East–West borrowing and adaptation, intra-Asian contact, and local evolution" (Jackson 2004, 227). In other words, the expectation that US ideas and culture flow unimpeded into Thailand is misguided – not only are the ideas changed in circulation, other nations also contribute to the Thai conglomeration of transnational and national popular culture. ILGA and IGLHRC will be unable to recognize their losses until they acknowledge that GLBT is not a unified concept, even if every culture has men who love men, women who love women, and people who defy normative gender or sexual regimes.

As venues for Thai gay clientele proliferate in Thailand, abroad, and online, conversations about rapidly changing identity rage. This effects not only how identity is understood by Thai gay men, but also by those who come into contact with them, whether through intimate relationships or formal encounters, such as inter-governmental organizational endeavors. Internet communication facilitates these dialogues, functioning intrinsically with other forms of communication including mobile audio devices, various print and image media, and face-to-face interactions. The consistent mishandling of Thai voices has led some Thais – such as members of SiamWEB.org – to shout online. This lack of specificity, seemingly a hallmark of western-based NGOs and websites such as Gay.com or Google.com has inspired some Thai gay men to engage in other methods of digital creolization. These subjects are not voiceless, but despite their growing conversations, they are increasingly undetectable.

Gay.com

Increasing internet access in Bangkok over the past ten years has created new opportunities for Thai gay men to forge non-Thai friendships and experience non-local depictions of gay life and practices. However, no information is available regarding Thai gay men's use of the internet to refine their sense of what constitutes a gay identity and how online and offline interactions coincide. Most analysis of online participation takes for granted that websites targeting a specific audience simplistically reflect that audience's uniform beliefs and priorities. In contrast, this study compares websites visited by Thai gay men and charts the changes in both viewing habits and the website content itself. This population's widespread internet use leads to diverse enunciations of desire, resources for matchmaking, and articulated resistance to dominant practices of identification. Several interviewees stated that they expect their online interactions to lead to face-to-face meetings, which can be said of many gay online encounters. Despite early studies of computer-mediated communication that focused on how users behaved differently online and offline, clearly the two are not considered to be discrete spaces for many users. This section will discuss the range of content used by Thai gay men in June 2004, which marks a moment when many began defecting from Gay.com.

Gay.com is the first result when either the term "gay" or "Thai gay" is entered into Google search engines – both the default and the Thai versions. While almost every man I interviewed had visited Gay.com, most did not have much to say about it except that they would no longer use it when it started charging a fee.[29] In contrast to "universal" gay sites such as Gay.com, the men I interviewed then reported visiting local websites. These Thai-based sites cannot be found by search engines like Google. Instead, word-of-mouth and links between sites serve to spread knowledge of their existence. Furthermore, unlike Gay.com, the content and layout of these websites illustrate processes of negotiation that challenge "gay" as a fixed set of socio-behavioral practices or identifications. Thai gay men's defection from Gay.com demonstrates a shift from a global gay identity to Thai-specific gay identities that are in dialogue with, but separate from, western conceptions of gender and sexuality.

Gay.com, through its parent company, Planetout.com, claims "to be the most extensive multi-channel, multi-platform network of gay and lesbian people in the world".[30] This description attempts to attract people who identify with these categories to their websites. By attracting eyeballs and optimizing stickiness (time spent at a particular domain), the company can argue for the buying power of its community of users. The quantification of a consumer group is crucial to start-up success, as defined by US venture capitalists.[31] On its 2004 homepage, the site itself proclaims: "Gay.com is the world's largest destination for chat, personals, health information, news and entertainment for the GLBT community."[32] In the hopes of appealing to the broadest consumer-base possible, Gay.com offers different geographically and linguistically based entry points with different features based on one's "default" physical location (i.e. the place a user reported occupying when creating the account). However, because of the centrality of US gay culture and its understanding of gay identity, many US-specific generalizations are proliferated. These include: the role of English, the site's geographical center and periphery, what constitutes a gay and lesbian identity, and what users desire when connecting with one another.

Rather than positing cyberspace as exceeding geopolitical borders, Gay.com relies on a linguistically arranged framework to situate the user in a postcolonial

Gay.com insists users make language choices (image from 1984, when my interviews were conducted).

world. In 2004, the second page a user encountered upon enrolling required a "default Gay.com location" premised on national language. When registering, visitors chose a language in order to determine how their "experience" (mostly, the default menu options frame that appears on every page) would be presented. English was and is the default language and is first in the list of choices. Other languages follow in three columns of options, each appearing in native form rather than as a language listed in English on an English-language page. In other words, Deutsch follows English, and the rest of the languages are offered in alphabetical order: Español, Français, Italiano and Portugués. This apparent linguistic sensitivity is ambiguous in effect; these six choices all refer to languages that originated in Europe. Each of the nations of origin for these languages recall former imperial powers that colonized vast regions of the world and insisted on language conformity (the Dutch and Japanese, also strong colonial forces, did not push for language assimilation to the same degree). Consequently, languages not employed by the colonizers or the colonized, such as Thai, simply do not exist, even as an all-encompassing catch-all "other." The remnants of colonialism are the organizing force that contextualizes place for Gay.com. The site ushers in the formerly colonized countries surrounding Thailand: Burma and Malaysia were part of the British Imperial Crown, and Laos and Cambodia comprised, along with Vietnam, French Indochina. Meanwhile, Thai-language speakers, or English-speaking Thais, are invisible. This omission persists even though Thailand is so frequently marketed as a gay paradise.

Colonialism's continued resonance is legible in the radio buttons under these language choices. The "Planet Out" posited by Gay.com is once again broken down into uneven geo-political correspondences. French is posited from the onset as existing beyond the boundaries of its "mother" country. Consequently, the term *francophone* implies that a person speaking French can be located anywhere: *pays* is both singular (meaning country) and plural (meaning countries). So while there is only a single choice under the language "Français," *Pays Francophone* recognizes that a user might inhabit any former French territory – French need only be his/her national language in order to provide a match. Likewise, *Portugués* offers only one choice: "Paises de lingua Portuguesa" (translated as "Portuguese-speaking countries"). The suggestion that Portuguese may be spoken in a number of countries recognizes the outspoken gay culture present in Brazil, which serves an iconic function in mainstream US gay culture because of its widely publicized, gay-friendly, Carnival celebrations. The choices under Spanish and English, however, are broken into regional categories. The Spanish choices make a distinction between Latin America, Argentina, and Mexico (yet do not mention Spain), which suggests the importance of the American continent. Meanwhile English, despite functioning as Gay.com's default language, is reduced to three radio buttons: the United States and Canada, the United Kingdom, and Australia. Speaking English in Thailand is not an option. English speakers beyond the pale of the site's linguistically articulated world are not locatable, even as English is the supposed lingua franca of both Gay.com and the World Wide Web.

Identity is proscribed through the many dialogue boxes that must be navigated on the site. User-submitted photographs and requests to "select a city" are, as with many social-networking sites, ways in which physical bodies can be linked to online identities. Bangkok, however, is not one of the cities available on the dropdown list of locations offered, once again erasing the presence and possibility of Thai membership. A default zip code option further reminds the user that the site is highly legible for US and Canadian users, while logging on from other locations takes a secondary screen of required information. Each box demands that one make a choice; the range of options is predetermined and arranged in a seemingly hierarchical default with one choice "naturalized" through its placement as first. Moreover, only one selection can be made, as opposed to the more fluid "check all those that apply" approach. In order to use the site's most popular functions, chat and member viewing, one must mark oneself through a series of either/or identifications that cannot be changed once the account is established.

Before 2004, when Gay.com was still popular among Thai gay men, one could have multiple names and descriptions within a single user account. That feature was eliminated, and now each member must have only one screen name and one personal description, anchoring users to accounts in a one-to-one correspondence. To substantiate one's corporeal claims, images are encouraged; for popularity to be achieved, the site warns, one must upload photographs. The "personals" search feature offers a pre-ticked box that limits searches to members who have uploaded photographs. This is similar to many social-networking websites – rather than presenting a new means for self-description or identification, visual verisimilitude represents honesty and worthiness for interaction. This takes for granted that an image offers some sort of physical proof – surprising in a day where Photoshop is widely available and often used, not to mention that a plethora of applications for photo enhancement are pre-installed on new computers and come with most digital cameras. Furthermore, Google Images has insured that images can easily be located on the World Wide Web; it is not at all difficult to present an image found on the Web as one's own.[33] This presuming by Gay.com that each account represents a singular, unified subject and that this subject is adjudicated a corresponding corporeal facsimile discourages the play supposedly facilitated on the site.

The construction of desire is also a "default" built into the Gay.com framework. For many Thais, *"kathoey"* is a main reference point for self-definition in addition to male and female. *Kathoeys* are biological men with female genders; they are expected to display feminine attributes and express attraction to men. In the Thai gender/sex/sexuality system, *kathoeys* occupy a distinct category that is just as "natural" as male or female designations. The categories "male" and "female" are no longer oppositions once *"kathoey"* is introduced, because one can "be" a man, but not be "masculine." The feminine-gendered *kathoey* can desire men without transgressing traditional Thai sex/gender/sexuality regimes. A *kathoey* might be understood as an additional sex, or an alternative to the endpoint suggested by the designation MTF (Male-to-Female).

When a user creates a personal profile, Gay.com requires a choice among five "gender" options – male, female, MTF, FTM (Female-to-Male) – and "prefer not to say." When searching for others to meet, one must also select one of the four "gender" categories. Only since the twentieth century have labels such as "gay" appeared in language and culture as a way to complicate the correspondence between gender conformity and same-gender object desire, yet by the twenty-first, they no longer suffice. This range of choices does not account for *kathoey*, who do not consider themselves to be MTF, yet might prefer to say that they are gendered female and desire masculine men. The *kathoey*, who is neither a man nor a woman, nor at the conclusion of a transition process suggested by the designations MTF or FTM, has no applicable boxes. More appropriate would be the gender-choice "feminine" – as opposed to female – but such flexibility is unavail-

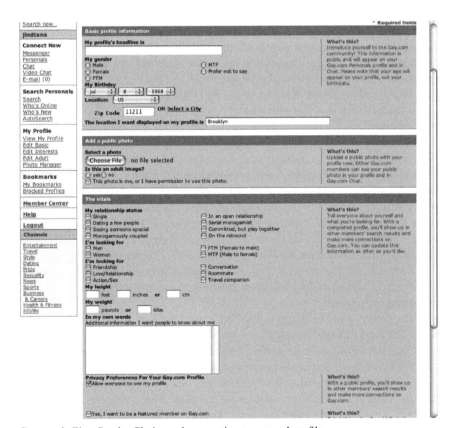

Gay.com's Five Gender Choices when creating a personal profile.

Gay.com's Gender Choices when searching for a match.

able in this network.[34] Similarly, the "gender" boxes supplied by Gay.com do not recognize the dominant Thai gender/sex framework: men who are masculine and desire masculine men disrupt this gender-based system more than masculine men with feminine "men." The word "gender," rather than "sex," makes marking the boxes particularly difficult for a Thai gay men where feminine and masculine gender pairings, such as those between *kathoey* and men, may not be celebrated, but do fall within the gendered understanding of desire. Thus Gay.com's supposed "world" consists of a series of predetermined choices that require its members to conform to a version of a gendered gay identity where "global" still carries the vestiges of colonialism, accompanied by imperial notions of the English language, and a US-centered conception of identity. The particular instantiations of a Thai gay audience, Thai women who love women, and *kathoey* are simply not visible.

"Googling" Gay

A search of "Thai gay" or "Thailand gay" on Google.com, might lead one to believe that most Thai gay men are located on porn sites and in porn videos, waiting to be watched.[35] Once this amorphous Web "genre" is omitted, several

English-language websites consistently appear in the top ten results. These sites also appear in the Thailand Google search results, although there are far fewer links to pornography.[36] Given that Google's success is attributed to its ability to quickly locate an array of potential results for any search term, the results for "gay" and "Thai" are surprisingly narrow.

While US-based users increasingly rely on Google's search services and trust its accuracy, only a few of the Thai men I interviewed mentioned visiting the sites listed in either Google's top-20 search results. The two named by Thai gay men were Utopia-asia.com and Dragoncastle.com – the latter was reported only once. No respondents named the many other similar sites targeted at western men interested in meeting Thai men. Between 2004 and 2008, the sites' content, their omissions, and their depictions of gay identity changed, but, consistently, they reach for an audience similar to Google's assumed search agent: a gay, male westerner looking for Thai companionship.

Searches on both www.google.com and www.google.co.th suggest that Google's analysis algorithm PageRank, which aggregates quotations and references, and assigns a numerical weighting to each element in effect produces a judgment concerning the relevancy of site content and search elements. The company touts its ability to incorporate a variety of variables, using not only PageRank, but also Click Through Rates (CTRs), so that search requests are aligned according to choices made by previous users who conducted similar searches. This approach capitalizes on the schism between signifier and signified rather than presuming a fixed, one-to-one connection. To this end, traffic information about users conducting searches and visiting particular sites is more heavily monitored by websites that deploy Google's statistics-monitoring generator. Webmasters can optimize their site's likelihood of appearing in search results based on statistics tabulated from searchers' actions, rather than presumptions about searchers' intent. Suggestions and advice about rendering oneself visible to Google's search technology are provided free of charge, and optimization is encouraged. Thus Google uses a strategy of amalgamation, providing a broad spectrum of choices that reflect data gathered from their crawler, user choices, and embedded content. CTRs and conformation to Google's standards affect what website will appear and how, and each search conducted produces traces. Both the website developer and the user participate in this algorithmic function, insuring that the results and meanings generated from searches are not disembodied mathematical information. Coding and use provide lingering effects that influence future search results and project a logic surrounding particular terms.

As a result of the emphasis on inclusivity, searches on Google do not always result in such reductive outcomes. For example, when searching the word "gay" on Google.com, the first option for the past several years has been Gay.com, but definitions of the term (such as on Wikipedia: en.wikipedia.org/wiki/Gay), resources (for example, www.bestgayblogs.com), and sites advertising gay gatherings and nightlife all appear in the top-ten results. Consequently, gay men, search agents seeking to learn about the term, and users looking to connect with other people identifying as gay or gay-related topics, both online or offline, are all addressed as potential audiences. However, in an English-language search, the addition of the term "Thai" or "Thailand" attributes a specific set of attributes to the searcher. In other words, as a result of previous searches and other factors, the agent searching "Thai" and "gay" is presumed to be a gay-identified western man interested primarily in viewing erotic images of Thai men, and secondarily in meeting Thai men in Thailand who are interested in contact with gay men outside of Thailand. Each time a search is conducted using "Thai" or "Thailand" and "gay" and links are followed to websites that provide information for western gay men interested in meeting Thai men, the heavier the trace and the higher the sites will rank in future searches.

A Thai man identifying as gay will not find resources aimed at him on Google. com or Google.co.th when he searches "gay" and "Thai."[37] In this scenario, the attributes afforded by Thai gay men searching for sites and self-definitions are obscured. Accordingly, the men I interviewed do not report using Google as a way to find resources and communities, thus their presence as likely search agents is continually diminishing. Rather than a global gay image that reflects the vicissitudes of particular locations, social configurations, or temporalities, Google searches are, over time, reducing Thai gay men to objects for western consumption; the specificities of what constitutes being Thai and gay are increasingly less visible.

This is particularly noteworthy when examining claims made by websites that top the list of results in a Google or Thailand Google search of these terms. Several of the websites that have ranked in the top-ten results on Google.com for the past seven years (from 2001–2008) market "community" and claim to serve a cohesive audience with a globally understood sense of being gay, one that includes Thai locals. Some of these "top-ten" websites feature personal profiles depicting Thai men eager to meet western men. Several respondents from the Thai gay community in Bangkok, however, reported that these profiles are misleading. They described that many of the men on these websites are similar to those who work in Bangkok's gay brothels, providing sex services for western and Thai men without necessarily identifying as gay. Some of these men claim to do sex-work, particularly with westerners, in order to provide for their wives and children. While these specificities are spoken of in go-go bars, neither sexual identification nor family structure are provided in the profiles on these top-ten websites.[38]

Excluding pornographic sites, Utopia-asia.com was the top hit in 2004 for Google and Google Thailand searches on "gay" and "Thai"; it still ranks among the top three in terms of relevancy (and therefore number of clicks through).[39] The center, started in 1994 by John Goss, an American gay man living in Bangkok, grew from a GLBT center consisting of a bookshop, cafe, pub, and guesthouse. Utopia serves as a meeting place for Thais – particularly toms, dees, and members of the women's group Anjaree – as well as westerners. It hosts author readings, women's workshops, AIDS/HIV education, and fundraising events. It held

Bangkok's first International Lesbian and Gay Film/Video Festival; acted as a founding sponsor of the first Bangkok Gay Festival in 1999; and started publishing a series of GLBT-targeted travel guides to the countries it features on its website. Goss claims the complex is "Southeast Asia's first gay and lesbian center."[40] Launched in 1995, the associated website, "has grown over the last decade to become the internet's most respected GLBT resource for Asia".[41] Since its inception, Utopia has followed trends in World Wide Web functionality, particularly for gay subculture websites. In 2008, it attempts, like Gay.com, to provide on its own website as many resources as possible: a one-stop resource rather than a conglomeration or tool for finding outside goods and services. Unlike Gay.com, however, it is geared toward a very specific audience: a subset of the western gay (and, to a lesser extent, lesbian) population that is interested in Asia/Asians as defined by the countries showcased (the countries that constitute Asia on the website have increased as the website resources have grown). The site offers an introduction to gay culture for westerners; travel agency services; guides to country restrictions, attractions, religion, and culture; information on gay and lesbian events, news about GLBT-oriented issues in the region; and a place to meet Asian men.

In an attempt to move with the times, Utopia changes the self-description listed on its banner from year to year. It was not until 1997 that it billed itself as a provider of "Gay & Lesbian Resources." By 1998, it had added a qualifier: "Asian Gay and Lesbian Resources," followed by a list of featured countries. It also moved, during this time, from peddling Utopia T-shirts to offering a full-fledged gift shop. By 2002, in addition to being a resource, the site claimed "The Net's 1st Asian gay mega-portal, launched on Dec. 13, 1995," using size and Web duration as the qualifiers for its status. At the time, "portal" was not the primary designation for a website of this sort, but the term served Utopia's idea well: it functioned as a door into the countries featured on the website. Its image was rooted firmly in *terra cognito* – the countries of Asia to which a viewer might travel. From 2005's "Asia's Gay and Lesbian Resources" and "Celebrating 10 years of Service to Asia's Gay and Lesbian Community" (www.utopia-asia.com 2005), it has recast itself as "Asian Gay and Lesbian Resources, celebrating our 12th year" (www.utopia-asia.com 2007). The language used to explain Utopia-Asia.com has thus been altered from "Asia," a noun constructing a notion of a united landmass, to its adjectival form, "Asian." And Asia, a questionable term whose boundaries are not clearly demarcated, is still depicted on the site as a list of discrete countries on a growing sidebar. Although the website originates in Bangkok, a quality it presents as a claim to additional knowledge and authenticity, it nonetheless presents an "Asia" for non-Asians, with the tourist and sex-commerce-related potential visitor as the understood audience. As a result, the "global gay" issues discussed on the website do not necessarily correspond to the issues directly concerning the Thai gay men Utopia claims to serve through its physical center.

Utopia-asia.com's Special Report of Gay and Lesbian Commitment Ceremonies in Thailand. The lesbians are two American women.

While Utopia demonstrates that it is in dialogue with a Thai gay population in some respects, it is first and foremost tourist-oriented, dedicated to providing tour information and connections for visitors. The news items do not show sensitivity to issues of gay identity or what constitutes sexuality for a Thai person. The lead story on the Utopia site in June 2004, for example, was about same-sex couples participating in traditional northern Thai commitment/marriage ceremonies. While not a universal practice in Thailand (it is increasingly replaced by US- or Chinese-style weddings), this is the official ceremony marking a union for many northern Thai couples. The Utopia story dubs these participants "gay and lesbian couples," employing terminology unlikely for most same-sex Thai couples located in northern Thailand. As the article continues, it is revealed that the lesbian couple is actually two American women living in northern Thailand. While news is "about" events in Thailand (though not specifically about Thais), the "commitment" is, as can be seen on the left side of the page, to "Asia's gay and lesbian community." Cultural sensitivity is thereby erased in favor of celebrating what seems to be gay pride, coming out, or political activism from a western standpoint.

One of Utopia's persistent links has been for AIDS education and resources. Yet, while there are many Thai men living with AIDS, it is not considered a "gay" issue for Thais, who know it primarily as a heterosexual virus. The Thai government's response to the virus was an AIDS-awareness campaign that followed a different trajectory of categorization and education than that of the US, both in the attribution of its origin (Africa) and its spread (among men involved in same-sex activities). The Thai government announced that AIDS originated from foreign tourists, particularly westerners, who participated in the sex-work industry. The government also announced the presence of a particular strain of HIV in Thailand, one that was particularly virulent and originated from heterosexual, not same-sex, intercourse. In 1987, one government official even insisted "the general public need not be alarmed. Thai-to-Thai transmission is not in evidence."[42] Well-funded, government-backed educational programs were credited with reducing the number of new HIV infections from 143,000 in 1991 to 19,000 in 2003.[43] By 1991, AIDS prevention and control had become a national priority at the highest level. Anti-AIDS messages aired every hour on the country's 488 radio stations and six television networks, and every school was required to teach AIDS-education classes.[44] This meant political activism among gay-identified Thai men was not prioritized as it was elsewhere. Instead of drawing members of the gay community together to inform and protect its members, AIDS activism drew Thai nationals together to increase awareness of the threat of disease associated with foreigners and the ramifications of the thriving brothel culture for both Thai men and tourists. While some Thai gay men lament this as a lost unifying moment for men in Thailand, this can also be read as a telling instance where blame and fear is taken off of Thai same-sex men and put onto western tourists.[45] This approach provided Thais the opportunity to think more critically about the allure of westerners, globalization, and the increasing dependence on tourism for Thailand's Gross National Product. Thus, the prominent AIDS link on the Utopia homepage reveals that Thai gay men are not the population being addressed.

Utopia's shift from representing Asia to providing a service about Asian-related resources has been simultaneously marked by the creation of a "world" of "Utopians." In the beginning of November 2004, the site encouraged membership and asked for personal data. In the past two years, it has also become a member-based site, like Gay.com. One can join to "Get in touch with thousands of other Utopians ... and enter a world of new friends".[46] Much like Google's presumptions about its users, this Utopian world assumes that users from all over the world, rather than those located specifically within Thailand or Asia, look to Utopia-Asia.com for Asian gay and lesbian resources. English is the only language available and consuming Asian men is the primary reason for visiting the site. Thus, one "friend" in any friendship is assumed to be a western gay man.

Like Gay.com, Utopia-Asia.com actively depicts itself as *the* single website that meets all the possible needs of its growing community. It projects itself as the first, the farthest-reaching, and the most long-standing resource of its kind. Members can meet other Utopians, both Thais/Asians and westerners, with similar interests in gay and lesbian travel, culture, contacts, and communities. Yet, Thai men who identify as gay are not spending time on this site, nor are they considering themselves to be Utopians – confirming the fact that Utopia's gay Asia has been constructed for and reaches out to a primarily western audience.

Bangkok Boyonthenet

While most of the interviewees who discussed their online use grudgingly acknowledged that they had visited Gay.com, they were more enthusiastic about local websites.[47] Internet use was already widespread in Bangkok, but time spent online was increasing, and

Boyonthenet.com – this website is no longer active; its domain is now public. These sites rise and fall in popularity (source: www.boyonthenet.com/gdate/index.php).

the volume of gay-identified people who used the internet was growing daily. The websites reported to me rarely appear in the list of results provided by Google.com and Google.co.th (either in English or Thai language searches). Google's inability to recognize these sites as desired search outcomes does not illustrate a dearth in websites but rather suggests an oversight in the search engine's abilities. It also shows that Google does not provide universally satisfying search results, as it is often lauded. Instead Thai gay men used alternative procedures for discovering and sharing websites and online communities. They used word-of-mouth, spreading URLs in gay bars and discos; reviewed browser caches on computers in neighborhood internet cafes; and read about sites in magazines and on flyers distributed in the area.

The websites catering specifically to Thai men encourage discussion around topics mentioned by users, including the changing nature of the category "gay." Such websites are not the only factor enabling change, but they constitute a well-trafficked, easily accessible forum for these conversations to occur. Thus, while a gay identity for a Thai man on Silom Road in 1997 and 1998 included desiring a relationship with a western man, in 2004 this was not the case. The men who habituated the same locales no longer directly associated being "gay" with the desire for romantic engagement with a westerner. In fact, several men described their quest for Asian or specifically Thai partners and expressed clear disinterest in western men. Rather than seeing a compromised version of Thai gay identity in a "global" setting – such as on Gay.com – Thai men who identified as gay used the World Wide Web to reinforce their offline community and circulate local information. Websites such as Boyonthenet.com were successful precisely because they were responsive to these shifting parameters. They provided forums in English, Thai, or Tinglish, allowing increased ease of use and reflecting the particularity of their members' embodied lives. They not only served as a place to report information as timeless or fixed, but also fostered discussion and the spread of information in a rapidly changing scene. For example, a bar closing might be announced and commented upon and its implications debated in discussion forums just hours after a raid took place.

Boyonthenet.com, Thailandout.com, Palm-plaza.com, and other similar websites situate the internet and the World Wide Web as convenient convergence media – part of many overlapping media that allow users to exploit digital communication in ways best suited to their lifestyles and local conditions. In these instances, extensive participation in global media has not led to static definitions of gay identity or gay community. What constitutes being gay and Thai in Bangkok is changing in dialogue with the spread of digital media and access to information. Rather than encouraging universal practices leading to monolithic definitions, alternative websites and understandings of the function of the internet flourish alongside conventional participation. Groups have the opportunity to refine their priorities and craft their distinguishing characteristics through discussion that is both exclusive to its own particular membership and in dialogue with global and local beliefs. The websites that compromised this connecting group showed a general rise in the volume of visitors as well as the frequency of updates in 2005, suggesting a general move away from the "global websites" and toward a more specific set of websites produced by and for the men who congregated in this gay area of Bangkok.[48]

A website's "stickiness" is often touted as intrinsically valuable. Social networking sites like Gay.com or Manhunt.net that target a gay audience, as well as the more popular MySpace.com or Facebook.com, try to keep users in their own network, providing internal links rather than pointing them to other domains. The Thai gay websites reported to me, however, were not designed to provide Interest-based connections between members or to keep users within their borders. Instead, these websites are highly integrated with each other and refer users to similar, external sites. While, like Manhunt.com and Recon.com, they allow users to create profiles that can enable face-to-face encounters, this is not these sites' primary goal. And even as they target a specific ethnic population, albeit the dominant ethnicity of the region, they do not advertise according to the logic of American affinity portals, owned by Community Connect (www.CommunityConnect. com), that target hyphenated ethnicities and/or race such as BlackPlanet.com, AsianAve.com, and MiGente.com.[49] Finally, these websites do not follow the strategies or ideological and marketing practices of other sites like Gay.com or Utopia-Asia.com, which claim to address the Thai gay population.

Since 2004, some sites have displayed frequent updates with cutting-edge Javascript applications (such as Boyonthenet.com), others have introduced constant additions to a frame-based page (Thailandout.com), and some have showcased unique content features (such as animated dance numbers on Palm-Plaza.

com). In addition to constant webmaster updates, these sites provide easily accessible statistical data using open-source software, similar in function to the tools
Google markets to its advertisers. Detailed information, for example, is available on
Siamboy.com, including how many posts each person on the site contributes and
where members lurk and post. Statistics about the viewing and posting habits of
members are available to other users – both in English and in Thai – on Thailandout.
com and Palm-Plaza.com. Members can see where others are spending time, what
topics are of interest on particular sites, and which sites attract the most attention.

Boyonthenet.com, with its banner directing users to "contact single people
and make new friends," gives detailed user statistics in order to facilitate making
contact and developing friendships – more detailed than many other SNS – even,
notably, the RSS feed feature of Facebook.com. Boyonthenet.com tracks all
activities, such as downloading and posting, as well as any departures from the
default settings, and the activity logs are available to any interested users, including guests (see the user statistics for olo in the image below). Guests are thereby
made to feel integral to the community through inclusion in statistics and granting
of access to features that, on other SNS, are touted as members-only privileges.
Included are bar graphs, percentages, categories, and lists. The very first statistic
posted is the user's "time spent online," or the duration of their session. Posts,
threads started, polls created, and votes cast are then enumerated in descending

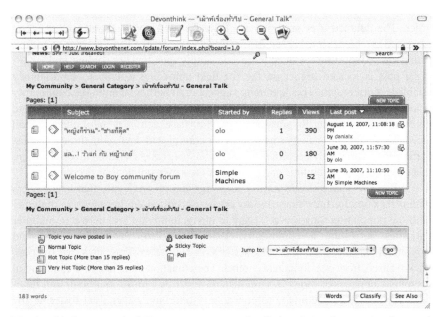

Membership is not required. Even a guest can see detailed statistics about topics discussed
and users contributing. Guests may also rank topics – such as marking them as "hot," "very
hot," or "sticky."

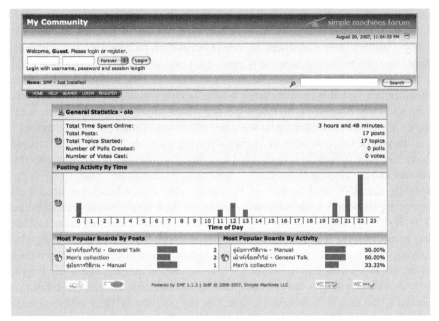

Certain kinds of participation count more than others, as demonstrated by Olo's profile. All of Olo's participation can be seen from a guest profile.

order. The detailed user statistics available for all viewers about each user are presented in a hierarchical order, delineating a value for the various types of participation tracked: posting is valued more than simply spending time online, and initiating a post is located higher on the list than uploading a reply to a previously established discussion. This hierarchy suggests that participation in the community is highly valued. Contributing to a discussion or starting a topic or poll are more noteworthy than voting for someone, yet all of these activities merit attention and are visible on the first statistics page. By encouraging and displaying these statistics, participation is not only encouraged, but the websites allow visitors to locate where other users are spending time and then tailor their own online time accordingly.

While the Thai sites do not try to merge into a single site that keeps users within its domain, they do strive to create an online environment in dialogue with the population they serve.[50] Easy to navigate among and between, together the sites constitute a community. Palm-Plaza.com, Thailandout.com, and Boyontheweb.com, among others, serve as social-networking sites that overlap, drawing users from one domain to another. They function more like non-commercial personal webpages or blogs, where links to websites with similar goals and functions are considered requisite to community building, rather than fostering the competitive isolation in which US-based gay sites exist. Links to resources supplemental to a particular portal or social-networking site are considered advantageous, not detracting. A comparable internet practice is the formerly popular webring, but these Thai websites do not maintain the formality most webrings do. While they consistently link to most of the other related sites, they are not connected to a set group of "members." Unlike webrings, they do not feature a consistent set of links or a link format between sites, and there is not an appointed moderator in charge of deciding who is granted membership into the charmed circle.

Between 2004 and 2008, these sites became less interested in involving non-locals (western men in particular), and they increasingly spoke to insiders rather than offering cultural explanations or other tourist-friendly services and goods. In contrast to the most highly studied sites on the World Wide Web and those geared toward westerners, they made no claims as to their size, their importance, their exclusivity, or their Web duration. Their geographical correlation was limited, referring, by and large, to specific venues within Bangkok, most of which were located in the Silom area. They offered and focused on Bangkok-based connections rather than presuming to address a world with one monolithic gay identity or a target audience of non-Thais attracted to images of Thai male bodies. Thailandout.com's links page, like that of Palm-Plaza.com, was featured prominently on its homepage. Similar local links appeared first and then a selected group of sites provided broader resources. The lists grew from local online communities to include Thai gay and lesbian resources used by western expatriates and tourists and sites claiming to represent the world on the Web, such as Gay.com.

Boyonthenet.com, Thailandout.com, and Palm-Plaza.com were, to varying degrees, bilingual – the sites attempted to attract visitors that could read and write in both Thai and English. Most of the sites started out primarily using English combined with some Thai in 2004 and, over time, they have all increased their usage of Thai and Tinglish. Between 2004 and 2008, the emphasis on cross-cultural communication and English as a "gay" language for Thai men to use to find western partners declined, as did the sites' interest in attracting non-Thai participation. Involvement in the local scene now occupies more of these men's online attention. English-use is diminishing while Thai is encouraged through options such as choosing between Thai and English as a default language, posting Thai-language-only content alongside English content, and responding to postings by Thais in Thai. This bi-lingual community suggests establishing a presence among these sites and then participating and learning to network between them. These websites require, overall, both English and Thai written comprehension – yet another instance of digital creolization using English.

The ability to read and write both Thai and English is necessary for participation in the digital-creolization strategies of these websites. English-language use is an integral part of the Thai middle-class, particularly Thai gay culture, and users must be able to handle the English on Palm-Plaza.com to even receive the Thai-only confirmation email required for the response that enables one to become a member of the community. This ensures that users have linguistic capabilities that are linked to social status, guaranteeing that they also meet class standards.

After the splash screen entry page, website users choose between watching Flash animations with either Thai or English pop songs. But to get past these initial pages, one must follow a Thai-only set up, including a confirmation sent via email. This could be a strategy to prevent culturally illiterate people from gaining access to these gay sites; westerners who can speak only some Thai are likely to be unable to respond to this message. These websites consistently mention specific venues such as bars, bathhouses, gay-owned or gay-friendly restaurants, local celebrities, and Thai politics without introduction. The required knowledge of Thai and English, as well as Bangkok-based references, posit an online community more specific in interests and abilities than even the real-world venues mentioned, which are often frequented by tourists, *kathoeys*, and people who do not identify as gay. Community-oriented and local, these websites enunciate desire and resistance to dominant practices of identification.

Those who are not gay are not encouraged to participate. The sites feature pictures that represent a Thai gay continuum – gay kings, gay queens, gay khwings – but they do not invite men who are uninterested in liaisons with other men. Furthermore, despite what seems to westerners as an obvious link between gay men and *kathoeys*, Thai gay men see themselves as a discrete group. Indeed, gay masculinity disrupts traditional notions of Thai gender; *kathoeys* do not. Accordingly, these websites do not encourage or incite *kathoey* participation, although *kathoeys* and others are not expressly excluded. Boyonthenet.com, for example, offers a search for "friends" with only "male" and "female" as choices. *Kathoeys* are mentioned neither on the pages nor in the links; however, many of the profiles seem to be gay queens who describe themselves in terms that overlap with traits associated with traditional *kathoey* identities.[51]

These sites illustrate online/offline convergence in ways specific to gay men in Bangkok, yet their functions exploit the popular machinations that take place on other gay-targeted websites. Each site offers ways to meet others – through chat, picture exchange, phone interaction, and physical encounters. IRC/chat is the most popular "feature" used on Gay.com and, according to my interviews, chat is also a crucial application on the Bangkok-based websites. This use of digital media marks intersection and union; online, offline, and specific media no longer need to be isolated. The websites function as an anchor, but the World Wide Web is not the only vehicle for providing interaction. For example, mobile-phone communication, available to Bangkok residents for a minimal charge, is increasingly popular. Small amounts of cash and general literacy are all that are required, yet much status is accrued through digital communication conducted on hand-held devices. Thailand and Singapore, in particular, have faster networks and more advanced handsets than those available to US consumers. The popularity of mobile telephony is reflected in the global market: some cell-phone models, particularly those by Nokia and Sony, are made exclusively for Asian markets and never reach the US, where digital consumer desire is less focused on cell-phone devices.[52] Digital telephony – both talk and SMS – is extremely popular in Thailand and, not surprisingly, cell-phone use among the middle-class is ubiquitous. As a "gay" identity often reflects the middle-class or middle-class aspirations, the websites respond to their target population by offering SMS and chat features as part of their services. Thus, Thai men performing identical online actions facilitate multiple community-formation practices: both the creation of a monolithic, global gay identity and the fracturing of what qualifies as gay in an exclusively local setting. Once again, digital creolization allows for a revision of the functions of websites that claim to articulate a definition of "gay," deploying all of the technologies available to serve their own members.

"Out links," as Thailandout.com presents them, are a useful pun. In this instance, being "out" not only refers to the western gay rallying term (recalling the prerequisite coming-out narrative and rights activism), but also functions as a form of digital creolization, putting the ubiquitous gay motto "out" to a specific, technology-based function. "Out links" represent convergence – reaching out of the World Wide Web and the internet to target other, digital communications media used by Thai gay men. "Outphoto" is first, and then there is "outchat" (an IRC feature on the website), and then, beyond the website itself, there is an "out-mobile" option for making calls to other members and an "outline" to call and talk to volunteers from the Web company. Because phone chatting is enabled by several of these websites, and men are quick to supply cell-phone numbers, the community transcends the online and offline divide articulated in the main Web page menu. In addition, Thailandout.com provides extensive sets of links on its homepage, serving as a general resource for Thai gay-related issues. This categorized set could be seen to function as the results list of a search conducted by Thai gay men who want to know more about their own community. Included are: NGO and government organizations relating to their community, resources concerning Thai popular culture, Asian and transnational gay resources, and worldwide gay websites such as Gay.com. The links, located in frames surrounding the bottom section of the page, move from the local, interconnected group, "out" to larger sets of gay-related and Asian-targeted websites.

A group of links lists Thailand-based NGOs addressing gay interests, if not the direct concerns of this particular gay-identifying group. One such site is Fridae.com. Originally, the site constructed a version of Asia that targeted an ethnic Chinese GLBT population, but it has grown to incorporate and welcome any participants in the region without providing a list of qualifying nation-states. Like Thai NGOs targeting gender and sexuality issues, these websites employ the umbrella term "Asian" more than before, but not by defining an ever-expanding list of qualifying countries as does Utopia-Asia.com. Some of the "Asian" websites are increasingly geared toward a specifically Thai population, and the specificity of Thai circumstances is reflected in the content of these sites. Similarly, worldwide issues, such as health concerns for gay men, are reflected by the websites' oft-changing content. For example, Boyonthenet.com advertises several discussion forums on its homepage, including one entitled "healthcare," but, unlike all of the western-oriented gay websites, this forum does not often include discussion concerning AIDS prevention or HIV awareness. It does, however, distribute information about healthcare options available to HIV-positive men.

Although many internet theorists debate the positive and negative consequences of global internet access, few question the contours of "global" media: global media presumes that communication occurs over long distances, and local interactions are incidental, if considered at all. Meanwhile, Thai gay men in Bangkok have created websites with diversified functions and services in order to create a local membership based on physical proximity. Furthermore, while the men I interviewed often frequent the same physical locales several times a week, their online visits shift as sites rise and fall in popularity. It is in this environment that men articulate their identities, concerns, and desires as they participate. Moreover, meanings and practices proffered by these websites reflect local circumstances and concerns. These websites mark a change in the Thai definition of being gay that is both in accordance with and contrary to global gay assessments by Binnie and Altman: community formation is a significant part of the global gay definition which emanates from post-Stonewall, US-originated ideologies. But, while conceptions of a global gay identity are inherently based on western histories and concerns, the centrality of westerners in "gay" identity-formation in Bangkok, both online and offline, is in flux. Overall, the websites centered on Thai gay men in the Silom area facilitated the ongoing process of crafting a particular Thai gay identity, including a sense of Asian-ness that suggests both the Thai gay and the tenuous and often western-glossed "gay Asian" are realities that are in dialogue with, but differ from, a global gay manifestation of gay identity.

Thai men are forming an identity that still relies on western notions of nonnormative sexual practices and gay identities. They still premise English as an important part of this identity, but it is no longer primarily based on physical involvement with western men or western countries. In fact, western interactions are being discouraged on these local sites as community members strive to create their identities among themselves – both in bars and online – in intersecting digital and analog transmissions. Thus, the sense of what constitutes being a Thai gay man has changed between 1998 and 2004, as well as between 2004 and 2008. Being Thai and gay in Bangkok extends hegemonic notions of what constitutes the spaces and practices of being gay and conceptions of language and physical/ digital location. Locating the changing function of virtual English on these websites elucidates the processes of queering these websites undertake to make their own versions of sexuality, ethnicity, community, and nationality.

Epilogue:
The Medium Massages

"Environmental Status Report"

In November 2006, consumers lined up at electronics stores in Japan, the United States, and Europe in anticipation of the release of Sony's PlayStation 3. People stood outside for up to four days to acquire the device. In Tokyo, residents were so enthusiastic that four days before the release date, stores held lotteries for the right to stand in line. When finally made available in the US and Japan, all PlayStation 3 units were sold out within minutes. Consumer demand was much greater than units available; only 100,000 machines were in stores in Japan and 400,000 in the United States.[1] Four months later, when PlayStations 3 hit the market again, its release was met with ennui.[2] Having dropped in status to the third most popular gaming device on the international market, Sony's European launch garnered almost no attention. Sony lured Londoners to the launch by offering free 46-inch televisions and taxi rides home with every purchase of PlayStation 3.[3]

The cause of the PlayStation shortage was a short-lived dearth of the elemental mineral tantalum (TA). Tantalum pentoxide in powder form is used to make capacitors, devices that regulate the flow of electricity within an integrated circuit. Tantalum was originally used for nuclear reactors, chemical-processing equipment, and aircraft and missile parts. More recently, electronic-chip manufacturers found that the metal was ideal for crafting small processing units. Its ability to withstand high temperatures and corrosion, inexpensive procurement price, and abundance made it an ideal material. As a result, it has become a popular element in the circuits of many digital communications devices.[4]

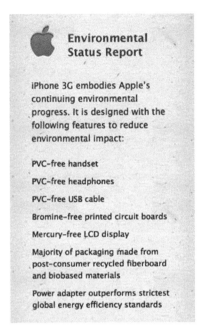

Green Apple. Apple's website proudly cites its commitment to caring for the environment. This box appears on the iPhone G3 tech specification page (source: www.apple.com/iphone/spec.html)

Tantalum compounds can be found in every PlayStation, iPod, mobile phone, and laptop computer, and they are also finding their way into the circuitry of hearing aids, video cameras, and digital cameras. The lack of tantalum for manufacturing PlayStation 3 was unexpected. Sales of PlayStation 1 and 2 had driven up the prices of coltan, as tantalum is known when mined in the Democratic Republic of the Congo. The Congo's mines produced 80 percent of the world's supply of coltan until the price spiked from $80/kilogram in 1999 to $200/kilogram in 2000. To control these price hikes and facilitate the booming electronics industry, in December of 2000 the United States government released their cache of the element, accumulated mainly for defense purposes. Subsequently, the market for coltan crashed to an $8/kilogram low. To complicate matters, in 2001, animal-rights activists lobbied for an international boycott on coltan mined from the Congo since the largest coltan mines were located in two of the Congo's national parks. According to a report released by the Dian Fossey Gorilla Fund and the Born Free Foundation in May 2001, the population of Eastern lowland gorillas in these protected zones has plummeted to less than 1,000 in the year 2000, an 85 percent decline in only nine years.[5] To ensure continued supply, Australia accordingly geared up production, and Canada, Brazil, China, Thailand, Malaysia, and other countries in Africa began mining tantalum as well.

Since the PlayStation debacle, the availability of tantalum has been carefully monitored from mine to market by numerous governments and independent agencies, assuring its steady procurement and refinement. New mines and markets for procuring and distributing coltan are constantly developing, so that neither corporations nor consumers will face such a crisis again.

On July 11, 2008, as I conclude this book, thousands of people around the world, including tens of thousands in the United States, are once again standing in line for hours, even days, to purchase today's momentous release, an iPhone G3. Despite moving over four million iPhones since its introduction a year ago, Apple is once again enjoying a consumer onslaught. Lines of eager customers wind for blocks around Apple and AT&T stores. For days after the release, iPhone sales in the US make news headlines around the world and the World Wide Web. What makes the iPhone so coveted? Convergence and speed. iPhones provide one small gadget where, only a decade ago, four were needed. Its wide-ranging capabilities have bridged what was, before last year, still often presumed to be four distinct realms: mobile phones, digital media players, digital cameras, and internet access. Ubiquitous internet access is the primary lure, convincing millions who already own a cell-phone, portable media device, and a computer to buy another titanium-based circuit appliance, which, according to Apple, "embodies Apple's continuing environmental progress" (www.apple.com/iphone/specs.html).

The newsworthiness of iPhone sales hearkens back to the release of the Play-Station 3, but Apple's and AT&T's media hype is billed as excess, not lack – reports on major news networks ask consumers why they gather in line for something readily available and easily purchased a week later. Where do they find the time? In addition, up-to-the-minute information is broadcast to the internet by those on hand, informing prospective customers whether the wait times predicted by retail workers are accurate, how many phones are available, and what is taking place in the community outside the stores. "Trendy," "cool," and "cutting-edge" are reasons given for the impulse to purchase the gadget immediately. Even after the lines diminish, plenty of iPhones will be available, because of free-market distribution of coltan that supposedly no longer comes from the Congo.

The miners in the DRC continue to mine. This, however, is not newsworthy. Officially, tantalum from the Congo makes up less than 1 percent of the world's available supply. This cannot be confirmed because the compound mixture in coltan can easily be shifted before marketing, rendering it no longer traceable to these mines. But journalists are not picking up this story; there is the continual war in the regions surrounding the newer mines (much of which has to do with acquiring the miners' products and moving the muddy resin to other locations), and new mines are no longer situated in areas shared by the okapis and gorillas whose lives were threatened.

Since 2005, when the "successful" boycott of coltan from the Congo was conducted (and Belgian-run airlines no longer flew to the nation), the miners' profits have fell precipitously. Earlier in the decade, industrious miners could make up to $80 per month for their labor and could afford not only food and shelter, but also luxuries like cigarettes, beer, and sex-workers. Before the creation of efficient transportation infrastructures, war erupted in neighboring Uganda, Burundi, and Rwanda, and prospects for further benefits from prosperity, such as healthcare and education, have dried up. Now, African miners continue to labor without prospects for healthcare, education, or even enough calories to sustain themselves. Yet these producers of coltan – no longer officially recognized and no longer considered essential to the burgeoning electronics market – are also no longer newsworthy. Although North Americans imagine that borders and boundaries are falling with the development of the award-winning iPhone, we as first-world consumers have, in fact, been intimately affecting the lives of thousands of residents of the DRC, Uganda, and Rwanda as they wage wars and conduct illicit trade to insure that there is always a cell-phone or PlayStation to spare. The borders, boundaries, and individual subjects are the motivating specters that drive the tech journalists' headlines and inspire our gadget lust.

A World Wide Web?

In their cyber-spiritual, utopian drive to imagine a better world through the interactions of individuals online, hardware and software innovators who persist in imagining discrete online and offline worlds inevitably fail to recognize the complexities of our digital boundary crossings. The flow of information and exchange of ideas are neither unidirectional nor innocent. Innovators, such as Nicholas Negroponte, developer of "One Laptop Per Child" (OLPC), perpetuate digital inequities and serve as gatekeepers, despite ideologies that tout the opposite. Their projects prescribe who internet users are; how they can be classified or embodied; what digital access, skills, and education they need; and how hardware and software will be used. As these pages have illustrated, powerful changes can by triggered by digital access, even among those who do not use English as a first language or those who are not considered part of the imagined netizen constituency. Communications visionaries cannot delimit every user and his/her/its intents, and the modern liberal human subject position is not available to all under current global capitalist paradigms, especially where coltan is an essential element for digital transmissions.

Negroponte's OLPC encourages US and Canadian citizens to buy laptops for deprived, at-risk children in faraway, impoverished lands. The purchase is tax-deductible: a good deed. Giving a laptop to a child on the other side of the digital divide is a noble act; nothing more is suggested. The campaign rests upon the notion of childhood worthiness and inherent innocence, a recent invention that has only existed in the US and Europe since the nineteenth century. The laptops are designed with underprivileged children in mind, and, according to the website description, those who will receive these laptops are good, eager, third-world children.

Worthiness through the inherent innocence of children cannot be disentangled from a capitalism-inspired fear: fear that the parents of the laptop recipients could exploit their children's resources for their own ends. Thus small keyboards have been installed that are difficult for adults and older children to use, particularly adult males and teenagers who constitute the majority of the "large-finger" demographic. Yet the developers premise their product as a vehicle that will provide access – the key to the best of the world: "The laptop not only delivers the world to children, but also brings the best practices of children and their teachers to the world" (http://laptop.org/children). The website's presentation suggests that the OLPC laptop provides children with ways to explore, express, and learn that are unquestionably superior to those otherwise available: without these

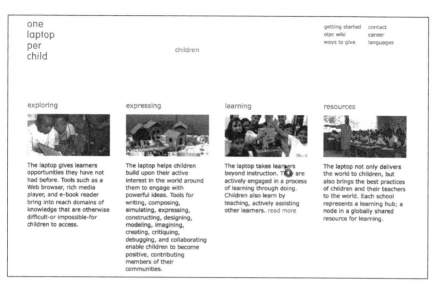

The kinds of children who will receive "One Laptop Per Child" and what it will do for them (source: http://laptop.org/children).

laptops, children would have less access to the "world" and would not be able to share their "best practices." While every child pictured on the site is racialized and presumed to be located in poverty-stricken regions of the third world, who actually produces these "best practices" is not necessarily tied to the image above it. The wording renders these best practices' site of origin decidedly vague. Since participating in the program means that schools become part of a "global hub," the "best" may be brought from wherever the reader imagines it, but this implies that the "best," like the laptops, originate in the savvy, well-educated, computer-filled first world.

Although initially touted as an open-source, not-for-profit global initiative built on the ideology of free knowledge, OLPC ran into problems when it refused to allow countries to adjudicate changes to the hardware/software combination. As a result, many countries balked at such US-controlled product rules and regulations: another form of imperialism? The complaints voiced by governments were many: with its proprietary keyboards, it was too difficult to adapt to local language constraints and too small to be easily used even by youth. In addition, there were too many requirements from its creators, yet no technical support. The organization's aim also continued to shift: the operating platform, Sugar, originally ran an open-source, Linux-based operating system, but in 2007, it was moved to a proprietary Windows environment.

The belief that parents would exploit their children's resources rather than use them to improve the lives of their families began with the movement for child labor laws in the UK, but Europe is no longer the focal point for child labor violations.[6] The International Labour Organization (ILO) has targeted developing

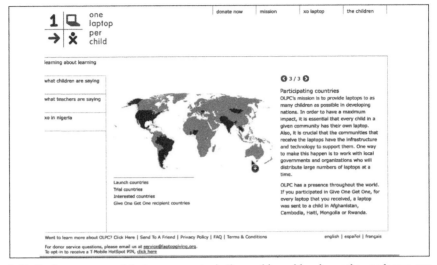

Initially, it was presumed that every country in the world would embrace the one laptop per child initiative. Yet as of July 2008, only the countries highlighted above have agreed to participate. The US and Canada's participation comes in the form of the "Give one Get one" campaign – where donors bought two and donated one for $399. The donation-only based campaign generated little interest in North America. (source: www.laptopgiving.org/en/learning-around-the-world.php#slode03)

countries – the same audience expected to purchase Negroponte's small laptops. The ILO reports that 218 million children between the ages of five and 17 work: 122.3 million children in the Asia-Pacific region, 49.3 million in Sub-Saharan Africa, and 5.7 million in Latin America and the Caribbean (http://hrw.org/children/labor.htm).[7] Innocent children and women will necessarily be the unintended digital laborers – women are more likely to have hands that can navigate a miniature keyboard than men.[8] In the end, One Laptop Per Child offers corporate-run operating systems on adult-proof computers that cannot respond to local circumstances. And for each of these laptops, non-white, poverty-stricken men and boys have illegally stood in mud-filled holes scraping, gathering, and selling dirt, while the girls and women who sustain them suffer from war, rape, and the rampant spread of HIV.

Language, Interface, Icons

Marshall McLuhan's *The Medium is the Massage: An Inventory of Effects*, a manifesto co-created with graphic designer Quentin Fiore and coordinated by Jerome Agel, was first published by Bantam Books in 1967.[9] Quipped, quoted, and endlessly reprinted, it functions as a sort of proto-technological-determinist tract, a rationale for internet development. McLuhan's notion of a global village is a presumed verity, predicating initiatives similar to the one I developed – described at the onset of this book – when working for Urban Technologies Incorporated. Its ideas are reflected in marketing – from Microsoft's "Where do you want to go today?" campaign[10] to the rationale for Negroponte's one laptop per child project. The book became a bestseller and a cult classic. According to Eric McLuhan, the use of the word "massage" rather than "message" in the book's title is actually a printer's mistake. However, McLuhan purposefully approved the misprint and, since publication, the word has been interpreted as a pun meaning alternately "massage," "message," and "mass age." Marshall McLuhan's original title is now a cliché – the Medium is the Message; few quoting it reproduce the "misprint." Still, this misspelling has accrued the status of an inside joke.

Indeed, the medium is the message and the message is the medium, but the medium is also the massage, both as a noun and a verb. The verb "to massage" refers to rubbing and kneading or the manipulation toward a desired end.[11] Both definitions recall the necessary motion involved in media. Like Deleuze and Guattari's "becoming," metaphor,[12] movement is embodied by medium – there is no fixed state, nor by analogy, can there be static, clearly defined identity categories (Tamil Eelam citizens, Thai women, or gay men) that are embodied through media and communication. Media function as movement – whether through facial distortions and vocal-chord vibrations, the creation of sound waves, or the rapid switches of electronic flows. All messages require manipulation of medium, and neither the medium, the message, nor the massage are distinguishable elements separate from one another. The insertion of "massage" recognizes the kinetic energy embedded in these nouns and the impossibility of their disconnection from each other. Digital communication cannot provide us with clean boundaries or distinct designations. How information is read, perceived, and interpreted is of primary importance to its impact. The medium is the massage and the message; one is no longer separable from the latter; interface functions to inscribe the medium's legibility.[13] The potential for expression through digital networked communication cannot be reduced to utopian/dystopian figurations that disregard the specificity of users and their aims.

The Whorf–Sapir Hypothesis suggests that different language speakers understand the world differently; thus every language provides speakers with linguistic frameworks from which to interpret the human–culture–technology interface, different linguistic maps for making meaning. Operating systems that represent this interface function as another level of language: the analog interface constructed by Mac OS offers a different lexicon than Windows Vista, or, importantly, Sugar, the original interface on an OLPC laptop. Furthermore, interface is only one of the ways in which language and the digital intersect; the notion of digital creolization suggests the complexity of meaning-making and the rich paths for strategic intervention. Digital communication is not only a question of bytes transferred, but also the paths by which they travel, their endpoints, and the hardware and software that render them legible. The internet and, more specifically, interactions that occur on, and beyond, the World Wide Web are highly mediated events. They change English as a language just as HTML deploys XML to better manipulate the organization of data and provide an ever-expanding language field with increasing forms of digital creolization. Furthermore, the Web is a space of convergence: not only has digital communication always already exceeded the boundaries of the computer screen and telephone lines, but it has provided means for creative convergence of digital communication devices, intersecting inter-faces, and alternative literary imaginings, all reflecting a complex interplay of medium, users, and contemporary concerns. Language is inherent both to the cre-ating of an interpretable online text and to the ability to speak to and for a wide range of constituencies, with innumerable geo-political and cultural concerns.

   In order to recognize queer internets, we must listen to others and retain historical awareness. Lila Abu-Lughod states, in order to hear across cultures, people in privileged positions must: "break with the language of alien cultures, whether to understand or eliminate them. Missionary work and colonial feminism belong in the past. Our task is to critically explore what we might do to allow all people "safety and decent lives."[14] To this end, my exploration assumes that all languages are alien and that they are involved with all cultures with which they come into contact with. As Gloria Anzaldúa so potently writes:

> Ethnic identity is twin skin to linguistic identity – I am my language.... Until I am
> free to ... switch codes without having always to translate ... and as long as I have
> to accommodate the English speakers rather than having them accommodate me, my
> tongue will be illegitimate.
>
>   (Anzaldúa 1987, 59)

Languages, particularly English, are potentially, yes virtually, alien, and threaten its code switchers with illegitimacy. In our transnational climate, every major language is necessarily accompanied by minor languages. The examples of digital creolization I have provided in the previous chapters illustrate that local contexts are essential elements of computer-mediated communication.

   To avoid the default standard English that might accompany the embedded language in all digital communication, we must, as Vron Ware urges: "remember that what is really required is a form of dialogue that depends on a readiness to speak *to* as well as an ability to listen."[15] To see, hear, communicate, and experi-ence more than what is predicted requires the persistent awareness of the embed-ded privileges of whiteness, linguistic competency, western and secular models of knowledge production, material wealth, and an understanding that these position-alities, even when recognized, continue to serve as overseers for interpretative acts. The medium of an information system consists of meaningful wires and plugs, bits and bytes, conventions of language deployment, political representation, and information dispersal. The medium is the message, certainly, and it is also the case that all readings reflect the technical, political, text, context, subject, and object. Critical inquiry and queer readings must endeavor to disrupt presumptions of a universal subject with singular identities and desires, all the while remaining attentive to the spatial, cultural, geo-political, and material circumstances embedded in every instantiation of virtual English.

Since digital technologies occupy center stage in the present and future of communication and knowledge production, it is imperative that we include those participants inhabiting the off-ramps of the "Information Superhighway." The exponential spread of digital media has certainly reinforced systemic inequities and incited nationalist passions. Dubbing disparity a "digital divide" assumes an a priori lag in knowledge and access, in effect expanding the crevice through its deployment. Divergent practices can be overlooked because of geo-political constraints, perceived standardization of applications, and the dominant way in which English use is understood as information. The tension between the localities and ideas of global, interconnectedness in unexpected configurations, exploitation when freedom is premised, and the reification of racial and global inequities remain, and these seeming contradictions must be brought to the foreground in our understandings of virtual English. This suggests that alternate boundaries and non-binary formulations between divergent translations can be made legible, foregrounded, accommodated, and integrated. Destabilizing the binary of global and local with more than a nod toward the "glocal," and highlighting the contradictions and vicissitudes of boundary crossings both refused and enabled by digital communication moves toward queering our internet.

A queer account challenges us to account for the material effects of internet use to reaffirm national boundaries and geo-political formulations while simultaneously unearthing the instances where they are destabilized, where nationalism, gender, and sex vality (sexuality) are strategically reimagined and adapted via digital communication. This study of digital creolization highlights a few moments where seemingly stable English-language notions are redefined and reassembled as new configurations of communities that recodify binaries and boundaries; hopefully, there is more to come.

Notes

Chapter 1

1. "Dirty Laundry" is an episode of "On the Reel," the animated portion of the *Youth Leadership Academy* (New York: Urban Technologies, Inc. 2007) materials produced and distributed by Urban Technologies, Incorporated.
2. National Urban Technologies, Inc. changed their name to National Urban Technology Center. For more information, see McLelland 2005.
3. Nelson *et al.* 2001.
4. www.youthradio.org; www.teenvoices.com; www.harlemlive.org.
5. In India, television programs geared toward the middle-class combine Hindi and English, called "Hinglish." While the use of English is longstanding in India as a former British colony, the way it is used is changing. Instead of English words being placed higher, or as Fanon would say, closer to the white man, on a chain of hierarchies, Hinglish is being deployed as a form of code-switching, or creolization, where it attempts to engage Indian middle-class viewers rather than work toward the emulation of proper English. I have noted this in my visits to Thailand. These programs are broadcasted via satellite to Thailand. The music channel "V" and Star TV from India are popular alternatives (there is a large Non-Resident Indian [NRI] population in Bangkok). Fernandes also mentions this phenomena in her study (2000, see pages 621–622).
6. This is not to discourage interface-specific considerations – which should use terms as specifically as possible. At this point, studying "internet use" may be too broad; World Wide Web or Internet Relay Chat (IRC) or mobile-to-mobile SMS, located in a particular moment and among specific users speak more to the point. This study, however, bridges many of these divides when considering the way digital communication is imagined, described, and deployed. Thanks to Hans Lee and others for contributing to a conversation that helped me think about these terms on the AoIR listserv. My query, "CMC, ICT, digital communications" was posted July 24, 2006.
7. Technology is a common misnomer for digital communication, yet I will continue to use it in its popular form. The *Oxford English Dictionary* provides the following definitions for technology (and these are its first three): 1. a. A discourse or treatise on an art or arts; the scientific study of the practical or industrial arts. b. trans f. Practical arts collectively. c. With a and pl. A particular practical or industrial art. "Technology," *Oxford English Dictionary*, http://dictionary.oed.com/cgi/entry/50248096?single=1&query_type=word&queryword=technology&first=1&max_to_show=10.

8. Deleuze and Guattari 1993, 156. Francoise Verges makes a similar argument about the function of deterritorialization by what she terms "cosmopolitan creoles," linking the practice specifically to the historical Creole movement. She writes that, after World War I,

> Cosmopolitan Creoles asserted their emerging autonomy through the process of "deterritorialization" – the process whereby there is a subversion of discourse conventions that wrench the hegemonic language from the possession of its cultural overlords. Their movement announced the postcolonial and postmodern practices of creolization.
>
> (Vergès 2001, 173)

9. Samuel Delany's important interview with Mark Dery was one of the first instances that exposed the conceptual problematics of the digital divide, remarking on the artificiality of attributing the "white boxes" of technology, i.e. computers, to white populations and "black boxes" – portable stereos, aka "boom boxes" – as the technological domain of African-Americans (Dery 1996). I am also referring to the contributions of others who have articulated the racisms encoded in digital communications. These include Kolko *et al.* 2000; Gajjala 2002; Manovich 2001; Foster 2005; Nelson, *et al.* 2001; Thuy Linh Nguyen Tu 2003; Nguyen 2003; Chun 2006; White 2006.
10. See these works for more detail: Sassen 2002; Mitra 1997; Kumar 2001; Green 2002.
11. Many New Media scholars initially asserted that creating one or multiple virtual persona that can participate in a wide range of activities and websites ameliorates social constraints in the realm of the virtual. The following vacillate between endorsing and refuting this: Stone 1995; Haraway 1991.
12. Gajjala 2001; Mitra 2001; Berry *et al.* 2003.
13. Hebdige 1979; Hall and Du Gay 1996.
14. Eng *et al.* 2005.
15. For example, Aijaz Ahmad provides a seminal discussion about postcolonial critics such as Homi Bhabha, Edward Said, or Gayatri Spivak, and postcolonial theory in general, foregrounds its inherently western epistemological grounding and US-centered material rewards. See Ahmad 1994.
16. Mohanty *et al.* 1991.
17. Carby 1987, 15; Gajjala 2001.
18. Much of this work appears in journals like *New Media and Society* and *Social Text*, and in recently published edited collections. Particularly valuable have been: Jones 1997; Kolko *et al.* 2000; Boellstorff 2008; Lee and Wong 2003; Berry *et al.* 2003.
19. Elia *et al.* 2003, 392.
20. Butler 1993. See especially the chapter titled "Critically Queer." See also Warner 1997.
21. Berlant and Warner 1995.
22. Warner and Berlant's preferred nomenclature.
23. See, in particular, many of the contributions to black queer theory, particularly: Cohen 1999; Johnson and Henderson 2005; Delany 2004.
24. hooks 1990, 153.
25. Sedgwick 1993, xii.
26. See Halberstam's discussion of her own methodology (1998).
27. Lancaster and Di Leonardo 1997, 4–5.
28. See, for example, Patton and Sánchez-Eppler 2000; Grewal and Kaplan 2000; Cruz and Manalansan 2002.
29. Sang 2003, 9.

30. Wakeford 2000a, 413.
31. Thailand was pressured by the British, French, and American governments. Britain considered taking over Thailand when they colonized Burma, but the Thai king was able to present Thailand, Thai culture, and Thai people in terms appreciated by the British colonizers, enabling Thailand to remain discrete. For an excellent account and analysis, see Winichakul Thongchai 1994. During the Vietnam War, US troops were based in Northern Thailand and the beach area south of Bangkok served as the premier Rest and Relaxation site for American troops in Southeast Asia.
32. McClintock *et al.* 1997, 11.
33. Chow 1998, 151.
34. For an analysis of Charles Taylor's conclusions about postcolonial studies, see Afzal-Khan and Seshadri-Crooks 2000, 3.
35. Spivak 1993, 65.
36. Seshadri-Crooks and Afzal-Khan 2000.
37. Gajjala 2008.
38. For a discussion of feminism's inability to deal with trans women (MTF) and their femininity that suggests an analogous situation, see Serano 2007.

Chapter 2

1. Busia (n.d.).
2. This is the title of a painting made by Franci Barraud of his brother's dog Nipper in 1899. Painted three years after Nipper's death, the work commemorated Nipper's habit of peering into a phonograph machine's horn, seemingly confused about the disembodied sounds it produced. The painting, like the other examples in the section it names, illustrates the process of globalization of New Media. On a visit to London, German-born, US-based Emile Berliner, inventor of the flat disc record and the gramophone, saw the painting, bought it, patented it, and passed it onto his partner, the owner of the victor talking machine. This advertisement was used in the United State, Great Britain, Europe, Central and South America, Asia, India, and Japan, and the Victor Gramophone machine enjoyed worldwide popularity, as did Nipper. The veracity of the phonograph's sound is embodied in this image, and this image still resonates – linked to RCA Victor, as well as the dog name Nipper. For a full account of the patent history, see Hafner and Lyon 1996.
3. Here I invoke the language of early cyber-utopians like Howard Rheingold.
4. In mechanical jargon, "certain connector designs (such as the SAE connector, and jackhammer air hose connectors) involve paired identical parts each containing both protrusions and indentations. The term hermaphrodite (or hermaphroditic) is used for such devices, along with combination (and combo), two-in-one, two-way, and others." See "Gender of Connectors and Fasteners," Wikipedia (http://en.wikipedia. org/wiki/Gender_of_connectors_and_fasteners; accessed September 4, 2006). For the constructed nature of gender, see foundational texts such as Butler 1990, 1993. For constructions of masculinity see Halberstam 1998; Johnson and Henderson 2005; Bordo 1999.
5. Kittler 1999. Also, Manovich (2001) tries through the theorizing of CUI (computer–user interface) to theorize a way to understand digital technology beyond the realm of visual, cinematic representation in particular, but ultimately reaffirms the centrality of cinema in his consideration.
6. Imken 1999, 92–106.

7. "Booting Up," in *Oxford English Dictionary* (accessed August 28, 2006).
8. "Bootstrapping," Wikipedia (http://en.wikipedia.org/wiki/Bootstrapping; accessed May 2, 2006): "Wikipedia is a multilingual Web-based free-content encyclopedia. It exists as a wiki, written collaboratively by volunteers, allowing most articles to be changed by anyone with access to a web browser and an Internet connection" (see Wikipedia, http://en.wikipedia.org/wiki/Wikipedia).
9. Said 1978, 2, 4.
10. Raspe (n.d.).
11. This legend is consistently attributed to the English version by Raspe or a later edition of the English tales. German sources attribute it to the English version of the tales, as well. The anonymous writer of the introduction to the fifth English edition of the adventures states that the tales were not, in fact, translated from the English, but were instead also the versions recounted by the Baron himself or by his spokesperson (see www.gutenberg.org/etext/3154). Yet online accounts, in this case, seem to create truth: the influence of Wikipedia cannot be understated. Students look up entries on Wikipedia covering topics we are discussing in class. Wikipedia's entry on bootstrapping reports that the term arose from the tales about Baron von Munchhausen. This entry in Wikipedia is also quoted verbatim on many online websites dedicated to culture and technology. See, for example, Wikipedia, "Bootstrapping," and Joseph Ransdell, www.welchco.com/03/00050/60/00/07/2801.HTM#2520. For illustration, see "Antiquity Project: Baron Munchausen: Gustave Dore Illustrations" (www.ironorchid.com/clipart/baron/index_01.htm).
12. In a bookkeeping manual, Henry Bryant writes:

> The person competent to construct a system of philosophy on such a basis, would be able to show how a man might lift himself by his own boot-straps, or get rich by taking money from one pocket and putting it in the other.

These sources mark its meaning as either doing something impossible (like making money by moving it from one pocket to another) or doing something with little resources. Still, attributing a US-based meaning for the term is a subject of debate.
13. Washington 1970.
14. Washington (n.d.).
15. "By His Bootstraps" is a science-fiction short story by Robert A. Heinlein published under the pseudonym Anson MacDonald. Initially, it appeared in the magazine *Astounding Science Fiction* in October 1941. The story, in which the phrase does not actually appear, is about time travel. For the full text, see Heinlein 1941.
16. For instance, the NNDB, or Notable Names Database, writes of Heinlein that he "was actually most prolific, and perhaps most influential upon the genre of science fiction, with his short fiction, he was also the first science fiction author to produce a best selling novel." And:

> But Heinlein's influence was hardly limited to the genre of science fiction, or to his fellow writers. He also managed to insert himself into mainstream popular culture – influencing language ("waldo" and "grok"), politics, sexuality, and even spirituality. His 1962 Hugo-winning *Stranger in a Strange Land* was not only a kind of guidance manual for the 1960s free love counterculture but it actually spawned a number of imitative churches. To a lesser but no less noteworthy extent his 1966 *The Moon is a Harsh Mistress* is credited with drawing many young people to Libertarianism and to the Libertarian party itself.
>
> (Soylent Communications 2006)

17. See Delany's description where "white" computer boxes are contrasted to the "black" sound boxes used by African-Americans (Dery 1994, 201).
18. Greg Lanier, personal email, March 2, 2006.
19. In English, the relationship between master and slave has been the subject of much philosophical consideration rooted in a mistranslation of Hegel. The position of a master to a slave and that, described by Hegel, between a master and a servant, is dramatically different – especially from the perspective of former slave-based economies such as that of the US. Although recent translations no longer portray Hegel's musing as regarding master and slave but rather master and servant (Lord/Bondsman), the terminology, and the resultant way of considering subjectivity and the relations constructed through servitude, endure. In the other direction, digital creolization could be said to exist in German "mistranslations" of English words for new technologies. For example, the German term for mobile phone is "handy" and the German word for a PowerPoint projector is "beamer." Both of these words reflect their English roots – a cell-phone can be held in the hand and can be, in fact, quite handy. A "beamer" does beam light from one source to another – and it recalls *Star Trek*'s Captain Kirk's infamous matter-transfer request: "Beam me up, Scottie." Scottie, a Scotsman, is able to use technology to transfer matter from one place to another, moving the televisual image of Kirk, precisely what a "beamer" does for images.
20. Derrida 1976, 16.
21. Manovich 2001, 70.
22. Saussure's description of semiotics, where signs consist of signifiers and signifieds, recognizes that the names (signifiers) are, in fact, more stable than what they represent. Syntagms are sequential, and thus temporal, but they can represent spatial relationships. See de Saussure 1974, 70.
23. Henry 2000.
24. Phillipson 1992; Pennycook 1998. See also Suresh Canagarajah, Julian Edge, and Adrian Holliday, for example.
25. Crystal 1997.
26. Pennycook 1994.
27. Brutt-Griffler 2002, 8. Alistair Pennycook, for example, aptly describes the colonialism embedded in English and the teaching of ESL. However, these ideologies are seen as inflicted upon "others" and unproblematically "adopted." The notion of creole troubles this, as does work by Bhabha and others illustrating that the process of mimicry necessarily includes resistance.
28. For further discussions of some of the problems of Bhabha's important work on mimicry and ambivalence, see Chambers and Curti 1996; Belnap 1993.
29. The work of Mary Louise Pratt's *Imperial Eyes* (1992) usefully describes these cultural collisions in her discussion of the contact zone, to which my argument here draws greatly from. Antoine Meillet noted in 1906: "'social change' is the ultimate, 'most often mediated and indirect' root of linguistic change" (quoted in DeGraff 1999, 11). Creoles, according to linguists, are created when pidgins are acquired as primary languages. Pidgins are second languages used between speakers of two or more non-mutually-intelligible languages.
30. See Vergès 2001, 172.
31. Bickerton 1981.
32. Silc and National Clearinghouse for ESL Literacy Education 1998.
33. Rushdie 1991, 64.
34. See Crystal 1997, 101–102, 55, for discussions of Indian, Sri Lankan, and Nigerian

Englishes. See also Achebe (1975) about Nigerian English and Rushdie (1991) for Indian English.

35. See the collection by Michel DeGraff (1991), especially his introduction where he contextualizes all the recent work being done in Creole studies.

36. Glissant 1989, 127. Edward K. Braithwaite attributes the birth of Creole to the Caribbean plantation system.

37. Later work has complicated this picture. Antoine Meillet, Michel DeGraff, Salikoko Mufwene, and John Lumsden argue that developments of Caribbean Creoles are in response to both external and internal factors, corresponding to processes accompanying both language change and language acquisition. See DeGraff 1999b.

38. Françoise Vergès writes an excellent account of creole as it is deployed transnationally. She remarks on the work of Fanon – his shifting of the understanding of creole to revolutionary ends – and Glissant's later redeployment of creolization. Of the Fanonian expression of creole revolutionary universalism, she argues that it "performed exclusionary practices that have been described elsewhere, such as in feminist critique of nationalism and socialism, in the queer critique of sexual politics, or in the critique by ethnic minorities of the national narrative" (2001, 178).

39. Fanon 1967, 18.

40. Edward K. Braithwaite attributes the birth of Creole to the Caribbean Plantation system. John Thornton argues that cultural change comes about through constant interaction with other cultures, attributing creole development to West Africa, where trade necessitated communication even before the Caribbean Plantation system.

41. See Deleuze and Guattari 1987.

42. Bernabe 2007, 98.

43. Walcott 1992. Here Walcott notes the echoes of cultural intersections with creoles renamed nouns and new metaphors as well as fragments of old, epic vocabularies. One exception would be Wilson Harris, who, Henry argues, finds the path not through resistance but recovery. For this discussion, see chapter 4, "Wilson Harris and Caribbean Poeticism," in Henry 2000. Paget Henry writes of two discursive strategies in the Caribbean intellectual tradition: the poeticist and the historicist (Henry 2000, 93, 120–121). Edouard Glissant, Derek Walcott, Sylvia Wynter, and Carole Boyce-Davies are poeticists. Fanon transitioned "from the poeticist to the historicist school" (2000, 93). Henry convincingly posits Wynter not as the bridge between historicist and poeticist, the dominant placement of her work, but as making an "epistemic turn within the poeticist tradition" through her discussion of the "liminal categories of totalized discourses" (2000, 124).

44. For example, Davies 1994: Glissant and Wing 1997; Glissant 1989; Henry 2000.

45. Ahmad 2007, 15–16.

46. Ahmad 2007, 19. The quote from Achebe also appears in Achebe 2007, 429.

47. Like Lacan's jouissance, language play exceeds the words that invoke it. Homi Bhabha writes: "the institution of the word in the wild is Entstellung – deformation, discipline, desire, mimesis and repetition yet it creates, in Derrida's words, 'the immediate vision of the thing, freed from the discourse that accompanied it'" (Bhabha 1994, 32).

48. Dor 2004, 97–118.

49. David Crystal notes that the recent globalization of English accelerates its change, making it conform increasingly to what is understood as processes unique to creoles. Rather than being "imposed," English-language acquisition facilitates new practices that are "not easily forecast" or "externally controlled" (Brutt-Griffler 2002, 8).

50. Balibar and Wallerstein 1991, 98.

51. Spivak discusses this term intermittently in her corpus. At one point, she states the *Oxford English Dictionary* definition of catachresis as

    "Improper use of words, application of a term to a thing which it does not properly denote, abuse of perversion of a trope or metaphor." My usage: a metaphor without an adequate literal referent, in the last instance a model for all metaphors, all names.

    (Spivak and Harasym 1990, 154)

    Spivak writes more about catechresis in the following: Spivak 1988a, 84; 1990, 4, 42; 1993; Spivak *et al.* 1996.
52. Spivak 1993, 65.
53. Bal 1996.
54. See Bradley 2004.
55. The software has evolved greatly since these initial categories. Now, social movements are created through this social-networking site. In addition, students have mobilized recently in response to a new feature on the site that alerts users any time a member of their network of friends updates her/his account. Thus the site has become a place for student activism, both within its confines (where one can join a group that condemns "barebacking" or supports a particular political candidate) and off (where live demonstrations are occurring against the recent modifications. For an interesting discussion on the recent addition of update feeds, see the listserv archives from September 6–8, 2006, of AoIR.
56. This is not to suggest in any way that I *know* what Web 2.0 is. For an excellent discussion of the meme function, yet unclear constitution of the idea, see www.oreillynet.com/pub/a/oreilly/tim/news/2005/09/30/what-is-web-20.html.
57. Michel DeGraff suggests that recent creole-specific studies may indeed reflect language development in other arenas. He concluded the Introduction to his edited collection with the following caveat: "this volume has a more ambitious, probably overly ambitious, goal: to promote cross-fertilizing alliances among subfields of linguistics, in search of the (common) constraints and processes that may underlie language creation and change" (DeGraff 1999a, 22). Versions of US-based English are deployed via the globalized commodification of cultural productions in English, particularly Hollywood films, contemporary American music, and internet communication. In addition to electronic conversations that take place in English (for mixtures of political, personal, and business purposes) that, in their current formulations, assume US and English-language centrality, Business English has become the dominant language of communication even in environments where English is not the primary language of any of the participants. While ideological apparatuses, to some extent, accompany the acquisition of any language, the presence of many vernaculars in the global marketplace and the acceptance of modifications of English practices render it particularly responsive and dynamic.
58. Carol Boyce Davies, Cheryl Wall, and Abena Busia, for example, not to mention the more recent New Media-specific work concerning race and gender from Chela Sandoval, Lisa Nakamura, Alondra Nelson, and others.
59. See Abril Trigo's history of the use of this term and its changing parameters, as well as its dubious replacement by the seemingly more transnational (i.e. less Latin American-specific) term, "hybridity," as employed by Homi Bhabha (Trigo 2000, 85–111).
60. "A Cyborg Manifesto" in Bell and Kennedy (2000, 312). Haraway writes, although not unproblematically at this point:

The nimble fingers of "Oriental" women, the old fascination of little Anglo-Saxon Victorian girls with doll's houses, women's enforced attention to the small, take on quite new dimensions in this world.... . Ironically, it might be the unnatural cyborg women making chips in Asia and spiral dancing in Santa Rita jail whose constructed unities will guide effective oppositional strategies.

(Bell and Kennedy 2000, 295)

While she privileges the positions of women of color to deploying the linguistic strategies necessary for her cyborg policies, she cannot help but orientalizing herself. Her quotation marks do not deflect the romanticization of Asian labor in hardware construction. Ai-hwa Ong recounts women workers being possessed by spirits, or hantu, on the workfloor or in the restrooms. They were legitimized by scientific notions of female maladjustment as well as requiring spirit-banishment procedures. Ong suggests that they also served as "ritualized rebellion" (1987, 210):

When production targets seemed unbearable, or a foreman had been especially harsh, operators registered their private vengeance by damaging the very components that they had painstakingly assembled. Others stalled the machines and thus interrupted production. The cumulative effect of countless subversive acts, as evidenced in thousands of defective components at the end of the month, constituted an anonymous protest against mounting work pressures rather than a collective action with specific demands on the management.

(1987, 211)

For more about spirit possession and Asian women factory workers, see Ngai 2000.
61. Fanon 1968.
62. Here I draw from both Benedict Anderson's notion of imagined communities and Mary Louise Pratt's conception of the contact zone. See Anderson 1983; Pratt 1992.
63. Warschauer 2002, 7.
64. Hall 1997, 11.

Chapter 3

1. Hopkinson 2000.
2. Mosley 2000, 405.
3. Leary 2000, 534–535.
4. Hopkinson 2000.
5. In *Neuromancer*, Gibson describes a Rasta or Dred society called Zion created by the construction workers of the Freeside tourist resort who had refused to return to Earth. Terms he uses to depict the conditions on Zion pull from Jamaican Rastafarian mythology; dub, for example is "a sensuous mosaic cooked from vast libraries of digitalized pop; it was worship ... Zion smelled of cooked vegetables, humanity, ganja" (Gibson 1984, 104). Similarly, in *Count Zero* and *Mona Lisa Overdrive*, Gibson uses Voudoun Loa such as Legba and Ezili Freda, as well as Dnabala Wedo, Ougou Feray, and Baron Samedi, to create a sense of exotic strangeness and street-gang syntax similar to Hollywood invocations of the religion: Gibson writes of Voudoun as "a street religion" that "came out of a dirt-poor place a million years ago" (Gibson 1987, 77). There are many studies examining at length Gibson's use of Caribbean language and religion. See, for example, George Slusser, who writes, "The Voodoo religion, it would seem, has all the potential to become a media event."

Gibson, in fact, employs voodoo gods in his novel *Count Zero*. His "livewire voodoo" is a version of the internet where voodoun deities such as Legbause practice their traditional maneuvers via cyberspace. See also Sponsler 1992; Stockton 1995.

6. Hopkinson, www.sff.net/people/nalo/nalo/index.html (accessed April 4, 2002).

7. This work might be considered in dialogue with the corpus of Bruce Sterling.

8. "Afrofuturism" refers to the recurring futurist themes found in black cultural production and the ways in which technological innovation is changing the face of black art and culture. For more information, refer to www.Afrofuturism.net or Alondra Nelson's introduction to the special issue of *Social Text* dedicated to Afrofuturism (Nelson 2002).

9. The globalization in cyberpunk refers to the post-industrial, postmodern flow of capital described by Frederic Jameson as "late capitalism." This moment, according to Jameson, began in the 1960s when, empowered by new technology, capitalism shifted from mass to flexible production (Jameson 1991). Anthony Giddens describes globalization as a consequence of modernity, locating its origins in the nineteenth-century European nations' deployment of force to conquer and colonize, while Roland Robertson dates globalization's first phase from the onset of exploration in 1400 (Giddens 1990; Robertson 1992). Hopkinson's novel recalls the traditions of the native Taino population, suggesting that, for her, globalization may even predate the Caribbean colonial enterprise.

10. Douglas 1987, 193–194.

11. Ross 1991b, 141.

12. In an interview with Mark Dery (1994, 201), Samuel Delany discusses the sway held by dominant cyberpunk figures. He recalls a 1987 incident where a young editor putting together a collection on and about cyberpunk was "quashed" by prominent author and cyberpunk aficionado Bruce Sterling. The construction of the canon and the works that were circulated were not a result of serendipity.

13. Hayles 1993, 176.

14. Hayles 1999, especially pp. 20–24.

15. Stone 1995, 35.

16. Lenoir 2000, 305.

17. Gibson coined "cyberspace" for the first time in his short story, "Burning Chrome" in the collection by the same name, but *Neuromancer* is generally credited, because of its widespread popularity, as the originary moment of the term. See Gibson 1986, 168–191.

18. Delany 1994, 165. See, also, essays in Delany 1977. For a thorough discussion of the changes in Delany's argument about the linguistic characteristics of science fiction, and responses to it, see chapters 2 and 5 in Broderick 1995.

19. Stockwell 2000.

20. Westfahl 1992.

21. Named for Toussaint L'Ouverture, whose revolution made Haiti, if only briefly, the first free black republic in the New World.

22. Glave 2003, 149.

23. Sterling 1991; Leonard 1998.

24. Leonard 1998.

25. Responses to and critiques of cyberpunk's sexism have come from writers such as Pat Cadigan, Lisa Mason, Melissa Scott, Kathy Acker, and Gwyneth Jones. Further critiques discussing its racism have been launched by Lisa Nakamura, Wendy Chun, Thomas Foster, and Samuel Delany: both in fiction and essay form. See Delany 1975, 1996, 2000.

26. The Jonkanoo festival on Toussaint is a continuation of a number of similar festivals that take place in the Caribbean and in the American South (as recounted in Jacobs and Child 1861). Called "Johnkankus" in Jamaica and "Jukanoo" in the Bahamas, Irene Smalls finds that it originated along the West Coast of Africa and was spread to the West Indies and the southern coast of America (Smalls n.d.).

27. Hopkinson n.d.

28. For discussions of race and gendered inequities in technological development, see Norris 2001; Green 2001. For considerations about the "whiteness" of cyberpunk, see Dery 1994.

29. Rifkin 2000.

30. Hart 2008. The Jargon File states:

> there is far less overlap between hackerdom and crackerdom than the mundane reader misled by sensationalistic journalism might expect. Crackers tend to gather in small, tight-knit, very secretive groups that have little overlap with the huge, open poly-culture this lexicon describes; though crackers often like to describe *themselves* as hackers, most true hackers consider them a separate and lower form of life.

31. US Congress 2000. For a similar take on hacker ethics, see Wark 2004.

32. US Congress 2000.

33. www.sff.net/people/nalo/nalo/index.html (accessed June 2003). The Mordecai terminology comes from a personal email in which Hopkinson discusses her choice of creoles and her strategy for use in many interviews and online conversations, including Rutledge 1999; Hopkinson 2000; Soyko 2002.

34. Hopkinson n.d.

35. Association of Research Libraries 2000.

36. While Hopkinson recognizes and strategically deploys the Rastafarian stereotype, she does not fetishize Rastas or Rastafarianism. Her treatment of Rastas can be thought of in direct contrast to *Neuromancer*, in which Gibson depicts Rastas as also choosing to leave Earth. In his scenario, however, they serve as cheap labor in the construction of alternative societies in space as well as happily assisting the protagonist in his quest. Gibson also uses Voudou, complete with loas and house eshus, in *Count Zero* and *Mona Lisa Overdrive*, but his depictions do not reflect the histories of these practices.

37. These specific instances of creole are noted by Hopkinson. She writes of this passage: "In fact, 'seen' is specifically Rasta talk [as far as I know], which I guess makes it oppositional squared when I have the runners use it" (Hopkinson, October 19, 2006, in an email message to author).

38. Hopkinson n.d.

39. Fodor's Travel Publications Inc. 1998, 369.

40. For more on Marryshow, see Steele 1995.

41. Wynter 1990, 363.

42. Hortense Spillers, Sylvia Wynter, and Carol Boyce Davies have provided important arguments about femininity's and female sexuality's vexed relationships to slavery. See Spillers 1987; Wynter 1990; Davies 1994.

43. Walter Ong 1982, 6–7, 8. Ong describes further the important inextricability of writing and sound:

> Written texts all have to be related somehow, directly or indirectly, to the world of sound, the natural habitat of language, to yield their meanings. "Reading" a text means converting it to sound, aloud or in the imagination, syllable-by-

syllable in slow reading or sketchily in the rapid reading common to high-technology cultures.

While Ong ultimately asserts that writing enhances sound, rather than the other way around, his premise that sound is intricate and essential to language is one shared by Hopkinson.

44. The eshus resemble the foglets championed in Kurzweil 2000, 145. (Kurzweil gets this idea from J. Storrs Hall.) While Kurzweil imagines foglets as hardworking, Steven Shaviro critiques the notion as seen in other representations. Foglets, Shaviro writes, inspire Fog People to act as "virtual aesthetes and dandies, who pass the time by having impalpable sex" (Shaviro 2003, 127).

45. On one occasion, Hopkinson writes:

> Today the a.i. had chosen to show itself as a dancing skeleton. Its bones clicked together as it jigged, an image the eshu was writing onto Antonio's optic nerve. It sweated robustly, drops the size of fists rolling down its body to splash *praps!* on the "ground" then disappear. "What I could do for you?" The eshu made a ridiculously huge black lace fan appear in one hand and waved it at its own death's head face.
>
> (Hopkinson 2000, 5)

The eshu's image evokes death and servility with humor and sarcasm, simultaneously resisting and acquiescing to the conditions of servitude. Invoking slavery's history, the eshu reverses its terms, fanning itself like a stereotypical white southern lady when called on to serve.

46. Gates 1988, 6, 21. Eshus are masters of figurative language: "Esu, god of indeterminacy, rules the interpretative process; he is god of interpretation because he embodies the ambiguity of figurative language." See Gates' chapter, "A Myth of Origins: Esu-Elegbara and the Signifying Monkey," for an extended discussion of Eshu mythology and scholarship that explores its past. Sometimes Eshu is rendered feminine, the wife of Onrokore.

47. This acceptance of the corporation contrasts sharply with Octavia Butler's *Parable of the Sower*, in which the corporation Olivar is seen as the last safe haven, but one that is racist, overcharges its members, and provides small apartments for those who used to own houses. Almost like a precursor to Hopkinson's world, Lauren, the protagonist, dreams of moving to another planet and starting a new community premised on non-violence, racial equality, and respect for the planet.

48. Rodowick 2001, 234.

Chapter 4

1. Here I refer to Deleuze and Guattari's model of assemblage in *A Thousand Plateaus*. Rob Shields (particularly in Shields 2000, 145–160) has done a remarkable job expanding and troubling the network metaphor – perhaps unintentionally – through his examination of indexing and links.
2. Lévy and Bononno 2001.
3. Jameson and Miyoshi 1998; Soja 1989.
4. Pile and Keith 1997, 2.
5. Imken 1999, 94.
6. Abbate 1999, 13.
7. Dodge and Kitchin 2001, 2.

8. Internet and communication networks are not overlooked entirely. For example, both Hardt and Negri (2000) and Shaviro (2003) link information and networks in terms of cyberspace. Shaviro draws from Deleuze and Guattari, writing: "Cyberspace is what Deleuze and Guattari call a 'haptic' space, as opposed to an optical one: a space of 'pure connection,' accessible only to 'close-range vision,' and having to be navigated step by step" (2003, 7). He links space and connectivity, arguing further that time is what is flexible on the internet.

9. See Benedikt 1993; Imken 1999; Manovich 2001; Sardar 2000; Stratton 2000.

10. Deleuze and Guattari 1987; Castells 2001.

11. Latour 1993.

12. Here, I mean "virtual" in its philosophical sense – as a state of precondition and potentiality, rather than for that which exists in a digital, as opposed to physical, state.

13. Massumi 2002, 87.

14. Stephenson 1992; Gibson 1984.

15. McClintock 1995, 27–28.

16. Winichakul Thongchai 1994, 132.

17. As quoted in Steinberg and McDowell 2003, 52.

18. Maiti 1999.

19. Halavais 2000, 22.

20. Recently (October 2007), the current.tv website was emptied of its content. Now, the URL automatically redirects to current.com. Perhaps this was in response to Gore's or his associates' recognition of the contradictions of using a country code TLDN with no regard for the country to which it recalls.

21. See Maney 2004.

22. www.tamilcanadian.com/page.php?cat=52&id=458 (accessed October 14, 2007).

23. Mintz 2002.

24. This appeared on the eelamweb.com home banner until 2004, when it was replaced. Now it can be found at www.eelamweb.com/introduction/eelam_demand.html. This was a quote from the "Heroes Day Speech" of 2001 by the Tamil Tiger leader.

25. Maya Ranganathan writes: "The argument is that the Western historians have erroneously attributed the invention to the Sumerians, who merely 'adopted it at a later stage'" (2006b).

26. Bhabha 1990, 112. Aijaz Ahmad's critique of Bhabha (Ahmad 1994) renders both this discussion of the construction of national imaginings and the use of the western press, the internet, and English by Tamil Eelam websites a capitalist capitulation that enjoys the fruit of individual materialism rather than moving toward Marxist-based reformulations of current conditions.

27. www.tamilnet.com, www.eelamweb.com, www.tamilcanadian.com, and www.sangam.org.

28. Ranganathan 2006a, 288. Ranganathan goes on to give several examples of how the land is depicted as developing.

29. Here I am thinking in particular of Paul Gilroy's assertions in *Against Race* where he argues that Bob Marley was a "planetary figure" built through "the seemingly universal power of a poetic and political language that reached out from its roots" (2000, 131). He writes: "His enduring presence in globalized popular culture is an important reminder of the power of the technologies that ground the culture of simulation" (2000, 130), rendering, in effect, the network of diaspora in contradistinction to the "webs of planetary popular culture … in the digital era" (2000, 132). Arguing that the internet and transnational communication only function to flatten out cultural

specificities rather than providing opportunities for them to arise is a common position vis-à-vis the rise of a networked world.

30. For instance, on soc.culture.thai, on August 11–14, there was conversation about this attack, including one message that included email accounts that were to be spammed. All messages posted by "rajaram2" invited people to contact an address in order to enlist themselves as Internet Black Tigers: http://groups.google.com/groups/profile?enc_user=1ocsYxAAAAD-ODotWT2bELVXxkhgbUzv (accessed October 3, 2007).

31. The MIBT Terrorist Knowledge Base states:

> the [Internet Black Tigers] are infamous for being the first known organization to carry out an act of cyber-terror against a nation. In August 1997, IBT attacked the email systems of several Sri Lankan embassies throughout the world. By flooding these accounts with over 800 emails a day, the IBT was able to disable embassy networks for nearly two weeks. The emails sent by IBT identified the group as an "elite department" of the LTTE, specializing in "suicide e-mail bombings." The group said the attack was an effort to counter Sri Lankan government propaganda. Although this incident was more of an annoyance then [sic] anything else, for many terrorism experts the attack represents a highly significant development in the future of cyber-terrorism and terrorist methods.
> (www.tkb.org/Group.jsp?groupID=4062; accessed October 10, 2007)

The "Cybercrime" website reports: "The messages contained 'We are the Internet Black Tigers and we're doing this to disrupt your communications.' It was called the first known attack by terrorists against a country's computer systems by Intelligence authorities" (http://library.thinkquest.org/04oct/00460/cyberterrorism.html; accessed October 3, 2007).

32. See Anderson 1983. This oft-invoked text links language and the spread of print capitalism to the developing sense of nationalism and national identity.

33. Agamben 1993, 11.

34. The site no longer exists. It was taken down in 2004.

35. TamilNet, www.tamilnet.com (accessed October 2004).

36. Whitaker 2004.

37. Ilankai Tamil Sangam, www.sangam.org (accessed December 2003).

38. Ilankai Tamil Sangam, www.sangam.org (accessed December 2003).

39. TamilCanadian, www.tamilcanadian.com (accessed June 2008).

40. EelamWEB, www.eelamweb.com/map 2003 (accessed December 2003).

41. Tamil Eelam homepage, http://eelamweb.com (accessed June 2008).

42. Jeganathan 1997, 528.

43. Ilankai Tamil Sangam, www.sangam.org/Mission.htm (accessed December 18, 2003).

44. Ilankai Tamil Sangam, www.sangam.org/Mission.htm (accessed December 18, 2003).

45. EelamWEB, www.eelamweb.com/people (accessed December 18, 2003).

46. EelamWEB, www.eelamweb.com/people (accessed December 18, 2003).

47. Ruth Frankenberg and Lati Mani (1993). "Crosscurrents, Crosstalk: Race, 'Postcoloniality' and the Politics of Location." In *Cultural Studies* 7(2): 292–310.

48. Kitalong and Kitalong (2000) describe a situation where Paluans in the US cast votes and organize politically in order to affect laws and decisions made by leaders located in their island nation of Palua. Like the citizens of Tamil Eelam, many Paluans have no plans on returning to their homeland, but their connections remain strong in their imaginations, in their local communities, and via the World Wide Web.

Chapter 5

1. http://lovetours.com/whytour.asp (accessed June 25, 2001).
2. Gaew posted this in the response section following SiamWEB.org's essay, "Thai Sisters are Doing it for Themselves," by Od Busakorn (www.siamweb.org.org/news-culture/women/). Patpong refers to the infamous area of Bangkok where the oldest and most well-known brothels catering to foreigners are located.
3. Bishop and Robinson prove, through meticulous archival work, that "[t]he stereotype of Thailand as the playground of the Western World dominates the public imagination outside the country and is continually reiterated in the popular media" (1998, 16).
4. Boonchalaksi and Guest (1994, 8) attribute economic growth, at least in part, to the commercialization of Thai women's sexuality: "The bodies of Thai women have become one of the bases of growth of the Thai economy." Whether Thailand is referred to as an "economic miracle" or as the country that triggered the Southeast Asian financial crisis, gendered images of the nation are constantly recycled.
5. While many competing images of Thai women emerge from the Thai press, the majority of depictions of Thai women by the western media, as Robinson and Bishop show, create an international memory consisting of two extremes.
6. Appadurai 1996, 32. Although eagerly anticipated, his book does not push past anecdotal evidence, nor does it display the rigorous analysis he called for in his 1990 essay, "Disjuncture and Difference in the Global Cultural Economy."
7. SiamWEB, www.siamweb.org.org/content/index/aboutus_eng.php.
8. SiamWEB, "Siamweb.Org," www.siamweb.org. From February 26 until November 22, 1993, the site was located at www.eskimo.com/~putt/siam/. On November 23, 1995, it moved to the www.siamweb.org URL and server.
9. SiamWEB, www.siamweb.org/content/About_Us/104/index_eng.php.
10. SiamWEB, www.siamweb.org/member/index_eng.php.
11. I use the term "homosocial" to diffuse the focus on sex acts inherent in the term "homosexuality" and its post-Stonewall deployment. Also, homosociality, along the lines of Eve Sedgwick's use of the term, designates a continuum incorporating homosexuality and same-sex (male, in Sedgwick's instance) bonding. "Homosocial" and "homoerotic" are both terms I've employed in this context to incorporate the desire articulated by both "toms" and "dees." They gesture toward a range of same-sex-centered activities that may or may not be read as explicitly sexual.
12. Standards of appropriate Thai womanhood vary greatly between classes in Thailand. The majority of configurations for adult womanhood include mothering, running the household and controlling the money, looking and acting "ladylike." What they do not entail is strong female bonds between non-relatives, gender non-conformity, and articulations of same-sex desire.
13. "Toms" and "dees" might also be said to correspond loosely with butch and femme models of western culture. The similarities are more superficially visual than culturally manifested, however. Furthermore, toms are not women, nor are they imitating men. For a nuanced discussion of the intricacies of tom and dee identities, consult Sinnott 2004.
14. This is a term coined by Anjana Suvarnananda, the founder and president of the Thai organization of the same name. For a longer discussion of Anjaree and the meanings of "women who follow nonconformist ways," see Enteen 1998.
15. One can also be a "man" – another adapted term that applies specifically to incarcerated women who have sex with inmates labeled "women" but do not assume the prescribed masculine attire and attributes of toms.

16. Paik and Mardon 2003.
17. Pasuk Phongpaichit and Baker 1998, 3.
18. For a thorough account of the economic and cultural changes in Thailand during this decade, see Pasuk Phongpaichit and Baker 1995, 1998.
19. I am not asserting that these media are without agendas that affect the way in which the information is presented. For example, sites on the internet exist in order to create desires for consumption, form certain types of international gay communities, create women-centered and/or feminist communities, change political policies, initiate friendships, etc.
20. One interesting result is the popularity of *luk krung* (biracial Thais, literally "half children"). A large number of singers and actors in Thailand's prolific music, television, and movie industries are of mixed race, and a significant number of them have been raised outside of Thailand. This marks a huge ideological shift; *luk krung* used to be vociferously rejected by Thai society because they symbolized a woman's involvement with a westerner, which alluded to prostitution. Until recently, *luk krung* were not considered Thai citizens and were not entitled to government-mandated education or healthcare.
21. Sen and Stivens 1998, xi.
22. See Jackson 1995; Sinnott 2004; Wilson 2004; Thongthiraj 1994. For discussions about the effect of English use on the articulation of genders and sexualities, see Enteen 1998, 2001.
23. Pleasuretours.com describes Asian women without differentiation and offers tours to Thailand, the Philippines, and Cambodia that are indistinguishable in description, varying only in the dates of travel ("Our next group tour leaves in November. Individual tours available with dates of your choice all year round!" [www.lovetours. com; accessed April 23, 2005]). However, they do distinguish between the countries of origin of potential customers: "Although the majority of our customers are from North America, we also have tour members from many other countries as well" (www.lovetours.com; accessed April 23, 2005).
24. Gaew, "Response To "Thai Sisters Are Doing It for Themselves" By Od Busakorn," www.siamweb.org.org/news-culture/women/ (accessed October 2007).
25. Feminist cultural work of many kinds has focused on the gendered aspects of national discourses and the way in which these representations may be constructed by alternate practices. For a concise tract outlining the links between nationalism and feminism, see Grewal and Kaplan (2000); Rajeswari Sunder Rajan (1993) provides extensive theoretical background. McClintock (1995) shows moments where the nation is inscribed on women's bodies while the body of the nation is raced and gendered.
26. Brutt-Griffler 2001, 32.
27. Here I am referring to Chomskyan linguistics, which lacks a theory of development of language change. Brutt-Griffler (2001) fully clarifies the unidirectionality of this approach.
28. SiamWEB, www.siamweb.org.org/us/index.html.
29. Rheingold 1993, 5.
30. SiamWEB, www.siamweb.org.org/us/index.html.
31. SiamWEB, www.siamweb.org.org/us/index.html.
32. Turkle 1995; Sullivan and Bornstein 1996; Bruckman 1996.
33. See The Turing Game for an example of non-MUD or IRC gender-swapping activities (www.cc.gatech.edu/elc/turing; accessed March 19, 2000).
34. Watson 1997, 107.

35. In addition to Turkle, Donna Haraway, and Alluquere Rosanne Stone were the most influential feminists arguing for the fluidity of identity in online environments. See Haraway 1991; Stone 1995.
36. Miller 1997.
37. For the classic, most referenced discussion of online rape in Moo and MUD environments, see Dibbell 1998.
38. For a forceful overview of the way in which western feminist assumptions and practices lead to the oppression of non-western women, see Mohanty *et al.* 1991. For nuanced critiques of white western feminist assumptions, see Guha and Spivak 1988; Spillers 1991, 2003.
39. Nakamura 2002, 94.
40. Mitra 1997, 2001; Gajjala 2001; Kitalong and Kitalong 2000. Many of these essays are from collections such as Landzelius 2006; Chung and Wong 2004.
41. Stone 1995, 17. While Stone does usefully remind us that a user at the keyboard with HIV still has HIV while at the computer, much of Stone's important discussion insists on the difference of the user's subjectivity and body in online environments.
42. Serano 2007.
43. Yujira 1997.
44. Chumsai 1997.
45. For an outline of the hierarchies and expectations of Thai society and modernized Bangkok in particular, see the first chapter of Jackson 1995.
46. Chumsai n.d.
47. Kandiyoti 1994, 382.
48. www.siamweb.org.org/joinus/; Negroponte 1995.
49. Thongchai Winichakul 1994, 130.
50. Anderson 1998, 152.
51. Wyatt 1984, 78.
52. SiamWEB, www.siamweb.org/content/NewsCulture/154/index_eng.php.
53. SiamWEB, www.siamweb.org/content/NewsCulture/154/index_eng.php.
54. SiamWEB, www.siamweb.org/content/NewsCulture/154/index_eng.php.
55. SiamWEB, www.siamweb.org/romance/yeah_right.
56. SiamWEB, www.siamweb.org.org/news-culture/women/index.htm.
57. SiamWEB, www.siamweb.org.org/content/News-Culture/155/index_eng.php.
58. SiamWEB, www.siamweb.org.org/content/News-Culture/155/index_eng.php.
59. SiamWEB, www.siamweb.org.

Chapter 6

1. http://boyonthenet.com/gdate/index.php (accessed December 18, 2007). Since 2008, the domain name is no longer owned and the site is no longer available.
2. Logo and disclaimer at http://palm-plaza.com (appears after splash page) (accessed December 21, 2007).
3. When discussing Thai men who identify as gay, I use "Thai gay men" to underscore the discontinuities among US and Euro conceptions of a gay identity and contemporary (meaning between 1996 and 2007) use among Thai men in Bangkok of the term "gay." This local conception cannot be clearly delineated, however, since it is dynamic, flexible, at times contradictory, and by no means monolithic. "Thai gay" highlights the specificity of this identity as it is articulated by specific texts, bodies, and linguistic practices.

4. There are commentaries from scholars around the world that work to particularize gay experiences, in particular, D'Emilio 2002. For the transnational turn in queer theory scholarship and sexuality studies, see Dinshaw 2006; Herdt 1994; Manalansan 1994; Alonso and Koreck 1989. There are also excellent essays about the lack of considerations of race in queer theory. See particularly the essays in *Black Queer Studies*, Johnson and Henderson 2005 (eds).

5. See arguments by Altman 2001; Binnie 2004. There are many others who presume a gay identity that is from the west/US exists identically in other places, and almost every tour guide produced outside of Thailand does this as well.

6. "Cissexual" is a term used in western Trans Theory to denote people who take for granted the match between their gender and sex. Like racism or heterosexism, the term is meant to show that there are embedded assumptions encoded in expecting this seamless conformity. I have chosen to use this word because the majority of Thais do not unquestionably match sex and gender. For several centuries, Thai religion, law, and culture has recognized the legitimacy of *kathoeys*, people whose biological sex do not match their inherent gender.

7. In June 2004, I interviewed over 100 Thai men. I asked each man if he identified as "gay" and, if so, if he used the internet. If the answers were affirmative, I inquired about which sites he visited and whether they were in Thai or English (or, as it is called, "Tinglish"). The men willing to talk to me reported, by and large, two categories of websites: US-based sites that cater to "global gay" audiences (i.e. Gay.com) and local sites that use a constantly shifting mix of Thai and English, reflecting the changing circumstances of Thailand-based events and conceptions surrounding sexual and gender identity.

8. Some studies that posit the overlap of gay communities online and off: Dawson 1996; O'Riordan and Phillips 2007; Campbell 2004; Thomas 2002; Shaw 1997; Lee 2005.

9. See Altman (1997) for a description, at times critically engaged and at other moments unreflexive, of the proliferation of gay discos, nightclubs, and bars. For some of the many critiques of queer theory's US centrality, see also the conversation surrounding Altman's post in the *Australian Humanities Review* by David Halperin, Gary Dowsett, Michael Tan, Donald Morton, Christopher Lane, Fran Martin, and Chris Berry (www.lib.latrobe.edu.au/AHR/archive/Issue-July-1996/altman.html [accessed July 14, 2008]).

10. As in Chapter 2, I invoke Pratt when I employ her useful construction of the contact zone (see Pratt 1992).

11. See Enteen 1998.

12. For a brief but interesting history of these two small alleys near the infamous heterosexual sex area Patpong, see Allyn and Chaiyana 2000, 45–46.

13. For some ethnographies that discuss what it means to be homosexual or gay in Thailand, see Enteen 1998; Jackson and Sullivan 1999; Costa and Matzner 2007.

14. A large number of Thais, particularly from Bangkok, consider themselves ethnic Chinese with Thai nationalities. Although many Chinese families have lived in Thailand for many generations, they still consider themselves to be overseas Chinese. Many Chinese living in Thailand maintain connections with extended family in China, Taiwan, or in other locations around the world.

15. Jackson notes that *phet* can refer to "male," "man," or "masculine." In general, *phet* is, in terms of men/masculinity, something that positions laymen from Buddhist clergy. Men have *phet*; monks, who must take a vow of celibacy, are linguistically without/opposite *phet*, having no sex, gender, or sexuality (Jackson 2004, 206–210).

16. There are many studies that confirm this, though histories and interpretations vary. See, for example, Allyn 1991; Jackson 2004; Morris 1994; Jackson and Cook 1999; Jackson and Sullivan 1999: Costa and Matzner 2007; Thongthiraj 1994.

17. This was reported to me constantly by both my students and the sex-workers I taught at the Thai-run NGO EMPOWER between 1992 and 1993. In fact, the sex-workers were eager to learn English-language terms for genitals and sexual positions, but if I so much as said the word "vagina" in Thai, I was scolded for being improper and impolite. A native-English speaker speaking these words in English was more acceptable – and not seen as impolite – but speaking the words in Thai carried a much greater sense of impropriety.

18. English phrases like "I am what I am" or "I don't give a damn" have also been used in several popular Thai pop songs, and "Bar-a-go-go" is the Thai word for Go-go bars. Thomas Fuller writes in the *International Herald Tribune* (2007):

> For as long as people here can remember, children have been given playful nicknames – classics include Shrimp, Chubby and Crab – that are carried into adulthood. But now, to the consternation of some nickname purists, children are being given such offbeat English-language nicknames as Mafia or Seven – as in 7–Eleven, the convenience store.

19. Koshy 1999, 11.

20. For example, although Asian governments and NGOs agreed on the validity of human rights, for the UN World Conference on Human Rights, Asian NGOs produced their own declaration of intent that differed from that of Asian governments (see Koshy 1999, 10–18, especially 12).

21. Allyn 1991.

22. This was given as a reason to me by Surang Janyam, manager of EMPOWER's former Patpong branch in a personal conversation at EMPOWER on June 16, 2004. Surang was working closely with other sex-related NGOs and their spokespeople. At the time, she was quitting EMPOWER to develop the new Thai-run NGO, SWING.

23. This is a term coined by Anjana Suvarnananda, the founder and president of the Thai organization of the same name. For a longer discussion of Anjaree and the meanings of "women who follow nonconformist ways," see Enteen 2001.

24. Taywaditep *et al.* 1998, 1235.

25. www.iglhrc.org/site/iglhrc/section.php?id=76.

26. ILGA writes of itself:

> The International Lesbian and Gay Association is a world-wide network of national and local groups dedicated to achieving equal rights for lesbian, gay, bisexual and transgendered (LGBT) people everywhere. Founded in 1978, it now has more than 560 member organisations. Every continent and around 90 countries are represented. ILGA member groups range from small collectives to national groups and entire cities.
>
> (www.ilga.org/aboutilga.asp; accessed September 10, 2007)

27. For an excellent discussion of statements by directors of the ILGA's teleological project of creating western versions of gay and lesbian, see Massad 2002.

28. Both women discussed their refusal to join ILGA in separate private conversations. Anjana discussed ILGA in an interview I conducted with her in October 1997. Surang described this in June 2004 (personal conversation).

29. In November 2005, Gay.com initiated "premium membership," which required a USD 19.95/month charge for full access to features, including the ability to view

multiple photographs of a member (once again, photographs are premised to be highly desirable anchors to the online experience) or enter a chat room already designated as "full." Payment for premier membership, however, is no longer required for members whose "default" location is outside the United States and Canada. Perhaps this change is in an attempt by Gay.com to attract more international members.

30. www.planetinc.com/company/.
31. The history according to the company site is worded as follows:

> In April 2004, PlanetOut Partners Inc. became, simply, PlanetOut Inc. Today, more than 3.5 million active members on PlanetOut's flagship sites, Gay.com and PlanetOut.com, make up a virtual metropolis that is bigger than the city of Chicago. The LGBT community now represents a reported buying power of $485 billion annually in the United States alone and FORTUNE 500 advertisers are taking notice. Companies like General Motors, Bristol Meyers Squibb, Wrigley's and Universal are among many reaching what the company believes is the largest network of gay and lesbian people in the world through Gay.com and PlanetOut. com's specialized content channels and community areas.
>
> A leading media company serving the LGBT market, PlanetOut's Gay.comGay. com website also compares favorably to mainstream websites by certain statistical measures. At more than four hours per month, the average time a user spends on Gay.com is better than all but one of the approximately 3,200 websites measured by Nielsen NetRatings in June 2004, including Yahoo!, eBay, MSN, and Google. By delivering on its mission to "connect, enrich and illuminate gay and lesbian people everywhere," PlanetOut keeps members connected to and engaged on its sites, with visitors returning to Gay.com almost every other day (Nielsen NetRatings, June 2004).
>
> (PlanetOut Inc., "Company History," http://planetoutinc.com/company/history. html; accessed September 10, 2007)

32. www.gay.com; accessed June 28, 2004.
33. www.images.google.com.
34. Interestingly, the options of choosing MTF and FTM have dropped out with the addition of the feature "fast search." In a fast search, one must choose "men" or "women," placing transgendered categories more deeply hidden within the site options (one must do an advanced search) at a time when, arguably, transgender presence is increasing in both western and transnational contexts.
35. The results are actually highly inconsistent. I have been conducting regular searches of these terms since 1997 (before Google, I searched on other popular search engines), and there seems to be no clear pattern of the ratio of websites selling pornography to those geared for western men interested in meeting Thai men. Between October and November 2007, for example, there was an increase in the top-ten results of the number of porn items available. A search on December 13, 2007, however, revealed not a single "pornography" site on google.com's top ten (www. google.com/search?source=ig&hl=en&rlz=1G1____ENUS243&q=thai+gay&btn G=Google+Search). I would conjecture that these changes reflect the nebulousness of the term in general, not the rise or fall in numbers of sites available or user click-through results.
36. A certain amount of censorship is exercised by the Thai government, and the production of pornography within Thailand (as opposed to the reproduction and sale of western pornography) was, until recently, strongly sanctioned, so little pornographic

material appears on the Thailand Google site. Particular attention is paid to the production of images that could be interpreted as child pornography, which is both highly illegal and socially condemnable in Thailand. Since Thailand's popular press consistently links pedophilia to homosexuality, "gay" pornography faces closer scrutiny than pornography supposedly targeted at heterosexual consumption. Although what constitutes gay pornography as opposed to images circulating under the auspices of social networking has not been clearly defined by the Thai legal system or, for that matter, by scholars or journalists. These circumstances mean that concern and ambivalence accompany homosocial images on the internet that originate from Thailand and feature Thai youth. Images that could fall under the classification of pornography are often available for viewing, but, in cases, forbid general access to these images, requiring enrollment in the website's community as a prerequisite for consumption. In the process of registration, these websites routinely ask for a date of birth or acknowledgement that the person creating the account is at least 18 years of age.

37. When conducting interviews about where men went online in June 2004, I asked several of them how they began using the internet. Most of them responded that they performed a search on Google for "Thai" and "gay."

38. This is said by male sex-workers to researchers as well as to western and Thai clients in go-go bars and brothels. It may function as a way of distancing oneself from one's career in sex-work. The accuracy of this claim has not been researched, as far as I know. It is noteworthy, however, that wives, children, and families are not mentioned in online personals.

39. www.utopia-asia.com.

40. www.amazon.com/Utopia-Guide-Singapore-Malaysia-Indonesia/dp/1411690095; accessed December 12, 2007. This was the first GLBT center in Southeast Asia started by an American and geared toward an English-language-speaking population.

41. www.amazon.com/Utopia-Guide-Singapore-Malaysia-Indonesia/dp/1411690095.

42. World Bank 1997, 275–276.

43. Porapakkham Yawarat and Aids Control and Prevention Project Family Health International 1996. This may no longer be the case since the campaign has declined in public attention and funding since 2004.

44. The high-profile campaign was initially unpopular with the influential tourism industry, and tourism temporarily declined. However, once AIDS had a prominent place on the national agenda, opposition to the measures gradually faded and support increased. The xenophobia behind the campaign provides an interesting twist on the generalizations so rampant about AIDS concerning Africa and Haiti (see Patton 2002). Simultaneously, NGOs were hard at work. Both EMPOWER and FACT (Fraternity for AIDS Cessation in Thailand) focused on the Thai sex-worker population. Natee Teerarojjanapongs of FACT created the successful "White Lines Dance Troupe" to highlight the risks faced by gay male prostitutes. His action-oriented NGO offered a path for government recognition and action. Rejecting the idea that AIDS was a heterosexual or non-Thai disease, the government began a massive program to control the spread of HIV through widespread condom-use campaigns; it ultimately achieved a substantial reduction in new infections.

45. See Rakkit Rattachumpoth in the Introduction to Jackson and Sullivan, eds 1999.

46. www.utopia-asia.com.

47. The most popular URLs provided to me were: Boyonthenet.com, Thailandout.com, Palm-plaza.com, Gboysiam.com, AboutG.com, and Gthai.net. Others, like

Gayguidebkk.com, and *Sticky Rice* (www.stickyrice.ws/?view=home) were linked to magazines or flyers.

I cannot determine whether or not the men I interviewed were pointing to these websites on my list because I provided them access to the list and they felt compelled to choose, or if they needed to see the URLs in order to recall the website's name. Their desire to see the list – something many interviewees requested when they saw it – might be another way in which the knowledge of these sites was circulated. The claim of familiarity does indicate an interest in them, I would argue, even if it is not quantitative evidence of previous knowledge of the existence of these websites.

48. Popularity was uneven between the websites. More men spent more time on these sites in general, but different sites had more visitors than others at any given moment. I was able to track this data because most of these websites, as I discuss later, provide details about how many users were online at any given moment or how many members were actively posting. I could track how often they updated the sites by using the data provided by the Wayback Machine at www.archive.org.

49. Community Connect also owns a site under development, Glee.com, which targets GLBT communities and hopes to compete with Planet Out/Gay.com.

50. In retrospect, it would have been useful to think about the websites in conjunction and develop questions accordingly.

51. Here I want to extend Turkle's and Stone's (1995) claims about the liberatory and non-normative effects of not grounding gender in sex. The online play of gender cannot be severed from the body it occupies, nor is it simplistically related. The relationship of gender play on real-life sexual identity is both monolithic and fractured, and online sexual cultures such as the ones I describe here provide another basis for theorizing and practicing cybersex and virtual personhood.

52. The popularity of Blackberries, Apple's iPhone, and their clones may soon render this assertion about the United States' cell-phone interests obsolete.

Epilogue: The Medium Massages

1. News reports about the Sony PlayStation 3 can be found in all major US newspaper archives. The BBC and Bloomberg feature international stories detailing the debut and sell-out: "PlayStation 3 Sells Out at Launch." (http://news.bbc.co.uk/2/hi/technology/6135452.stm) and Michael White, "Sony PlayStation Debuts in U.S., Sells out in Minutes (Update 3)" November 17, 2006 (www.bloomberg.com/apps/news?pid=20601101&sid=a0Yh1BT8uDfo&refer=japan). Accessed July 14, 2008.

2. Lack of availability is not the only reason PlayStation 3 has decreased in popularity. It's prohibitively high price means that fewer games are available. While it has the most advanced graphics of the three most popular gaming systems, Microsoft's Xbox 360 cost $500 less and had no compatibility issues with games from earlier versions. Furthermore, Nintendo's Wii, available for only $150–$180, offers many games. Although the graphics are limited, the Wii has become the "non-gamer's" gaming device. Accessed July 14, 2008.

3. "Playstation 3 European Launch," March 23, 2007 (http://news.bbc.co.uk/2/hi/technology/6474045.stm). Accessed July 14, 2008.

4. For more information about Tantalum use, consult www.tanb.org/tantalum1.html, www.tanb.org/coltan.html, and www.grandviewmaterials.com/tantalum/industry.html. Accessed July 14, 2008.

5. For a full account of the mining of coltan in the DRC, see Johann Hari. "Congo's tragedy: The War the World Forgot," May 5, 2006 (www.independent.co.uk/news/world/africa/congos-tragedy-the-war-the-world-forgot-476929.html) ; Blaine Harden, "The Dirt in the New Machine," August 12, 2001 (http://query.nytimes.com/gst/full-page.html?res=9D0DE1D7113CF931A2575BC0A9679C8B63&sec=&spon=&partner=permalink&exprod=permalink) and David Barouski, " 'Blood Minerals' in the Kivu Provinces of the Democratic Republic of the Congo," zmag.org, June 1, 2007 (www.raceandhistory.com/historicalviews/2007/2106.html). Accessed July 14, 2008.

6. The Human Rights Watch, a US-based international NGO writes:

> Children's physical and intellectual immaturity makes them particularly vulnerable to human rights violations. Their ill-treatment calls for special attention because, for the most part, children cannot speak for themselves, their opinions are seldom taken into account and they can only rarely form their own organizations to work for change.
>
> (http://hrw.org/doc/?t=children; accessed July 14, 2008)

7. "The ILO was founded in 1919, in the wake of a destructive war, to pursue a vision based … upon decent treatment of working people. The ILO became the first special-ized agency of the UN in 1946." According to the ILO:

> Work is central to people's well-being. In addition to providing income, work can pave the way for broader social and economic advancement, strengthening indi-viduals, their families and communities. Such progress, however, hinges on work that is decent. Decent work sums up the aspirations of people in their working lives.
>
> (www.ilo.org/global/About_the_ILO/lang–en/index.htm;
> accessed July 14, 2008)

The current leader, since 1999, is from Chile. All other leaders of the organization have been from Europe.

8. The "nimble fingers of 'Oriental' women" – as Donna Haraway writes, creating, in effect, an imagined, feminized worker, laboring to produce every chip essential to a computer's function, reappears once again – these small fingers are imagined, in a different context, to be users of this machine (from Haraway 1991, 153).

9. McLuhan and Fiore 1967.

10. See Nakamura 2002, particularly the excellent critique in the fourth chapter.

11. From "Dictionary." Version 2.0.1 (51.1), Apple, Inc. 2005–7. "Massage: verb [trans.] 1 rub and knead (a person or part of the body) with the hands." From "Massage," in *Oxford English Dictionary* (accessed May 24, 2008). "Verb: trans. In extended use.

   a. To manipulate so as to achieve a desired effect (lit. and fig.); to flatter, gratify, indulge.

   b. To manipulate (data, figures, etc., or their presentation), esp. in order to give a more acceptable result.

12. Deleuze and Guattari 1987.

13. McLuhan and Fiore 1967.

14. Lila Abu-Lughod 2002, 790.

15. Ware continues: "instead of objectifying women on the basis of nationality, geogra-phy, religion, or ethnicity" (2006, 548).

Bibliography

Abbate, Janet. 1999. *Inventing the Internet, Inside Technology*. Cambridge: MIT Press.

Abelove, Henry, Michèle Aina Barale, and David M. Halperin, eds. 1993. *The Lesbian and Gay Studies Reader*. New York: Routledge.

Abu-Lughod, Lila. 2002. Do Muslim Women Really Need Saving? *American Anthropologist* 104 (3): 783–790.

Achebe, Chinua. 1975. *Morning Yet on Creation Day: Essays*. Garden City: Anchor Press.

——. 2007. The African Writer and the English Language. In *Rotten English: A Literary Anthology*. New York: W.W. Norton & Co.

Afzal-Khan, Fawzia and Kalpana Seshadri-Crooks. 2000. *The Pre-Occupation of Postcolonial Studies*. Durham and London: Duke University Press.

Agamben, Giorgio. 1993. *The Coming Community*. Minneapolis: University of Minnesota Press.

Ahmad, Aijaz. 1994. *In Theory: Classes, Nations, Literatures*. London: Verso.

Ahmad, Dohra. 2007. Introduction. In *Rotten English: A Literary Anthology*. New York: W.W. Norton & Co.

Allyn, Eric. 1991. *Trees in the Same Forest: Thailand's Culture and Gay Subculture*. San Francisco: Bua Luang Publishing Co.

Allyn, E.G. and Samorn Chaiyana. 2000. *TMOT 7: The Men of Thailand Listings: Thailand's Gay Venues 1999–2000*. 7th edn. Bangkok: Floating Lotus Press.

Alonso, Ana Maria and Maria Teresa Koreck. 1989. Silences: "Hispanics," Aids, and Sexual Practices. *Differences* 1 (1).

Altman, Dennis. 1996. On Global Queering. *Australian Humanities Review*. Online, available at: www.australianhumanitiesreview.org/archive/Issue-July-1996/altman.html.

——. 1996. Rupture or Continuity: The Internationalization of Gay Identity. *Social Text* 14 (3): 77–94.

——. 1997. Global Gaze/Global Gays. *GLQ: A Journal of Lesbian and Gay Studies* 3 (4): 417–436.

——. 2001. *Global Sex*. Chicago: University of Chicago Press.

Anderson, Benedict. 1983. *Imagined Communities: Reflections On the Origin and Spread Of Nationalism*. London: Verso.

——. 1998. *The Spectre of Comparisons: Nationalism, Southeast Asia, and the World*. New York: Verso.

Anzaldúa, Gloria. 1987. *Borderlands, La Frontera: The New Mestiza*. San Fransisco: Spinsters/aunt lute.

Appadurai, Arjun. 1996. *Modernity at Large: Cultural Dimensions of Globalization*. Minneapolis: University of Minnesota Press.

Association of Research Libraries, Office of Scholarly Communication. 2000. *Directory of Scholarly Electronic Journals and Academic Discussion Lists*. 1st edn. Washington, DC: Office of Scholarly Communication, Association of Research Libraries.

Azim, Firdous. 1993. *The Colonial Rise of the Novel*. Routledge.

Baker, Christopher John and Phongpaichit Pasuk. 2005. *A History of Thailand*. New York: Cambridge University Press.

Bakhtin, Michel. 1981. *The Dialogic Imagination*. Texas: University of Texas Press.

Bal, Mieke. 1996. Critical Response. *Critical Inquiry*.

Balibar, Etienne and Immanuel Maurice Wallerstein. 1991. *Race, Nation, Class: Ambiguous Identities*. London and New York: Verso.

Bell, David and Barbara M. Kennedy, eds. 2000. *The Cybercultures Reader*. New York: Routledge.

Belnap, Jeffrey Grant. 1993. *The Postcolonial State and the "Hybrid" Intellectual*. California: U.M.I.

Benedikt, Michael. 1993. Cyberspace: First Steps. In *Cyberspace: Some Proposals*, edited by M. Benedikt. Cambridge: MIT Press.

Berlant, Lauren and Michael Warner. 1995. What Does Queer Theory Teach Us About X? *PMLA* 110 (3): 343–349.

Bernabe, Jean, Patrick Chamoiseau, Raphael Confiant, and M. B. Taleb-Khyar. 1997. *In Praise Of Creoleness*. Paris: Gallimard.

Berry, Chris, Fran Martin, and Audrey Yue, eds. 2003. *Mobile Cultures: New Media in Queer Asia, Console-ing Passions*. Durham: Duke University Press.

Bhabha, Homi K. 1990. *Nation and Narration*. London and New York: Routledge.

———. 1994. *The Location of Culture*. London and New York: Routledge.

Bhaopichitr, Kirida. 1998. Thailand: The Road to Economic Crisis. *Third World Resurgence* (89): 13–14.

Bickerton, Derek. 1981. *Roots of Language*. Ann Arbor: Karoma.

Binnie, Jon. 2004. *The Globalization of Sexuality*. London: SAGE.

Bishop, Ryan and Lillian S. Robinson. 1998. *Night Market: Sexual Cultures and the Thai Economic Miracle*. New York: Routledge.

Boellstorff, Tom. 2008. *Coming of Age in Second Life: An Anthropologist Explores the Virtually Human*. Princeton: Princeton University Press.

Boonchalaksi, Wathinee and Philip Guest. 1994. *Prostitution in Thailand*. Nakhon Pathom, Thailand: Institute for Population and Social Research, Mahidol University.

Bordo, Susan. 1999. *The Male Body: A New Look at Men in Public and in Private*. New York: Farrar, Straus and Giroux.

Bradley, Phil. 2004. *Meta Tags – What, Where, When, Why?* Online, available at: www. philb.com/metatag.htm (accessed July 26, 2006).

Brathwaite, Edward Kamau. 1971. *The Development of Creole Society in Jamaica, 1770–1820*. Oxford: Clarendon Press.

Broderick, Damien. 1995. *Reading by Starlight: Postmodern Science Fiction*. London and New York: Routledge.

Bruckman, Amy S. 1996. Gender Swapping on the Internet. In *High Noon on the Electric Frontier*, edited by P. Ludlow. Cambridge: MIT Press.

Brutt-Griffler, Janina. 2001. *English as an International Language: The Remaking of English through Language Spread and Change*. Clevedon: Multilingual Matters.

——. 2002. *World English: a Study of its Development*. Clevedon and Buffalo: Multilingual Matters.

Burniske, R.W. and Lowell Monke. 2001. *Breaking Down the Digital Walls: Learning to Teach in a Post-Modem World*. Albany: State University of New York Press.

Busia, Abena P.A. n.d. Caliban. *Poetry Daily*. Online, available at: www.poetrydaily.org (accessed June 21, 2004).

——. 1993. Performance, Transcription and the Languages of the Self: Interrogating Identity as a "Post-Colonial" Poet. In *Theorizing Black Feminisms: the Visionary Pragmatism of Black Women*, edited by S.M. James and A.P.A. Busia. London and New York: Routledge.

Butler, Judith. 1990. *Gender Trouble: Feminism and the Subversion of Identity*. New York: Routledge.

——. 1993. *Bodies That Matter: On the Discursive Limits Of "Sex."* New York: Routledge.

Butler, Octavia E. 1993. *Parable of the Sower*. New York: Four Walls Eight Windows.

Cadigan, Pat. 1992. *Fools*. New York: Bantam Spectra.

Campbell, John Edward. 2004. *Getting It On Online: Cyberspace, Gay Male Sexuality, and Embodied Identity*. New York: Harrington Park Press.

Carby, Hazel V. 1987. *Reconstructing Womanhood: The Emergence of the Afro-American Woman Novelist*. New York: Oxford University Press.

Card, Orson Scott. 1977. Ender's Game. In *UnSo: The Future at War*, edited by R. Bretnor. New York: Ace.

Castells, Manuel. 2000. *The Rise of the Network Society*. Edited by M. Castells. 2nd edn. Oxford and Malden: Blackwell Publishers.

——. 2001. *The Internet Galaxy: Reflections on the Internet, Business, and Society*. Oxford and New York: Oxford University Press.

Chambers, Iain and Lidia Curti, eds. 1996. *The Post-Colonial Question*. London: Routledge.

Chauncey, George. 1994. *Gay New York: Gender, Urban Culture, and the Makings of the Gay Male World, 1890–1940*. New York: Basic Books.

Chow, Rey. 1998. *Ethics After Idealism: Theory, Culture, Ethnicity, Reading*. Bloomington: Indiana University Press.

Chumsai, Areeya. 1997. A Definition of a Strong Woman. Online, available at: www.siamweb.org/sanook/star_profile/pop (accessed April 25, 2005).

Chumsai, Areeya. n.d. Labels. Online, available at: www.siamweb.org/content/Sanook/203/labels/index_eng.php (accessed April 25, 2005).

Chun, Wendy Hui-Kyong. 2006. *Control and Freedom: Power and Paranoia in the Age of Fiber Optics*. Cambridge: MIT Press.

Chung, Rachel C. Lee and Sau-Ling Cynthia Wong, eds. 2004. Asianamerica.Net: Ethnicity, Nationalism and Cyberspace. *New Media and Society* 6(4).

Cobham, Rhonda. 1992. Misgendering the Nation: African Nationalist Fictions and Nuruddin Farah's Maps. In *Nationalisms and Sexualities*, edited by A. Parker *et al.* New York: Routledge.

Cohen, Cathy J. 1999. *The Boundaries of Blackness: Aids and the Breakdown of Black Politics*. Chicago.

Cornwall, Richard R. and Phanindra V. Wunnava. 1991. *New Approaches to Economic and Social Analyses of Discrimination*. New York: Praeger.

Costa, LeeRay M. and Andrew Matzner, eds. 2007. *Male Bodies, Women's Souls: Personal Narratives of Thailand's Transgendered Youth*. New York: Haworth Press.

Craig, Dorothy Valcarcel and Educational Resources Information Center (US). 1999. *A League of their Own Gender, Technology, and Instructional Practices.* Washington, DC: US Department of Education Office of Educational Research and Improvement Educational Resources Information Center.

Crang, Mike, Phil Crang, and Jon May, eds. 1999. *Virtual Geographies: Bodies, Space, and Relations.* London and New York: Routledge.

Cruz, Arnaldo and Martin F. Manalansan, eds. 2002. *Queer Globalizations: Citizenship and the Afterlife of Colonialism.* New York: New York University Press.

Crystal, David. 1997. *English as a Global Language.* New York: Cambridge University Press.

——. 2001. *Language and the Internet.* Cambridge and New York: Cambridge University Press.

Cummings, Dolan and Institute of Ideas. 2002. *The Internet: Brave New World?* London: Hodder & Stoughton.

Danet, Brenda. 2001. *Cyberpl@y: Communicating Online.* Oxford: Berg.

Davies, Carole Boyce. 1994. *Black Women, Writing, and Identity: Migrations of the Subject.* London and New York: Routledge.

Davis, Mike. 1992. *City of Quartz: Excavating the Future in Los Angeles.* New York: Vintage Books.

Dawson, Jeff. 1996. *Gay & Lesbian Online.* Berkeley: Peachpit Press.

de Saussure, Ferdinand. 1974 [1916]. *Course in General Linguistics.* Trans. Wade Baskin. London: Fontana/Collins.

DeGraff, Michel. 1999a. Creolization, Language Change, and Language Acquisition: A Prolegomenon. In *Language Creation and Language Change: Creolization, Diachrony, and Development*, edited by M. DeGraff. Cambridge: MIT Press.

DeGraff, Michel, ed. 1999b. *Language Creation and Language Change: Creolization, Diachrony, and Development.* Cambridge: MIT Press.

Delany, Samuel R. 1975. *Dhalgren.* Toronto and New York: Bantam Books.

——. 1977. *The Jewel-Hinged Jaw: Notes on the Language of Science Fiction.* 1st edn. Elizabethtown: Dragon Press.

——. 1994a. *Silent Interviews: on Language, Race, Sex, Science Fiction, and Some Comics: a Collection of Written Interviews.* Hanover: Wesleyan University Press: University Press of New England.

——. 1994b. Some *Real* Mothers...: The *SF Eye* Interview. In *Silent Interviews: On Language, Race, Sex, Science Fiction, and Some Comics: A Collection of Written Interviews.* Hanover: Wesleyan University Press: University Press of New England.

——. 2000. Racism and Science Fiction. In *Dark Matter: A Century of Speculative Fiction from the African Diaspora*, edited by Sheree R. Thomas. New York: Warner Books.

——. 2004. Some Queer Notions about Race. In *Queer Cultures*, edited by D. Carlin and J. DiGrazia. Upper Saddle River: Pearson/Prentice Hall.

Deleuze, Gilles and Félix Guattari. 1987. *A Thousand Plateaus: Capitalism and Schizophrenia.* Minneapolis: University of Minnesota Press.

——. 1993. Minor Literature: Kafka. In *The Deleuze Reader*, edited by C.V. Boundas. New York: Columbia University Press.

D'Emilio, John. 1982. Out of the Shadows: the Gay Emancipation Movement in the United States, 1940–1970. Doctoral dissertation. Online, available at: http://academic commons.columbia.edu:8080/ac/handle/10022/AC:P:1249

——. 1993. Capitalism and Gay Identity. In *The Lesbian and Gay Studies Reader*, edited by H. Abelove, M.A. Barale, and D.M. Halperin. New York: Routledge.

——. 2002. *The World Turned: Essays on Gay History, Politics, and Culture*. Durham: Duke University Press.

Derrida, Jacques. 1976. *Of Grammatology*. Baltimore: Johns Hopkins University Press.

——. 1998. *Monolingualism of the Other, or, The Prosthesis of Origin, Cultural Memory in the Present*. Stanford: Stanford University Press.

Dery, Mark. 1994. Black to the Future: Interviews with Samuel R. Delany, Greg Tate, and Tricia Rose. In *Flame Wars: The Discourse of Cyberculture*, edited by M. Dery. Durham: Duke University Press.

——. eds. 1996. *Escape Velocity: Cyberculture at the End of the Century*. 1st edn. New York: Grove Press.

Dibbell, Julian. 1998. *A Rape in Cyberspace*. Online, available at: www.juliandibbell.com/texts/bungle.html (accessed February 15, 2009).

Dinshaw, Carolyn. 2006. The History of GLQ, Volume One: LGBT Studies, Censorship, and Other Transnational Problems. *GLQ: A Journal of Lesbian and Gay Studies* 12(1): 5–26.

Dodge, Martin and Rob Kitchin. 2001. *Mapping Cyberspace*, 1st edn. New York and London: Routledge.

Dor, Danny. 2004. Englishization to Imposed Multilingualism: Globalization, the Internet, and the Political Economy of the Linguistic Code. *Public Culture* 16 (1): 97–118.

Douglas, Susan J. 1987. *Inventing American broadcasting, 1899–1922*. Baltimore: Johns Hopkins University Press.

Dozois, Gardner R. 1990. *The Year's Best Science Fiction: Eighth Annual Collection*. New York: St. Martin's Press.

Due, Tananarive. 2001. *The Living Blood*. New York: Pocket Books.

Elia, John P., Catherine Swanson, and Amanda R. Goldberg. 2003. More Queer: Resources on Queer Theory. *Journal of Homosexuality* 45 (2–4).

Eng, David L., Judith Halberstam, and Jose E. Munoz. 2005. Introduction: What's Queer About Queer Studies Now? *Social Text* 84/85: 1–18.

Enteen, Jillana. 1998. "Whiskey is Whiskey. You Can't Make a Cocktail from That": Self-Identified Gay Thai Men in Bangkok. *Jouvert: A Journal of Post-Colonial Studies* 2 (1).

——. 2001. Tom, Dii and Anjaree: Women Who Follow Non-Conformist Ways. In *Post-colonial, Queer: Theoretical Intersections*, edited by J. Hawley. New York: State University of New York Press.

Fabian, Johannes. 1983. *Time and the Other: How Anthropology Makes its Object*. New York: Columbia University Press.

Fanon, Franz. 1967. *Black Skin White Masks: The Experiences of a Black Man in a White World*. Translated by C.L. Markmann. New York: Grove Press, Inc. Original edition, Peau Noire, Masques Blancs.

——. 1968. *The Wretched of the Earth*. 1st Black Cat edn. New York: Grove Weiderfeld.

Featherstone, Mike. 1990. *Global Culture: Nationalism, Globalization, and Modernity: A Theory, Culture & Society Special Issue*. London and Newbury Park: Sage Publications.

Fernandes, Leela. 2000. Nationalizing "The Global": Media Images, Cultural Politics and the Middle Class in India. *Media, Culture & Society* 22 (5): 611–628.

Fodor's Travel Publications Inc. 1998. *Fodor's Caribbean: The Complete Guide to Choosing and Enjoying the Perfect Island Vacation*. New York: Fodor's Travel Publications, Inc.

Foster, Thomas. 2005. *The Souls of Cyberfolk: Posthumanism as Vernacular Theory*.

Edited by S.W. Mark Poster, Katherine Hayles. Minneapolis: University of Minnesota Press.

Foucault, Michel. 1979. Discipline and Punish: The Birth of the Prison. New York: Vintage Books.

——. 1988. *The History of Sexuality*. 3 vols. New York: Vintage Books.

Francoeur, Robert T., ed. 1998. *The International Encyclopedia of Sexuality*. New York: Continuum.

Freedman, Carl Howard. 2000. *Critical Theory and Science Fiction*. Hanover: Wesleyan University Press: University Press of New England.

Fuller, Thomas. 2007. Thais Ask: "What's in a Nickname?" *International Herald Tribune*, August 23. Online, available at: www.nytimes.com/2007/08/29/world/asia/29nickname.html.

Gajjala, Rhadika. 2001. Studying Feminist E-Spaces: Introducing Transnational/Post-Colonial Concerns. In *Technospaces: Inside the New Media*, edited by Sally R. Munt. New York: Continuum.

——. 2002. An Interrupted Postcolonial/Feminist Cyberethnography: Complicity and Resistance in The "Cyberfield." *Feminist Media Studies* 2 (2).

——. 2008. Conclusion: Moving On, Re-mixing It Up: Web 2.0, Offline/Online Intersections, Globalization through NGOs, Machinima, Mash-ups.... In *South Asian Technospaces*, edited by R. Gajjala and V. Gajjala. New York: Peter Lang.

Gates, Henry Louis. 1988. *The Signifying Monkey: A Theory of Afro-American Literary Criticism*. New York: Oxford University Press.

Ghashghai, Elham, Rosalind Lewis, and Rand Corporation. 2002. *Issues Affecting Internet Use in Afghanistan and Developing Countries in the Middle East*. Santa Monica: Rand.

Gibson, William. 1984. *Neuromancer*. New York: Ace Books.

——. 1986 *Burning Chrome*. New York: Ace Books.

——. 1987. *Count Zero*. New York: Ace Books.

——. 1989. *Mona Lisa Overdrive*. Bantam paperback edn. New York: Bantam Books.

Giddens, Anthony. 1990. *The Consequences of Modernity*. Stanford: Stanford University Press.

Gilroy, Paul. 1993. *The Black Atlantic: Modernity and Double Consciousness*. Cambridge: Harvard University Press.

——. 2000. *Against Race: Imagining Political Culture Beyond the Color Line*. Cambridge: Harvard University Press.

Gilster, Paul. 1996. *Finding it on the Internet: the Internet Navigator's Guide to Search Tools and Techniques*. Revised and expanded, 2nd edn. New York: Wiley.

Glave, Dianne D. 2003. An Interview with Nalo Hopkinson. *CALLALOO* 26 (1): 146–159.

Glissant, Edouard. 1989. *Caribbean Discourse: Selected Essays*. Translated by J.M. Dash. Edited by A.J. Arnold, *CARAF Books*. Charlottesville: University Press of Virginia.

—— and Betsy Wing. 1997. *Poetics of Relation*. Ann Arbor: University of Michigan Press.

Green, Venus. 2001. *Race on the Line: Gender, Labor, and Technology in the Bell System, 1880–1980*. Durham: Duke University Press.

Green, Lelia. 2002. *Technoculture: From Alphabet to Cybersex*. Sydney: Allen & Unwin.

Grewal, Inderpal. 1998. On the New Global Feminism and the Family of Nations. In *Talking Visions: Multicultural Feminism in a Transnational Age*, edited by E. Shohat. Cambridge: MIT Press.

—— and Caren Kaplan. 2000. Postcolonial Studies and Transnational Feminist Practices. *Jouvert: A Journal of Post-Colonial Studies* 5 (1).

Guha, Ranajit and Gayatri Chakravorty Spivak. 1988. *Selected Subaltern Studies.* New York: Oxford University Press.

Guven, Serhat. 1995. *The Future in Cyberpunk.* Computer Writing and Research Lab, University of Texas at Austin. Online, available at: www.cwrl.utexas.edu/~tonya/cyberpunk/papers/serhat1.html (accessed December 12, 2000).

Hafner, Katie and Matthew Lyon. 1996. *Where Wizards Stay up Late: The Origins of the Internet.* New York: Simon & Schuster.

Halavais, Alexander. 2000. National Borders on the World Wide Web. *New Media & Society* 2 (1): 7–28.

Halberstam, Judith. 1998. *Female Masculinity.* Durham: Duke University Press.

Hall, Stuart. 1997. Introduction. *Representation: Cultural Representations and Signifying Practices.* London: Sage.

Hall, Stuart and Paul Du Gay, eds. 1996. *Questions of Cultural Identity.* London: Sage.

Haraway, Donna Jeanne. 1991. *Simians, Cyborgs, and Women: the Reinvention of Nature.* 1st edn. New York: Routledge.

Harcourt, Wendy. 1999. *Women@Internet: Creating New Cultures in Cyberspace.* London and New York: Zed Books.

Hardt, Michael and Antonio Negri. 2000. *Empire.* Cambridge: Harvard University Press.

Harpold, Terry. 1999. Dark Continents: A Critique of Internet Metageographies. *Postmodern Culture* 9 (2). Online, available at: http://muse.jhu.edu/login?uri=/journals/postmodern_culture/v009/9.2harpold.html.

Hart, Michael. 2000. *The American Internet Advantage: Global Themes and Implications of the Modern World.* Lanham: University Press of America.

Hawthorne, Susan and Renate Klein. 1999. *Cyberfeminism: Connectivity, Critique and Creativity.* North Melbourne: Spinifex Press.

Hayles, Katherine N. 1993. The Seduction of Cyberspace. In *Rethinking Technologies,* edited by V A. Conley. Minneapolis: University of Minnesota Press.

——. 1999. *How We Became Posthuman: Virtual Bodies in Cybernetics, Literature, and Informatics.* Chicago: University of Chicago Press.

Hebdige, Dick. 1979. *Subculture: The Meaning of Style.* London: Methuen.

Heinlein, Robert A. 1941. By His Bootstraps. *Astounding Science Fiction.* Online, available at: www.xs4all.nl/~pot/scifi/byhisbootstraps.pdf#search=%22%22by%20his%20bootstraps%22%20macdonald%22 (accessed August 29, 2006).

Henderson, Mae Gwendolyn. 1989. Speaking in Tongues: Dialogics, Dialects, and the Black Woman Writer's Literary Tradition. In *Changing Our Own Words: Essays on Criticism, Theory, and Writing by Black Women,* edited by C.A. Wall. New Brunswick: Rutgers University Press.

Henry, Paget. 2000. *Caliban's Reason: Introducing Afro-Caribbean Philosophy, Africana Thought.* New York: Routledge.

Herdt, Gilbert H., eds. 1994. *Third Sex, Third Gender: Beyond Sexual Dimorphism in Culture And History.* New York: Zone Books.

—— and Andrew Boxer. 1993. *Children of Horizons: How Gay and Lesbian Teens are Leading a New Way Out of the Closet.* Boston: Beacon Press.

Hine, Christine. 2000. *Virtual Ethnography.* London and Thousand Oaks: Sage.

Hines, Alicia Headlam, Thuy Linh N. Tu, and Alondra Nelson. 2001. Introduction: Hidden Circuits. In *Technicolor: Race, Technology, and Everyday Life,* edited by A. Nelson, T.L.N. Tu, and A.H. Hines. New York: New York University Press.

hooks, bell. 1990. Choosing the Margin as a Space of Radical Openness. In *Yearning: Race, Gender, and Cultural Politics*. Boston: South End Press.

Hopkinson, Nalo. n.d. Nalo. *SFF Net*. Online, available at: www.sff.net/people/nalo/ (accessed April 4, 2002).

———. 2000a. A Conversation with Nalo Hopkinson. *SF Site*. Online, available at: www.sfsite.com/03b/nh77.htm (accessed May 5, 2007).

———. 2000b. *Midnight Robber*. New York: Warner Brooks.

Imken, Otto. 1999. The Convergence of Virtual and Actual in the Global Matrix: Artificial Life, Geo-Economics and Psychogeography. In *Virtual Geographies: Bodies, Space and Relations*, edited by M. Crang, P. Crang, and J. May. New York: Routledge.

Jackson, Peter. 1995. *Dear Uncle Go: Male Homosexuality in Thailand*. Bangkok: Bua Luang Publishing.

———. 2004. *Gay* Adaptation, *Tom-Dee* Resistance, and *Kathoey* Indifference: Thailand's Gender/Sex Minorities and the Episodic Allure of Queer English. In *Speaking in Queer Tongues: Globalization and Gay Language*, edited by W. Leap and T. Boellstorff. Urbana: University of Illinois Press.

—— and Nerida M. Cook, eds. 1999. *Genders & Sexualities in Modern Thailand*. Chiang Mai, Thailand: Silkworm Books.

—— and Gerard Sullivan, eds. 1999. *Lady Boys, Tom Boys, Rent Boys: Male and Female Homosexualities in Contemporary Thailand*. New York: Harrington Park Press.

Jacobs, Harriet A. and Lydia Marie Francis Child. 1861. *Incidents in the Life of a Slave Girl*. Boston: Published for the author.

Jagose, Annamarie. 1996. *Queer Theory: An Introduction*. New York: New York University Press.

Jameson, Fredric. 1991. *Postmodernism, or, the Cultural Logic of Late Capitalism*. Durham: Duke University Press.

—— and Masao Miyoshi. 1998. *The Cultures of Globalization, Post-Contemporary Interventions*. Durham: Duke University Press.

Jeganathan, Pradeep. 1997. eelam.com: Place, Nation and Imagi-Nation in Cyberspace. *Public Culture* 10 (3): 515–528.

Johnson, E. Patrick and Mae Henderson, eds. 2005. *Black Queer Studies: A Critical Anthology*. Durham: Duke University Press.

Jones, Steve. 1997. *Virtual Culture: Identity and Communication in Cybersociety*. London and Thousand Oaks: Sage Publications.

———. 1999. *Doing Internet Research: Critical Issues and Methods for Examining the Net*. Thousand Oaks: Sage Publications.

Judy, Ronald A.T. 1999. Some Notes on the Status of Global English in Tunisia. *boundary 2* 26 (2): 3–44.

Kandiyoti, Deniz. 1994. Identity and Its Discontents: Women and the Nation. In *Colonial Discourse and Post-Colonial Theory: A Reader*, edited by Patrick Williams and Laura Chrisman. New York: Columbia University Press.

Kendall, Lori. 2002. *Hanging Out in the Virtual Pub: Masculinities and Relationships Online*. Berkeley: University of California Press.

Kitalong, Karla Saari and Tino Kitalong. 2000. Complicating the Tourist Gaze: Literacy and the Internet as Catalysts for Articulating a Postcolonial Palauan Identity. In *Global Literacies and the World-Wide Web*, edited by G.E. Hawisher and C.L. Selfe. New York: Routledge.

Kitchin, Martin and Dodge, Rob. 2001. *Mapping Cyberspace*. 1st edn. New York and London: Routledge.

Kittler, Friedrich. 1999. *Gramophone, Film, Typewriter*. Palo Alto: Stanford University Press.

Kolko, Beth E., Lisa Nakamura, and Gilbert B. Rodman, eds. 2000. *Race in Cyberspace*. New York: Routledge.

Koshy, Susan. 1999. From Cold War to Trade War: Neocolonialism and Human Rights. *Social Text* 58.

Kumar, Amitava 2001. Temporary Access: The Indian H-1b Worker in the United States. In *Technicolor: Race, Technology, and Everyday Life*, edited by Alondra Nelson, Thuy Linh N. Tu, and Alicia Headlam Hines. New York: New York University Press.

Kurzweil, Ray. 2000. *The Age of Spiritual Machines: When Computers Exceed Human Intelligence*. New York: Penguin Books.

Laclau, Ernesto and Chantal Mouffe. 2001. *Hegemony and Socialist Strategy: Towards a Radical Democratic Politics*. 2nd edn. London and New York: Verso.

Lamming, George. 1984. *The Pleasures of Exile*. New York: Allison and Busby.

Lancaster, Roger N. and Micaela Di Leonardo. 1997. Introduction: Embodied Meanings, Carnal Practices. In *The Gender/Sexuality Reader: Culture, History, Political Economy*, edited by Roger N. Lancaster and Micaela Di Leonardo. New York: Routledge.

Landzelius, Kyra. 2006. *Native on the Net: Indigenous and Diasporic Peoples in the Virtual Age*. London and New York: Routledge.

Latour, Bruno. 1993. *We Have Never Been Modern*. New York: Harvester Wheatsheaf.

——. 1997. *On Actor–Network Theory: A Few Clarifications*. Online, available at: www.keele.ac.uk/depts/stt/stt/ant/latour.htm.

Leary, Timothy. 2000. The Cyberpunk: The Individual as Reality Pilot. In *The Cybercultures Reader*, edited by D. Bell and B.M. Kennedy. New York: Routledge.

Lee, Han. 2005. Race in Cyberqueer Space: Looking at Race in Online Personal Advertisements for Men Seeking Men. Chicago: University of Illinois.

Lee, Rachel C. and Sau-ling Cynthia Wong. 2003. *Asian America.Net: Ethnicity, Nationalism, and Cyberspace*. New York: Routledge.

Lefebvre, Henri. 1991. *The Production of Space*. Oxford and Cambridge: Blackwell.

Lenoir, Tim. 2000. All But War is Simulation: The Military–Entertainment Complex. *Configurations* 8 (3): 289–336.

Leonard, Andrew. 1998. *Is Cyberpunk Still Breathing?* www.salon.com/21st/books/1998/09/14books.html (accessed March 18, 2002).

Levinson, Paul. 1999. *Digital McLuhan: a Guide to the Information Millennium*. New York: Routledge.

Lévy, Pierre and Robert Bononno. 2001. *Cyberculture*. Minneapolis and London: University of Minnesota Press.

Liebowitz, Stan J. 2002. *Re-thinking the Network Economy: the True Forces That Drive the Digital Marketplace*. New York: Amacom.

Lipschultz, Jeremy Harris. 2000. *Free Expression in the Age of the Internet: Social and Legal Boundaries*. Boulder: Westview Press.

Logan, Robert K. 2000. *The Sixth Language: Learning a Living in the Internet Age*. Toronto: Stoddart.

Lovink, Geert. 2002. *Dark Fiber: Tracking Critical Internet Culture*. Cambridge: MIT Press.

Lush, David, Helliate Rushwayo, Fackson Banda, and Panos Southern Africa. 2000. *Into or Out of the Digital Divide? Perspectives on ICTs and Development in Southern Africa*. Lusaka, Zambia: Panos Southern Africa.

McCaffery, Larry, ed. 1991. *Storming the Reality Studio: a Casebook of Cyberpunk and Postmodern Science Fiction.* Durham: Duke University Press.

McCaughey, Martha and Michael D. Ayers. 2003. *Cyberactivism: Online Activism in Theory and Practice.* New York: Routledge.

McClintock, Anne. 1995. *Imperial Leather: Race, Gender, and Sexuality in the Colonial Conquest.* New York: Routledge.

——, Aamir Mufti, Ella Shohat, and Social Text Collective. 1997. *Dangerous Liaisons: Gender, Nation, and Postcolonial Perspectives.* Minneapolis: University of Minnesota Press.

McCrank, Lawrence J. 2001. *Historical Information Science: An Emerging Unidiscipline.* Medford: Information Today.

McHugh, Maureen. 1994. A Coney Island of the Mind. In *Isaac Asimov's Cyberdreams*, edited by G. Dozois and S. Williams. New York: Ace.

McLelland, Mark J. 2005. *Queer Japan from the Pacific War to the Internet Age.* Lanham: Rowman & Littlefield.

McLuhan, Marshall and Quentin Fiore. 1967. *The Medium Is the Massage.* New York: Bantam Books.

Maiti, Prasenjit. 1999. Banal Nationalism and the Internet. Online, available at: http://65.107.211.206/post/poldiscourse/maiti/11.html.

Manalansan, Martin. 1994. (Dis)Orienting the Body: Locating Symbolic Resistance among Filipino Gay Men. *Positions: East Asia Cultures Critique* 2 (1).

——. 1995. In the Shadows of Stonewall: Examining Gay Transnational Politics and the Diasporic Dilemma. *GLQ: A Journal of Lesbian and Gay Studies* 2 (4).

——. 2005. Race, Violence and Neo-Liberal Spatial Politics in the Global City. *Social Text* 23 (3–4): 141–155.

Maney, Kevin. 2004. Tuvalu's Sinking, But its Domain is on Solid Ground. *USA Today* April 27.

Manovich, Lev. 2001. *The Language of New Media.* Cambridge: MIT Press.

Marriott, Michel. 1998. The Web Reflects a Wider World: As More Non-English Speakers Log On, Many Languages Thrive. *New York Times*, June 18, G1+.

Massad, Joseph. 2002. Re-Orienting Desire: The Gay International and the Arab World. *Public Culture* 14 (2): 361–368.

Massumi, Brian. 2002. *Parables for the Virtual: Movement, Affect, Sensation, Post-Contemporary Interventions.* Durham: Duke University Press.

Mercer, Kobena. 1988. Diaspora Culture and the Dialogic Imagination. In *Blackframes: Critical Perspectives on Black Independent Cinema*, edited by M. Cham and C. Watkins. Chicago: University of Chicago Press.

Miller, Laura. 1997. *Sexing the Machine: Three Digital Women Debate Gender, Technology, and the Net.* Online, available at: http://archive.salon.com/sept97/21st/tech4970911.html (accessed February 19, 2003).

Mintz, Anne P. 2002. *Web of Deception: Misinformation on the Internet.* Medford: Cyber-Age Books.

Mitra, Ananda. 1997. Virtual Commonality: Looking for India on the Internet. In *Virtual Culture: Identity and Communication in Cybersociety*, edited by S.G. Jones. London: Sage Publications.

——. 2001. Marginal Voices in Cyberspace. *New Media and Society* 3 (1): 29–48.

Mixon, Laura. 1992. *Glass Houses.* New York: Tor Books.

Mohanty, Chandra Talpade, Ann Russo, and Lourdes Torres, eds. 1991. *Third World Women and the Politics Of Feminism.* Bloomington: Indiana University Press.

Morris, Rosalind. 1994. Three Sexes and Four Sexualities: Redressing the Discourses on Gender and Sexuality in Contemporary Thailand. *Positions: East Asia Cultures Critique* 2 (1): 15–43.

——. 2000. *In the Place of Origins: Modernity and its Mediums in Northern Thailand, Body, Commodity, Text*. Durham: Duke University Press.

Moschovitis, Christos J.P. 1999. *History of the Internet: a Chronology, 1843 to the Present*. Santa Barbara: Abc-Clio.

Mosley, Walter. 2000. Black to the Future. In *Dark Matter: A Century of Speculative Fiction from the African Diaspora*, edited by S.R. Thomas. New York: Warner Books.

Munt, Sally R. 2001. *Technospaces: Inside the New Media*. New York: Continuum.

Nakamura, Lisa. 2002. *Cybertypes: Race, Ethnicity, and Identity on the Internet*. New York: Routledge.

Nanda, Serena. 1991. *Cultural Anthropology*. 4th edn. Belmont: Wadsworth Publishing Co.

Negroponte, Nicholas. 1995. *Being Digital*. 1st edn. New York: Knopf.

Nelson, Alondra, ed. 2002. *Afrofuturism: A Special Issue of Social Text*. Durham: Duke University Press.

——, Thuy Tu, and Alicia Hines, eds. 2001. *Technicolor: Race, Technology, and Everyday Life*. New York: New York University Press.

Ngai, Pun. 2000. Opening a Minor Genre of Resistance in Reform China: Scream, Dream, and Transgression in a Workplace. *Positions: East Asia Cultures Critique* 8 (2): 531–535.

Nguyen, Mimi. 2003. Queer Cyborgs and New Mutants: Race, Sexuality, and Prosthetic Sociality in Digital Space. In *Asian America.Net: Ethnicity, Nationalism, and Cyberspace*, edited by R.C. Lee and S.-l.C. Wong. New York: Routledge.

Norris, Pippa. 2001. *Digital Divide: Civic Engagement, Information Poverty, and the Internet Worldwide*. Cambridge and New York: Cambridge University Press.

Novak, Marcos. 1993. Liquid Architectures in Cyberspace. In *Cyberspace: First Steps*, edited by M. Benedikt. Cambridge: MIT Press.

Ong, Ai-hwa. 1987. *Spirits of Resistance and Capitalist Discipline: Factory Women in Malaysia*. Albany: State University of New York Press.

Ong, Walter J. 1982. *Orality and Literacy: the Technologizing of the Word*. New York: Routledge.

O'Riordan, Kate and David J. Phillips, eds. 2007. *Queer Online: Media Technology & Sexuality*. New York: Peter Lang.

Paik, Won Kwang and Russell Mardon. 2003. Global Income Inequality in Developing and Less Developed Countries. *Pacific Focus* 18.

Paolilli, John C. 1995. Code-switching on the Internet: Panjabi and English on soc.culture. panjab. Paper read at Georgetown University Round Table on Languages and Linguistics, Pre-session on Computer-Mediated Discourse Analysis, March. Georgetown University.

Parker, Andrew. 1992. *Nationalisms & Sexualities*. New York: Routledge.

Pasuk, Phongpaichit and Christopher John Baker. 1995. *Thailand, Economy and Politics*. Kuala Lumpur and New York: Oxford University Press.

——. 1998. *Thailand's Boom and Bust*. Chiang Mai: Silkworm Books.

Patton, Cindy. 2002. *Globalizing AIDS*. Minneapolis: University of Minnesota Press.

—— and Benigno Sánchez-Eppler. 2000. *Queer Diasporas*. Durham: Duke University Press.

Paz, Octavio. 1992. *Theories of Translation*. Chicago: University of Chicago Press.

Pennycook, Alastair. 1994. *The Cultural Politics of English as an International Language.* London: Longman.

———. *English and the Discourses of Colonialism.* London and New York: Routledge.

Phillipson, Robert. 1992. *Linguistic Imperialism.* Oxford and New York: Oxford University Press.

Pile, Steve and Michael Keith. 1997. *Geographies of Resistance.* London and New York: Routledge.

Pongsapich, Amara. 1997. Theories and Praxis: Women's Social Movement in Thailand. In *Women, Gender Relations, and Development in Thai Society,* edited by W. Somsawat and S. Theobald. Chiang Mai: Women's Studies Center, Faculty of Social Sciences, Chiang Mai University.

Porter, David. 1997. *Internet Culture.* New York: Routledge.

Poster, Mark. 2001. *What's the Matter with the Internet?* Minneapolis: University of Minnesota Press.

Pratt, Mary Louise. 1992. *Imperial Eyes: Travel Writing and Transculturation.* London and New York: Routledge.

Rafael, Vicente L. 1988. *Contracting Colonialism: Translation and Conversion in Tagalog Society Under Early Spanish Rule.* Cornell: Cornell University Press.

Rajan, Rajeswari Sunder. 1993. *Real and Imagined Women: Gender, Culture, and Postcolonialism.* London and New York: Routledge.

Ranganathan, Maya. 2006a. The Internet and History: An Exploration of the Transmission of History by Political Websites. *South Asia: Journal of South Asian Studies* 29 (2): 279–292.

———. 2006b. *Nurturing Eelam on the Net: The Transmission of Nationalist Ideologies Through Sri Lankan Tamil Websites.* Clayton: Monash Asia Institute.

Raspe, Rudolf Erich. n.d. *The Surprising Adventures of Baron Munchausen.* Online, available at: www.gutenberg.org/etext/3154.

Rheingold, Howard. 1993. *The Virtual Community: Homesteading on the Electronic Frontier.* Reading: Addison-Wesley Publishing Co.

Rifkin, Jeremy. 2000. *The Age of Access: The New Culture of Hypercapitalism, Where All of Life is a Paid-For Experience.* New York: J.P. Tarcher/Putnam.

Robbins, Bruce. 1999. *Feeling Global Internationalism in Distress.* New York: New York University Press.

Robertson, Roland. 1992. *Globalization: Social Theory and Global Culture.* London and Newbury Park: Sage.

Rodowick, David Norman. 2001. *Reading the Figural, or, Philosophy After the New Media.* Durham: Duke University Press.

Rosenfeld, Louis and Peter Morville. 1998. *Information Architecture for the World Wide Web.* 1st edn. Cambridge and Sebastopol: O'Reilly.

Ross, Andrew. 1991a. Hacking Away the Counterculture. In *Technoculture,* edited by C. Penley and A. Ross. Minneapolis: University of Minnesota Press.

———. eds. 1991b. *Strange Weather: Culture, Science, and Technology in the Age of Limits.* London and New York: Verso.

Rushdie, Salman. 1991. Commonwealth Literature Does Not Exist. In *Imaginary Homelands: Essays and Criticism, 1981–1991.* London and New York: Granta Books, in association with Viking.

Rutledge, Gregory E. 1999. Speaking in Tongues: An Interview with Science Fiction Writer Nalo Hopkinson. *African American Review* 33 (4): 589–601.

Said, Edward W. 1978. *Orientalism.* New York: Pantheon Books.

Sandoval, Chela. 2000. *Methodology of the Oppressed*. Minneapolis: University of Minnesota Press.

Sang, Tze-lan Deborah. 2003. *The Emerging Lesbian: Female Same-Sex Desire in Modern China*. Chicago: University of Chicago Press.

Sardar, Ziauddin. 2000. alt.civilizations.faq: Cyberspace as the Darker Side of the West. In *The Cybercultures Reader*, edited by D. Bell and B.M. Kennedy. New York: Routledge.

Sassen, Saskia. 2002. *Global Networks, Linked Cities*. New York: Routledge.

Schiller, Dan. 1999. *Digital Capitalism: Networking the Global Market System*. Cambridge: MIT Press.

Schuyler, George Samuel. 1931. *Black No More; Being an Account of the Strange and Wonderful Workings of Science in the Land of the Free, A.D. 1933–1940*. New York: The Macaulay Company.

Scott, Melissa. 1994. *Trouble and her Friends*. 1st edn. New York: Tor.

Sedgwick, Eve Kosofsky. 1985. *Between Men: English Literature and Male Homosocial Desire*. New York: Columbia University Press.

———. 1990. *Epistemology of the Closet*. Berkeley: University of California Press.

———. 1993. *Tendencies*. Durham: Duke University Press.

Sen, Krishna and Maila Stivens. 1998. *Gender and Power in Affluent Asia*. London and New York: Routledge.

Serano, Julia. 2007. *Whipping Girl: a Transsexual Woman on Sexism and the Scapegoating of Femininity*. Emeryville: Seal Press.

Seshadri-Crooks, Kalpana and Fawzia Afzal-Khan. 2000. At the Margins of Postcolonial Studies I & II. In *The Pre-Occupation of Postcolonial Studies*, edited by Fawzia Afzal-Khan and Kalpana Seshadri-Crooks. Durham: Duke University Press.

Shaviro, Steven and ebrary Inc. 2003. *Connected, or, What it Means to Live in the Network Society*. Minneapolis: University of Minnesota Press.

Shaw, David. 1997. Gay Men and Computer Communication: A Discourse of Sex and Identity in Cyberspace. In *Virtual Culture: Identity and Communication in Cybersociety*, edited by Steve Jones. London: Sage Publications.

Sherman, Chris and Gary Price. 2001. *The Invisible Web: Uncovering Information Sources Search Engines Can't See*. Medford: CyberAge Books.

Shields, Rob. 1996. *Cultures of Internet: Virtual Spaces, Real Histories, Living Bodies*. London: Sage.

———. 2000. Hyptertext Links: The Ethic of the Index and Its Time-Space Effects. In Andrew Herman and Thomas Swiss, eds. *The World Wide Web and Contemporary Cultural Theory*. New York: Routledge.

Shohat, Ella, ed. 1998. *Talking Visions: Multicultural Feminism in a Transnational Age*. Cambridge: MIT Press.

—— and Robert Stam, eds. 1994. *Unthinking Eurocentrism: Multiculturalism and the Media*. London and New York: Routledge.

Silc, Kathleen Flannery and National Clearinghouse for ESL Literacy Education. 1998. *Using the World Wide Web with Adult ESL Learners*. Washington, DC: ERIC National Clearinghouse for ESL Literacy Education.

Silko, Leslie Marmon. 1991. Language and Literature from a Pueblo Indian Perspective. In *Critical Fictions: The Politics of Imaginative Writing*, edited by P. Mariani. Seattle: Bay Press.

Sinnott, Megan. 2004. *Toms and Dees: Transgender Identity and Female Same-Sex Relationships in Thailand*. Honolulu: University of Hawaii Press.

Slusser, George Edgar and Tom A. Shippey, eds. 1992. *Fiction 2000: Cyberpunk and the Future of Narrative*. Athens: University of Georgia Press.

Smalls, Irene. n.d. Johnkankus: The Roots of an African-American Christmas Tradition. *The Black Collegian On-line*. Online, available at: www.black-collegian.com/african/johnkankus1299.html (accessed April 2, 2002).

Soja, Edward W. 1989. *Postmodern Geographies: The Reassertion of Space in Critical Social Theory*. London and New York: Verso.

Sorensen, Lena and Wellesley College, Center for Research on Women. 1997. *"Reach Out and Touch Someone": Women Networking on the Internet*. Working paper series, no. 283. Wellesley: Center for Research on Women.

Soyko, David. 2002. Nalo Hopkinson Uses SF to Probe the Inner and Outer Worlds of Alienation. *Science Fiction Weekly* (Scifi.com). Online, available at: www.scifi.com/sfw/issue232/interview2.html.

Soylent Communications. 2006. Robert A. Heinlein. *Notable Names Database*. Online, available at: www.nndb.com/people/710/000023641.

Spillers, Hortense. 1987. Mama's Baby, Papa's Maybe: An American Grammar Book. *Culture and Countermemory: The "American" Connection*. The Johns Hopkins University Press.

———. 1991. *Comparative American Identities: Race, Sex, and Nationality in the Modern Text*. New York: Routledge.

———. 2003. *Black, White, and in Color: Essays on American Literature and Culture*. Chicago: University of Chicago Press.

Spivak, Gayatri Chakravorty. 1988a. Feminism and Critical Theory. In *In Other Worlds: Essays in Cultural Politics*. New York: Routledge.

———. 1988b. *In Other Worlds: Essays in Cultural Politics*. New York: Routledge.

———. 1990. Strategy, Identity, and Writing. In *The Post-Colonial Critic: Interviews, Strategies, Dialogues*, edited by Gayatri Chakravorty Spivak and Sarah Harasym. New York: Routledge.

———. 1993. *Outside in the Teaching Machine*. New York: Routledge.

——— and Sarah Harasym. 1990. *The Post-Colonial Critic: Interviews, Strategies, Dialogues*. New York: Routledge.

——— and Claire Sponsler. 1992. Cyberpunk and the Dilemmas of Postmodern Narrative: The Example of William Gibson. *Contemporary Literature* 33 (4).

———, Donna Landry, and Gerald M. MacLean, eds. 1996. *The Spivak Reader: Selected Works of Gayatri Chakravorty Spivak*. New York: Routledge.

Springer, Claudia. 1996. *Electronic Eros: Bodies and Desire in the Postindustrial Age*. 1st edn. Austin: University of Texas Press.

Steele, Beverly. 1995. Marryshow House – a Living Legacy. *Caribbean Quarterly* 41.

Steinberg, Philip E. and Stephen D. McDowell. 2003. Mutiny on the Bandwidth: The Semiotics of Statehood in the Internet Domain Name Registries of Pitcairn Island and Niue. *New Media & Society* 5 (1): 52.

Stephenson, Neal. 1992. *Snow Crash*. New York: Bantam Books.

Sterling, Bruce. 1991. Preface from *Mirrorshades*. In *Storming the Reality Studio: A Casebook of Cyberpunk and Postmodern Science Fiction*, edited by L. MacCaffery. Durham: Duke University Press.

Stockton, Sharon. 1995. "The Self Regained": Cyberpunk's Retreat to the Imperium. *Contemporary Literature* 36 (4): 588–612.

Stockwell, Peter. 2000. *The Poetics Of Science Fiction*. Harlow and New York: Longman.

———. 2003. Introduction: Science Fiction and Literary Linguistics. *Language and Literature* 12 (3): 195–198.

Stoicheva, Mila and ERIC Clearinghouse on Reading English and Communication. 2000. *The Digital Divide and its Implications for the Language Arts*. Bloomington: ERIC Clearinghouse on Reading English and Communication.

Stoll, Clifford, C-SPAN (Television network), and Commonwealth Club of California. 1996. *Technology & the Future*. Video (59 mins.).

Stone, Allucquère Rosanne. 1995. *The War of Desire and Technology at the Close of the Mechanical Age*. Cambridge: MIT Press.

Stratton, Jon. 2000. Cyberspace and the Globalization of Culture. In *The Cybercultures Reader*, edited by D. Bell and B.M. Kennedy. New York: Routledge.

Sullivan, Caitlin and Kate Bornstein. 1996. *Nearly Roadkill: An Infobahn Erotic Adventure*. New York: High Risk Books.

Sunder Rajan, Rajeswari. 1993. *Real and Imagined Women: Gender, Culture, and Postcolonialism*. London and New York: Routledge.

Sussman, Gerald. 1999. Urban Congregations of Capital and Communications: Redesigning Social and Spatial Boundaries. *Social Text* 17 (3): 35–51.

Suvin, Darko. 1979. *Metamorphoses of Science Fiction: On the Poetics and History of a Literary Genre*. New Haven: Yale University Press.

Taylor, Lucien. 1999. Creolite Bites: A Conversation with Patrick Chamoiseau, Raphael Confiant, and Jean Bernabe. *Transition* 7 (2): 124–161.

Taywaditep, Kittiwut Jod, Eli Coleman, and Pacharin Dumronggittigule. 1998. Sexuality in Thailand. In *The International Encyclopedia of Sexuality*, R.T. Francoeur. New York: Continuum.

Thomas, Allen Britton. 2002. Internet Chat Room Participation and the Coming-out Experiences of Young Gay Men: a Qualitative Study. Online, available at: www.lib. utexas.edu/etd/r/d/2002/thomasa022/thomasa022.pdf#page=3   http://wwwlib.umi. com/cr/utexas/fullcit?p3086714.

Thomas, Sheree. 2000. *Dark Matter: A Century of Speculative Fiction from the African Diaspora*. New York: Warner Books.

Thongthiraj, Took Took. 1994. Toward a Struggle Against Invisibility: Love Between Women in Thailand. *Amerasia Journal* 20 (1): 45–58.

Trigo, Abril. (2000) Unforeseeable Americas. In *Shifting Paradigms: From Transculturation to Hybridity: A Theoretical Critique*, edited by R. de Grandis and Z. Bernd. Netherlands: Rodopi.

Trinh, T. Minh-Ha. 1989. *Woman, Native, Other: Writing Postcoloniality and Feminism*. Bloomington: Indiana University Press.

Trinkle, Dennis A. and Scott A. Merriman, eds. 2002. *The European History Highway: A Guide to Internet Resources*. Armonk: M.E. Sharpe.

Tu, Thuy Linh Nguyen. 2003. Good Politics, Great Porn: Untangling Race, Sex, and Technology in Asian-American Cultural Productions. In *Asian America.Net: Ethnicity, Nationalism, and Cyberspace*, edited by R.C. Lee and S.-l.C. Wong. London: Routledge.

Turkle, Sherry. 1995. *Life on the Screen: Identity in the Age of the Internet*. New York: Simon & Schuster.

United States Congress. Senate Committee on the Judiciary. 2000. *Cybersquatting and Consumer Protection: Ensuring Domain Name Integrity: Hearing before the Committee on the Judiciary, United States Senate, One Hundred Sixth Congress, First Session, on S. 1255, a Bill to Protect Consumers and Promote Electronic Commerce* by Amending Certain Trademark Infringement, Dilution, and Counterfeiting Laws, and for Other Purposes, July 22, 1999. Washington: US GPO.

Valovic, Thomas. 2000. *Digital Mythologies: The Hidden Complexities of the Internet*. New Brunswick: Rutgers University Press.

Verges, Francoise. 2001. Vertigo and Emancipation: Creole Cosmopolitanism and Cultural Politics. *Theory, Culture and Society* 18 (2): 169–183.

Wachowski, Andy and Wachowski, Larry, dir. 1999. *The Matrix*, Silver Pictures.

Wakeford, Nina. 2000a. Cyberqueer. In *The Cybercultures Reader*, edited by David Bell and Barbara M. Kennedy. New York: Routledge.

——. 2000b. New Media, New Methodologies: Studying the Web. In *Web.Studies: Rewiring Media Studies for the Digital Age*, edited by D. Gauntlett. New York: Arnold.

Walcott, Derek. 1992. *The Antilles: Fragments of Epic Memory*. New York: Farrar.

Ware, Vron. 2006. Info-War and the Politics of Feminist Curiosity: Exploring New Frameworks for Feminist Intercultural Studies. *Cultural Studies* 20 (6): 526–551.

Wark, McKenzie. 2004. *A Hacker Manifesto*. Cambridge: Harvard University Press.

Warkentin, Craig. 2001. *Reshaping World Politics: NGOs, the Internet, and Global Civil Society*. Lanham: Rowman & Littlefield Publishers.

Warner, Michael, eds. 1997. *Fear of a Queer Planet: Queer Politics and Social Theory*. Minneapolis: University of Minnesota Press.

Warschauer, Mark. 2002. Languages.com: The Internet and Linguistic Pluralism. In *Silicon Literacies: Communication, Innovation and Education in the Electronic Age*, edited by I. Snyder. London: Routledge.

Washington, Booker T. n.d. The 1895 Atlanta Compromise Speech. *Africa Within*. Online, available at: www.africawithin.com/bios/booker/booker_bio1.htm (accessed March 2, 2006).

——. 1970. *Up from Slavery*. New York: Heritage Press.

Wathinee, Boonchalaksi, Philip Guest, and Mahawitthayalai Mahidon, Sathaban Wichai Prachakon l Sangkhom. 1994. *Prostitution in Thailand*. Nakhon Pathom, Thailand: Institute for Population and Social Research Mahidol University.

Watson, Nessim. 1997. Why We Argue About Virtual Community: A Case Study of the Phish.Net Fan Community. In *Virtual Culture: Identity and Communication in Cybersociety*, edited by S.G. Jones. London: Sage Publications.

Weeks, Jeffrey. 1977. *Coming Out: Homosexual Politics in Britain from the Nineteenth Century to the Present*. London and New York: Quartet Books.

——. 1995. *Invented Moralities: Sexual Values in an Age of Uncertainty*. New York: Columbia University Press.

Wertheim, Margaret. 1999. *The Pearly Gates of Cyberspace: A History of Space from Dante to the Internet*. 1st edn. New York: W.W. Norton.

Westfahl, Gary. 1992. Words of Wishdom: The Neologisms of Science Fiction. In *Styles of Creation: Aesthetic Technique and the Creation of Fictional Worlds*, edited by George Edward Slusser and Eric Rabkin. Athens: University of Georgia Press.

Whitaker, Mark P. 2004. Tamilnet.com: Some Reflections on Popular Anthropology, Nationalism, and the Internet. *Anthropological Quarterly* 77 (3): 469–498.

White, Michele. 2006. *The Body and the Screen: Theories of Internet Spectatorship*. Cambridge: MIT Press.

Wilson, Ara. 2004. *The Intimate Economies of Bangkok: Tomboys, Tycoons, and Avon Ladies in the Global City*. Berkeley: University of California Press.

Winichakul, Thongchai. 1994. *Siam Mapped: A History of the Geo-body of a Nation*. Chiang Mai: Silkworm Press.

World Bank. 1997. *Confronting Aids: Public Priorities in a Global Epidemic*. Oxford: Oxford University Press.

Wyatt, David K. 1984. *Thailand: A Short History*. New Haven: Yale University Press.

Wynter, Silvia. 1990. Beyond Miranda's Meanings: Un/silencing the "Demonic Ground" of Caliban's Woman. In *Out of the Kumbla: Caribbean Women and Literature*, edited by C.B. Davies and E.S. Fido. Trenton: Africa World Press.

Yawarat, Porapakkham and Aids Control and Prevention Project Family Health International. 1996. *The Evolution of HIV/AIDS Policy in Thailand, 1984–1994*. Arlington: AIDSCAP Family Health International.

Yujira. 1997. Ahem* We Are Not Horny Thai Girls! Online, available at: www.siamweb.org/romance/yeah_right.

Index

Printed and bound by CPI Group (UK) Ltd, Croydon, CR0 4YY

01/11/2024

01782627-0002